DANCING IN THE SKIES

T. E. JONSSON

GRUB STREET · LONDON

Published by
Grub Street
The Basement
10 Chivalry Road
London SW11 1HT

Copyright © 1994 Grub Street, London
Text and translation copyright © Tony Jonsson

Jonsson, Tony
Dancing in the Skies
I. Title
940.5442

A catalogue record is available on request from the British Library

ISBN 1-898697-03-5

Typeset by Pearl Graphics, Hemel Hempstead

Printed and bound in Great Britain by
Biddles Ltd, Guildford and King's Lynn

The author and publisher would especially like to thank Christopher Shores for
reading the manuscript, Reg Wyness for invaluable assistance in providing
photographs and caption information, and Daniel Balado-Lopez for the index.

CONTENTS

READY FOR TAKE-OFF

I started writing this book 45 years ago. On returning home to Iceland after the war my father, and various publishing houses, urged me to put my wartime memories on paper, mainly for the purpose of telling the good citizens of my country about the events in the life of a young lad who went off to the wars. Iceland has no armed forces and my fellow countrymen's knowledge of military matters is limited to what they read about them. Eventually I got around to completing the book and it was well received in Iceland, becoming the best-selling book in 1992. My publishers persuaded me to write a sequel, about my post-war experiences in civil aviation, and that book has also now become a best-seller.

This narrative is based on memory, jogged by my flying log book, snatches of diaries and the unstinting help of my old RAF pal of long standing, Alun Williams, to whom I am most grateful. Subject to the above it is as accurate as I can make it. This translated version differs somewhat from the Icelandic version in as much as I have left out various passages that would be mainly of interest to the Icelandic reader, such as a more detailed portrayal of my years of childhood and youth in Iceland.

Readers will probably notice that at times I describe in detail various military matters that may be obvious to people that have grown up in countries where things military are common. This was obviously done for the Icelandic reader, but I deliberately decided to leave these passages unaltered as so much has changed in recent years, and the descriptions contained therein may even come in handy for today's younger generations.

T.E.J.

HIGH FLIGHT

Pilot Officer John G. Magee, Jr.

Oh! I have slipped the surly bonds of earth
And danced the skies on laughter-silvered wings;
Sunward I've climbed, and joined the tumbling mirth
Of sun-split clouds—and done a hundred things
You have not dreamed of—wheeled and soared and swung
High in the sunlit silence. Hov'ring there
I've chased the shouting wind along, and flung
My eager craft through footless halls of air.

Up, up the long, delirious, burning blue
I've topped the wind-swept heights with easy grace
Where never lark, or even eagle flew—
And, while with silent lifting mind I've trod
The high untrespassed sancity of space
Put out my hand and touched the face of God.

PROLOGUE

It was April 18, 1940. I was standing on board a trawler that was about to set sail for England. I still kept wondering if I was dreaming. It seemed too good to be true. For months I had been waiting and striving for this moment, and with each passing day it seemed to be further away. Then suddenly there I was, standing on the bridge, impatiently waiting for the mooring ropes to be cast off! I kept looking at my watch. The time was half past eleven, and the *Oli Garda* was not due to sail until midnight. That meant another half-hour to wait—a whole eternity. Such a lot could happen to prevent me from getting away—or at least, I kept imagining so. I tried to keep my mind occupied by singing. The men working on deck were making so much noise themselves that my voice, fortunately, was drowned. After a while I grew tired of the same tune, and tried to think of a new one. That brought my thoughts back to the ship, and the time. Only five minutes left; surely nothing could happen now.

With a shock, I noticed two uniformed men coming on board. With relief I saw they were only customs officers and thought they would hardly concern themselves with me. They disappeared into the captain's cabin. Yet I was not at ease. Might they find some reason for obstructing my departure? Hardly, if the passport were in order, even though war had broken out. But they might ask me all sorts of awkward questions. Was I going to England to study? Had I any guaranteed job or occupation in England? Did I have any document to show that I would be allowed to disembark in Britain?

Just then I heard the skipper's voice:

'Thorsteinn, will you come in here a minute? The customs officers want a word with you.'

This is it! I said to myself. I entered the captain's cabin filled with apprehension.

'This is our passenger,' said the skipper. 'Take a seat, Thorsteinn.'

I sat down facing the customs officers, trying to hide my fear.

'So, you are going to England to join the Air Force.' I heard one of them say. 'You've got big ideas! Whatever makes you want to do such a crazy thing?'

I was getting tired of that question. I had been asked it so often during the last few months, and every time I tried to explain my reasons I felt a bit of a fool, as I could think of no tangible, or easy answer to it. And many times I had been told that I was a fool. 'You'll just go and get yourself killed,' my friends had said. 'You're just asking for trouble, and after all, this war is none of your business. Let them fight their own dirty war. The British Air Force is much inferior to the German Air Force, and it will get knocked out of the sky in no time. You will be led like a lamb to the slaughter.' And so on and on—an endless stream of discouragement.

'I have my reasons', I replied and could feel myself blushing. Perhaps that was a little too abrupt. Maybe I should show these men more respect; they might be able to stop me from going if they took an objection to me. Oh well... I didn't think they could stop me now. They didn't have the power to do that. Or did they?

'Well, you know your own mind best. May I see your passport?'

I handed it to him, feeling a little more at ease. 'Now let us see... Thorsteinn Elton Jónsson... Icelandic citizen... 18 years of age... hm... hm... this appears to be in order.'

Then my heart took a leap when I heard the next question, which was one I had been dreading. 'Have you anything to show that you will be admitted into the Air Force, or even allowed ashore when you reach England? You know they are very strict about those matters now.'

I handed him a letter from Commander Hawkridge, one of a group of friends of my father in England, who had written to the Air Ministry and asked whether I could be granted admission to the RAF. The Commander had attached the reply to the letter I handed to the customs officer.

I had read the two letters so often that I knew the wording of them by heart. The Air Ministry had stated that it was contrary to official policy to admit foreigners to the armed forces of the Crown, but Parliament had agreed to make an exception in the case of Mr. Jónsson, as his mother had been English, but subject to the condition that those recommending him would accept responsibility for him. The Air Ministry had also written that there was a long list of candidates awaiting air-crew training, and the schools were filled to capacity. 'If Mr. Jónsson comes,' the letter ran, 'he will be liable to have to wait a considerable time before being called upon for medical and educational examinations, and he should be warned that the standard required in both is very high. Mr. Jónsson will, for security reasons, have to pay his own passage to the United Kingdom.'

Commander Hawkridge had written in his letter to me that, if I came to England, he personally would see to it that I was allowed ashore. Surely those two letters were enough? It was most unlikely that officials here in Iceland could forbid me to join the Air Force. And yet...?

While the customs officer read the letters, I sat there letting my eyes roam around the cabin, trying to look as casual as I possibly could. I noticed my hand was shaking a little so I put it under the table. My heart beat so loud that I was sure everyone was bound to hear it, and my stomach muscles were cramped just like the time once when I was skiing on a high ridge and my companions were grinning at me, waiting for me to honour my thoughtless boast to take the steepest way down.

Oh, how long this customs officer was taking over the letters! I wondered if he could read English well enough to understand their contents.

'Well, my lad, this seems to be in order. But don't you have any pass or recommendation from the British Legation here in Iceland?'

'No, they were not very co-operative, I am afraid.'

'Well, was that so. I'm afraid you'll probably find that you need one,' continued the customs officer, 'but, however, there's no harm in trying. I wouldn't be surprised though, if you had to come back on the same ship. Anyway, I wish you the best of luck.'

'Thank you,' I said. 'Is that all then?'

'Yes, that's all; you may go now. Have a pleasant voyage.'

I could have embraced him. What a relief. I said good-bye and rushed out on deck again. I was bursting with joy. I wanted to jump and sing aloud. My dreams were coming true and it would not be long before I started flying in the blue sky! Hurrah! Hurrah!

Shortly after midnight the *Oli Garda* slipped silently out of the little port of Hafnarfjördur. I stood outside the bridge watching the lights of the town gradually disappearing. A long time would pass before I again saw lit-up human dwellings. The stars glimmered in a cloudless sky and I could only just trace the outlines of the mountains I knew so well, and which had become so much a part of me. It is during moments like this that it becomes obvious how deep one's feelings are for one's country. When would I see it again?

Midnight, and the sky was pitch-black. It was our second night out from port. The sea was running high, and the *Oli Garda* ploughed steadily through the waves, occasionally shuddering when she dug her bows into extra-large ones, and with the white spray—clearly visible in the blackness —pouring over the forecastle like snowfall. It was warm and peaceful here in the darkness of the bridge, where I leant against the rail in front of the windows and stared into the night. I was alone except for the quarter-master, who was standing silently before the wheel with the dull light from the binnacle occasionally shining on his face. The radio had been playing late-night dance-music from Reykjavík, but it was silent now. The only sounds came from the throbbing of the ship's engine, the whistling wind in the masts and rigging, the dull crashing of the waves, the spray thrashing against the windows, and the spasmodic clanging of the steering engine as the quartermaster moved the wheel. I liked these sounds and the cosy atmosphere in the wheel-house. One could just stand there and gaze uninter-rupted into the dark and think, or rather, let one's mind roam at will.

Now that the dream seemed to be coming true, thoughts unavoidably entered my mind that I might possibly be rushing headlong into a lot of foolishness, as so many had already pointed out to me, and doubts crept in. I was leaving behind loved ones, friends and a fatherland where everyone lived peacefully, and rushing off to a war and uncertainty. Nothing seemed to indicate that the war would soon end, and I would inevitably have to fight in it if I joined the Royal Air Force, and of course it could end with my . . . No, such thoughts were not allowed.

Just then I caught sight of a white light ahead of us, and shortly after-wards a red and a green light below it.

'Probably a trawler homeward bound from Britain,' said the quarter-master.

And so it was. The trawlers passed quite close to each other—one on its way to a safe harbour in Iceland, and the other heading for the dangers of U-boats, mines and even air attacks in the troubled seas around the coast of Britain.

But now the seaman had broken the tranquillity, and my train of thought. He became talkative:

'So, my lad. You are on your way to join the British Air Force to drop bombs on helpless women and children.'

Oh, how fed-up I was becoming with that hackneyed accusation from 'ignorant fools'.

'Not at all,' I answered. 'I hope to become a fighter pilot for the express purpose of preventing bombs being dropped on women and children.'

'Ah, but that means you'll have to kill Germans, and killing people is equivalent to committing murder,' the quartermaster continued. 'Who are you to judge whether a man is to be allowed to live or not? Don't you see that you might be killing someone who leaves a bereaved mother or wife and children behind—what right do you think you have to do that?'

How I was beginning to hate these arguments! How could people be so stupid—the same thoughtless questions all the time. I attempted to reply to the quartermaster.

'It is by no means certain that I shall ever have to kill Germans, but should it happen I would not have an excessively bad conscience. As I told you, I have in mind to become a fighter pilot, and as such my role will be to shoot down German bombers on their way to dropping bombs on women and children. Preventing that happening could hardly be called murder, even if I did kill a German or two in the process. If somebody should be accused of murder, it must be Hitler for sending these sons and husbands to war to kill or be killed. What right do you think he has to do that?'

The deck-hand was not to be put off so easily.

'But don't you think that the Germans consider their cause equally just as the British and the French declare theirs to be?'

'Of course they do,' I replied, 'but that is only because during the past few years Hitler has managed to get the Germans to believe that all their neighbours are wicked, and intent upon suppressing their innocent little country. He has got them to believe that they are a master-race, and, as such it gives them the right to alter Germany's borders at will. Anybody who is imprudent enough to oppose them should be mercilessly destroyed. The German youth has been brought up on military spirit and hatred, and peace will not be restored until such teachings have been discarded. Therefore the Nazis must be fought and beaten.'

This was a long speech for me, and I was somewhat pleased about it. I only wished the wretched man would change the subject or, better still, shut up and let me get on with my own thoughts.

He smiled teasingly at me.

'So, young fellow, you intend to give old Hitler a thrashing. Why do you want to get involved? Why on earth don't you stay safely at home in your own country, and let others do the job?'

There it was once again—that persistent question.

Yes, why...?

CHAPTER ONE

HOW IT BEGAN

I GROWING UP

An extract from my father's diary on the 19th October 1921 reads:

"The last Wednesday of summer. Very little wind, temperature above freezing, occasional light snow mostly turning into sleet, at least here in town. Florrie began to feel slight birth pangs late yesterday evening, and they started to become severe by early morning. The midwife arrived at eight o'clock, followed by the doctor after I had explained the situation on the phone. However, they left again, but by midday the labour pains had become so intense that I requested the doctor to return. At two o'clock a boy weighing 8lbs was born. At four-thirty I telegraphed the tidings to my parents-in-law: 'Fine boy all well', and the same telegram to Mrs. Wilkins. At seven-thirty I telegraphed mother: 'Son born today. All well. I went personally round to Mrs. Christine Sigurdsson, Mrs. Schram and Gudfinna. The boy appears to be strong and healthy.'"

I was born in Reykjavik on the 19th October 1921, as described by my father in his diary, the eldest of four siblings. I was given the names Thorsteinn Elton, and like most boys with the name Thorsteinn I was addressed by friends and family by the diminutive Steini. My parents were Annie Florence Wescott and Snæbjörn Jonsson, state-registered translator and bookseller. My father was of farming stock, and after finishing high school in Iceland he entered the Central Labour College in London in 1912 where he studied until the First World War broke out, and shortly after that he moved to Copenhagen to continue his studies. There he came under the guidance of Professor B. Melsted, and it was through his urging that my father later established his business, The English Bookshop, in Reykjavik in 1927. However, in 1916 he went back to England and was employed as a translator in one of the ministries in London until he returned to Iceland in

1920. It was during this period that he met my mother, who was a nurse, and they married in 1919. My maternal grandfather was Elton E. Wescott, headmaster of an elementary school in the village of Grasby in Lincolnshire, married to Elizabeth Leah. They had eight children, my mother being the only daughter. Three of her brothers lost their lives serving in the army in the great war.

Judging from old letters written by my parents it was obvious that during the first two or three years of my life I was an 'angel' in their eyes; but that of course was while my field of activities was rather limited. Gradually, as I became more mobile and unruly, my angelic wings began to wilt, and no doubt I then started to cause my parents a good deal of worry. For example, before I had reached the age of ten, I had twice given the police, boy scouts and other rescue organizations cause to mount large-scale searches for me as a missing person. It should also be mentioned in passing that, at a very early age, I had dealings with the media—nude photos of me appearing in newspapers before I had even reached my first birthday. The reason was that a certain milk-powder under the trade-name GLAXO was being marketed, and photos of me were used to advertise how beautiful babies could become if they were fed on this modern wonder-food!

When my parents moved to Iceland, they initially experienced great difficulties in finding suitable lodgings, and because of this I spent much of the first four years of my life with my grandparents in Grasby, often accompanied by my mother. However, by 1925 my father had built his house in the western part of Reykjavik, and there I grew up with my brother and sisters. Nonetheless, I had not completely taken leave of England, as for various reasons I was occasionally dispatched to stay with my maternal grandparents.

Usually the crossings were made on trawlers sailing with fish to Grimsby, but on one occasion, when I was three years old, I was sent on a steamship in the care of Mrs. Ingibjorg Thors, who many years later was to suffer the ordeal of becoming my mother-in-law. During my eighth year I spent thirteen months in England and I have very clear recollections of that period.

Grasby is a pretty and peaceful little village nestling on a hillside on the eastern border of the wide flatlands of Lincolnshire. It took pride in having a charming old Norman church, a small Methodist chapel, a village store that also served as a post office, an elementary school, a lime-quarry and two pubs. In those days it had neither electricity nor running water. Oil lamps and candles were used to provide light, and in my grandparent's back yard there was a water pump. Water was also collected off the roof into barrels. An orchard climbed the hill with apple, plum, and pear trees, and in addition Grandma (whom we children always called Nanny) kept some poultry and pigs. And, most important of all, there was Gyp, a beautiful Collie dog who was my bosom friend and playfellow. At the top of the orchard, behind some bushes and trees, Gyp and I had our secret hide-out.

On the road side of the house by the front door was the lounge, but I do not remember it ever being used by members of the family. It contained a piano on which Nanny gave lessons to fledgling musicians. The main room in the house was a spacious kitchen-come-living room. It had a large black cooking-range that kept the room warm and cosy. In one corner next to it stood Granddad's rocking chair in which he sat and listened to the news from a battery-powered radio with a large loudspeaker shaped like a funnel.

Sydney was the youngest of my uncles and the only one still living at home. At that time he was nineteen and I shared his bed in a little room above the kitchen, and I adored him. He owned a motor bike, and I loved to sit on its pillion with my arms wrapped around Syd's stomach as we roared along the narrow country lanes at (what seemed to me) breakneck speed. We wore goggles, and the peaks of our caps faced backwards in the same way as they were worn by the intrepid aviators in magazine pictures. At times I felt resentment at having to give up my seat to Dorothy, his sweetheart from the next village, but as I was also very fond of her, my resentment was short-lived.

The residents of the village were mainly lime-quarry workers, farm workers, carpenters, blacksmiths and wagon-builders, and the two most respected persons were the vicar and the head master, my grandfather.

Next door to us lived Mr. Andrews. He was a blacksmith and hammered red hot steel all day long. I used to love hanging around the smithy watching him and treading his bellows for him, no doubt influenced by the fact that he usually had some sweets tucked away in a leather bag that was proffered now and again. But there was one thing even more important about Mr. Andrews: he was the owner of a great big steam engine on wheels—two enormous ones at the back and two smaller ones in front—with a tall chimney and a large swing-wheel on one side. When running, this monster made a lot of noise and emitted hissing columns of steam, and it was extremely exciting to ride with Mr. Andrews when he drove his contraption into the fields towing the corn thresher. I can still keenly remember the very special smell that accompanies steam engines.

It seems that I developed an interest in the fair sex at an early age. When I was led into the class-room for the first time, I wasted no time in seating myself beside the prettiest girl in the class, a lass wearing a blue dress with red ribbons in her golden locks. However, I don't think I formed any special relationship with her as, inevitably, playing with the other boys was much more exciting for a lad of my age.

Uncle Reg, the eldest of my maternal uncles, lived a little further down the village, and three of his children, Enid, Ted and Mary were amongst my chief playmates.

Granddad owned an Austin 7, which I think was the only car in the village. It is debatable which of the two of us, Gyp or I, was more devoted to this car. I did have the advantage though of being able to sit in the driver's seat and pretend to drive, whereas poor Gyp had to suffice with being a mere passenger. I don't remember ever seeing the car with the top up. It was a fair-weather car and seldom taken out of the shed except on sunny holidays to drive us children to the sea-side at Cleethorpes—a heavenly place where we splashed in the sea and built castles on the white sand with our buckets and spades. In addition we were given rides on donkeys, taken on the roundabouts, the 'Big Wheel' and other exciting fairground machines. There were also stalls selling all sorts of chocolates, sweets, ice-creams and other goodies, but most of the time I had to reconcile myself to just staring at these delicacies. However, each trip to the sea-side was accompanied by a stick of 'rock' and, of course, fish-and-chips.

The days spent with Nanny and Granddad in England were enchanting.

But my childhood days home in Iceland were no less enchanting. There was no television to keep us occupied, but we certainly had no difficulties getting time to pass—rarely were the days long enough from our point of view. The west end of town, where we lived, was very far from being the built-up suburb that it is now-a-days. It was much more like a small fishing-village than a section of a city. Most of the houses bore names, were widely spaced on grassy lawns with flower beds and potato patches and were surrounded by stone walls. Many had patches laid with flat stones for sun-drying salted fish—the 'Baccalao'—that was mainly exported to the Mediterranean countries. We were right on the sea, and didn't have to travel far to reach enchanting places of adventure such as Effis Island, which could be reached along the breakwater, the main harbour, the Selsvor landing stage for small fishing boats, or Seltjarnarnes peninsula, which at that time was practically untouched countryside. Also, on fine autumn days we kids would go berry-picking on the Eskihlid hill, which now is well within the boundary of the city but was then far out in the country. We would travel over the Melar flatlands, which then stood bare, and traverse the Vatnsmýri (lake swamp) where the airport now stands. This was a considerable distance for short legs to cover, and as there were so many ditches on the way—some containing sticklebacks—to be explored, the trip invariably took the whole day. The West-end was certainly a wonderland for adventurous youngsters in those days.

Our home was a two-storied, re-inforced concrete house with a basement and attic. It stood on spacious grounds divided into a grass field (lawn would be too grandiose a word for it), vegetable garden and flower beds. There was also a chicken coop. As soon as I was old enough to handle the proper tools I was set to digging the garden in spring, pulling weeds during the summer and harvesting potatoes and other vegetables in the autumn. I had little love for these chores, but they were not to be avoided. Occasionally these duties became more bearable when I (like Tom Sawyer) managed to talk some of my playfellows into helping me. Our lawn was fairly large and produced a lot of hay, which an elderly lady in the neighbourhood, who kept a few sheep, would collect after our father had cut the grass with a scythe. It pleased us kids to give her a helping hand, as it was quite enjoyable working in the hay, and in addition she usually had a bag of sweets to offer us.

Quickly after she settled in Iceland, from the neighbours our mother learned many typically Icelandic culinary customs and practices such as using the innards of sheep for making black-pudding and liver-sausage (similar to Haggis), cooking singed sheeps' heads, smoked mutton, salted meat, lumpfish, fish-balls, salted, dried and hung fish to mention just a few. She also learned to knit sweaters, socks and mittens in the Icelandic fashion, which was very different from the way to which she had been accustomed. In return she taught the Icelandic ladies items of English cuisine and the art of making jams and other preserves, and the use of the English type of knitting needles. Our mother was a very keen and accomplished gardener, and taught her neighbours to grow various vegetables and cultivate plants they had not known before.

Life within our home was a mixture of English and Icelandic customs, but probably the English influence was the more prominent. And although our mother got along quite well with the Icelandic language English was always spoken in the home.

Our father, who was considered to be rather strict, played only a distant part in our upbringing. During the early days of our youth we did not see very much of him, as most days he was at work in various government departments, and later in his bookshop after that was established. When at home he spent his time behind closed doors in his study doing literary work and translations. It was mainly during meal times that we saw him, or at weekends when he might take us for walks.

In the beginning there were only the three of us children, as my younger sister, Kitty, was born so many years later. My sister Betty Amelia was nearly three years younger than I, and my brother Boyi (pronounced Boyih) Jon was more than five years younger. We were subjected to much stricter discipline than was customary in Icelandic homes. We were also unstintingly made to take part in the family chores, such as washing up, helping with house cleaning and many other jobs, both indoors and out, and it never occurred to us to voice objections, at least not within the hearing of our parents. Furthermore, our mother was fairly strict about us going to bed early and we often felt resentment when we were called in from play whilst the other kids were allowed to stay out longer.

As far as I can remember our parents got on well together in spite of their very divergent temperaments and personalities. Father was a very serious, intellectual person, but he certainly had a sense of humour and could at times be even playful. Although not a total abstainer he very rarely touched alcohol. He was little given to social life, and placed strict demands of moderation on himself as well as others. His playground was the world of literature and his toys were pen and paper.

My mother's personality differed greatly from his. Certainly she shared his interest in literature to a great extent, mainly the lyrical, but thenceforth their paths diverged. In spite of my father's objections she smoked heavily, and although she was far from being a drinker, she did appreciate a glass or two in good company. She could be serious when it was called for but most of the time she was cheerful and merry, with a keen sense of humour. Above all she was a devoted and loving mother who had a greater under-standing of our needs, and therefore stood closer to us, than our father. When the above-mentioned comparisons are kept in mind it is not surprising that the marriage was on occasions stormy, and that we children sometimes heard our parents quarrel, but even more memorable are their embraces, and without doubt love was the predominant feeling.

Our mother ran the household in an energetic and exemplary way. For instance she baked most of the bread for the family, made jams and preserved vegetables, and in addition to knitting she spent a good deal of time with her Singer sewing-machine making clothes for us. Furthermore, she took care of the garden and tended the chickens. She had brought some impregnated eggs from Grasby, and her hens aroused attention as they were brown, and laid brown eggs, something that was unusual in Iceland, where all chicken were white, and laid white eggs.

The Christmas festivities were mainly conducted in the Icelandic way, although the English influence was noticeable. For instance we children, contrary to our Icelandic counterparts, believed in Santa Claus and hung up our stocking on Christmas eve before going to bed. Next morning we always found them filled with all sorts of goodies. The living room was always decorated with paper-streamers from the chandelier to the four corners, and as we became old enough we were allowed to help mother decorate the Christmas tree. The main Christmas dinner was on Christmas eve in accordance with Icelandic custom, and usually consisted of either roast pork or roasted fowl of some sort, but the dessert was always a typical

English Christmas pudding. Also Christmas crackers were on the table, which was not a custom in Iceland. After dinner came the ceremony that we children had been impatiently awaiting—opening the Christmas presents. The most exciting parcels were the ones from Uncle Ásgeir, as we called him. Mr. Ásgeir Sigurdsson was the British Consul and, more importantly, owned the largest toy shop in town. He and his wife were close friends of our parents, and every Christmas a large parcel containing precious toys arrived from them. Mother was an accomplished piano player, so we did a lot of singing and dancing around the Christmas tree in the Icelandic tradition, especially on Boxing Day when our playmates in the neighbour-hood were invited to a party.

Whilst we were still small we were not allowed to roam far outside the walled grounds of our home, but we certainly weren't isolated. It was considered such a safe place that the mothers of our playmates were happy to know they were there.

Often, during sunny summer days, our mother would load a picnic basket and take us to the seaside. Within walking distance from home were sandy beaches where we could splash about in the sea. In the autumn she took us berry picking in the hills outside town, and I remember these group excursions to the country in box-cars, as they were called. These were Ford Model T lorries with boxes, containing benches for passengers, strapped to the platform. As I grew older I was allowed to accompany mother when she went mushroom-picking. Our neighbours shook their heads over this odd behaviour of Mrs. Jonsson—didn't she know that mushrooms could be deadly poisonous.

When the weather was not suitable for outdoor activities we always found plenty to keep us busy indoors. I was very attached to my Meccano Set (a very instructive toy which, sadly, is no longer produced) building cranes, aeroplanes, cars and many other things. We dabbled in all sorts of handicrafts and played various games and we were happy with our lot. There was no television to distract us, and there can hardly be any doubt that children of that era were called upon to use their imagination to a far greater extent than the children of today—something which was surely only to the good.

I was eight years old when I returned home from my last stay with my grandparents in England, and started attending the Reykjavik Mid-town Elementary School. Most boys of my age at that time wore knee-length trousers, but their legs were covered with full length woollen stockings held up by garters or suspenders. In England I had become used to wearing knee-length socks and refused to wear stockings. Because of this 'English-ness' I became known as Steini Boy. Admittedly my mother managed to persuade me to wear stockings on the coldest of winter days, but I never liked them and bared my knees whenever I could. My knees rarely seemed to feel the cold, even though my toes might be freezing.

We 'west-enders' had to pass the town lake on our way to and from school, and rarely did we have dry feet when we got home, especially if there was ice on the lake. Ice-floe-skipping was much too tempting! We were not very old when we started venturing further and further afield in search of adventures. A popular pastime was a trip to the harbour where there was always hustle and bustle. It was very exciting to 'acquire' a rowing boat (usually without the owner's consent) and row out to the French and Faroese fishing schooners lying at anchor and scrounge biscuits. We would go fishing for saith and plaice off the many wooden jetties, for the sea in the harbour was then clean and crystal clear, not polluted with oil and rubbish as it is now, and the fish therefore edible. Naturally we used hand-lines for in those days we did not own fishing rods like most young lads seem to now-a-days. Probably our mothers were not excessively enchanted with having catches of small fish dumped on their kitchen tables, but so as not to hurt the sensitive souls of proud young providers they were persuaded to produce tasty dishes from these 'best fishes ever caught!'

There were many other favoured fishing places along the coast, and the fact that a certain amount of danger was sometimes involved in reaching them only made them all the more exciting. I am sure that if our mothers had at times seen what we were up to they would have swooned, but we always managed to get home safely, if not always dry.

On Sundays we usually went to YMCA meetings, not, I suspect, from any great religious awakening, but rather because the kindly old vicar who ran it read to us an exciting serial, and it was also fun singing 'Onward Christian Soldiers' and other good YMCA hymns at the top of our voices.

Naturally, as everywhere in the world where groups of young lads get together, we played a great deal of football. We also played a ball game that has some affinity to American baseball. As we became old enough most of us acquired bicycles on which we roamed far and wide. Around about the age of ten I joined the Boy Scouts and for the next few years I derived much pleasure and adventure from my association with that excellent organization.

I have tried to draw a brief sketch of the idyllic and carefree childhood life I led until the age of fourteen. But then my mother died and great changes took place in my life. The reader will most likely have perceived that during those first fourteen years my mother played a dominant part in my upbring-ing. Without doubt I was an unruly and high spirited lad that needed a firm hand, but at the same time a great deal of understanding, and she had both of these attributes. Although my father had many eminent qualities, the necessary insight for bringing up children successfully was not one of them, and it was not long before we clashed. I will not go into details, but it is sufficient to state that our relationship became very difficult, and when I was sixteen I eventually left home. This came about in the following way.

At the end of May 1937 I graduated from the Reykjavik Grammar School, and our graduation class decided to go on a two-day camping trip into the country. My father refused me permission to go on this trip—most likely due to my rather poor showing in the examinations—and I was naturally bitterly disappointed, but forced to accept his decision. In the early morning when my classmates gathered at the school to board the bus transporting them into the country I turned up, still wearing my slippers, to wish them Godspeed. The upshot was that after much persuasion from my school fellows I decided to throw filial obedience to the wind and boarded the bus. On return I confronted my very irate father, and our conversation went something like this:

'Son, if you are unable to obey me you have no place in this house.'

'In that case father, good-bye.'

I managed to obtain a summer job in the herring industry up north, and in the autumn my father informed me that I had been enlisted in the High School of Akureyri, the main town of northern Iceland, as this school had boarding facilities.

I liked Akureyri and the school life there very much, 'though I had never been much of a scholar. I was not sufficiently studious (or too lazy) to do my homework as conscientiously as I should, and somehow there always seemed so many more interesting things to do. But there was an atmosphere, or spirit, about the old college, which I liked. No doubt every school has its own special morale, but I felt there could be none to equal ours. Most of all, I loved the school's ski-hut *Útgardur* up in the mountains above the town, where I had spent many a happy weekend skiing with my school fellows.

At school, the world war that had just broken out was naturally one of the most discussed subjects. Who was going to win? We talked and argued about it for hours on end, each one producing 'facts' or 'statistics' to back up his ideas and convictions. The majority of my school-mates were convinced that the Germans would win the war. This was something I simply could not agree on, but I always found my arguments overwhelmed by the opposition's figures and facts—some true, but others invented by the very effective Nazi propaganda machine. My handicap was, of course, that I had no convincing facts to show how the Allies were to succeed in winning a war against the powerful German war machine. Germany was armed to the hilt, and had been for years, driven on by a maniac's lust for power and

world domination, whereas the British and French were pitifully unpre-
pared for war. I had only my resolute faith in the stamina of the British
people to back up my belief in their ultimate victory. Later, when in
England, I realised that their special quality of refusing to even entertain
the idea of defeat—and treating the idea as a joke—was the quality that
unfailingly carried them through.

Often, during these arguments, I felt annoyed with the British for not
having shown the strength that I felt they should have done. So far in this
war, they had only won a single major victory in battle—the *Graf Spee*
action. But even this my school-mates managed to belittle, pointing out
that seven British warships were needed to overpower one German
'pocket' battleship. 'The British with their self claimed sense of fair-play!'
they mocked.

The theme of their debates used to be something in the following
manner:

What chance had the obsolete Allied armies against the modern and
powerfully mechanised German army? Especially with the Soviets
practically on the side of the Nazis. The Siegfried Line was much more
modern and much stronger than the Maginot Line, and the Allies could
never hope to break through it. If they decided to wage a sitting war they
were doomed to lose in the end because of the German U-boats, which
would relentlessly sink all ships sailing for British and French ports. The
Allied blockade of Germany was laughable and practically useless as
Germany had so many routes, untouchable to the Allies, by which she
could import all her necessary commodities. Also, Hitler had declared that
Germany had built up huge food reserves—enough to last at least three
years. Sooner or later the Italians would enter the war, and, with their large
fleet and air force, could close the Mediterranean to the Allies. Perhaps the
British were hoping that America would fight on their side, but those hopes
were doomed to failure. If the Germans wished to, they could crush the
Allied air forces in no time and then wipe out every city in France and Great
Britain. As Hitler had said: 'There are no islands now.' The French had
practically no air force, and although the RAF was a little larger it would
only be a slight nuisance to the Luftwaffe at first, and then would be
completely knocked out of the sky.

These remarks about the RAF irritated me most of all. From an early age
I had always been interested in flying, and my ambition from childhood was
to become a pilot, though I knew it was a goal far beyond my means and
reach. Since the beginning of the war in 1939 I had taken a great interest in
the RAF's activities, and felt a personal triumph when it beat the German
Air Force in an engagement over the Forth Bridge during that winter. I had
secretly toyed with the idea of trying to join the RAF, preferably as a pilot,

but failing that, as an air-gunner, but the obstacles had seemed too many and too great. I had been discouraged after making enquiries at the British Consulate in Akureyri. The Consul had gently, but firmly, told me that I might as well give up the idea, as only British subjects could be accepted in the British fighting forces. Even the fact that my mother had been English would be of no avail.

Other emotions influencing my ambition were of the type that were not spoken, as they lay deep in my heart. England was my deceased mother's country. Three of her brothers had died fighting the Germans in the last war, and although Iceland was my home, having my love and loyalty, I could not help wanting to support my mother's country in any way I could, in its struggle for survival. Furthermore I was convinced that England's cause in this war was just as much Iceland's, and if England fell it would also mean the end of Iceland as a sovereign state.

Unavoidably other thoughts also crept in; thoughts arousing apprehension. Should the unlikely happen and I somehow found ways of joining the Royal Air Force, was I not taking a great and unnecessary risk? Wasn't it possible that I might be shot down and be killed? Oh, no—I tried to convince myself—I would naturally be a skilful pilot and defeat all adversaries in aerial battles. Of course the possibility existed that a shell from an anti-aircraft gun might hit my aircraft... But I brushed all such thoughts aside. The optimism of youth had the upper hand.

Some of my friends learned about my longing to join the RAF, and once, during a discussion about the merits of the various air forces, one of them burst out: 'Well, as you have such a high opinion of the mighty British Air Force, and you pretend you are so keen on joining it, why don't you have the courage of your convictions, and do so?'

That decided it! I just *had* to join the RAF!

There was no time to be wasted; I simply must go to Reykjavik and try to find some means of getting into the Air Force. I went to the headmaster and told him my decision. He tried unsuccessfully to point out what a terrible mistake I was making, but I was not to be moved. I was determined to find some way to make my dreams come true. I would go to the British Legation in Reykjavik and try to persuade the Minister to help me. Surely it would be to my advantage that I was half English.

My classmates and a few of the teachers threw me a good-bye party. They were sceptical about the wisdom of my decision but wished me Godspeed. As soon as I reached Reykjavik I visited the British Legation and asked for an interview with the Minister, Mr. John Bowering. He received me cordially but emphasized that he did not consider there was any possibility of my being accepted in the British Armed Forces. However, he promised to write and make enquiries to the appropriate authorities regarding my application. After a long delay the reply arrived, and it was in accordance with what the Minister had expected. Because of my nationality I was unacceptable to the RAF.

Now I was faced with what seemed to be an insurmountable obstacle, but I was more determined than ever to find some way out of the impasse. I considered the possibility of going to my grandmother in England, to make an attempt from that side. My grandfather had died but possibly some of my uncles or other relatives might be able to help me. I had, however, to admit to myself that this was not very probable. They were common folk who were not likely to have much sway with people in authority.

As I have already related, my father and I had not parted on the best of terms, but I now decided that I must swallow my pride and go to him for assistance. He had influential friends in England who might be able to help me. He, already aware of what I was up to, said he was not exactly overjoyed with it, but added that if I was firmly resolved to go through with it he would try to help me. He wrote to some of his friends in Britain and after a few weeks the results appeared in the aforementioned letter from Commander Hawkridge.

And now, in the black night I stood on the bridge of *Oli Garda* gazing into the darkness, letting my mind roam into the past, and thinking with excitement and not a little apprehension of our arrival at Fleetwood in three days time.

CHAPTER TWO

THE DREAM COMES TRUE

I   BANANAS AND GENERAL PEP

On the high tide of April 23rd we glided slowly into Fleetwood fishing docks. It was a grey morning with haze all around the horizon limiting visibility to only a mile or so. The shore had come into view as a thin, indistinct line, broken only by high factory chimneys and cranes. As we drew nearer I was surprised to see how flat the countryside was—not a hill in sight. How different it was from my own country. However, I did not pay a great deal of attention to this; I was too excited and impatient. Very soon my worries would begin again. I did not even know if I would be allowed ashore, but somehow I would have to contact Commander Hawkridge. But who would give me the necessary permission? The skipper was doubtful whether the ship would stay in port longer than 48 hours, and that gave me very little time to accomplish anything.

At about midday we tied to a wharf and I jumped ashore. At last I was back in England again. More than ten years had passed since I was there as an eight year old child. At least I had achieved this much!

I looked around me. We were in a small square-shaped dock containing many trawlers, and some of them, I noticed from the flags painted on their sides, were Icelandic. The dock was surrounded on three sides by large open sheds, or warehouses, in which the fish were stacked in boxes, and people were everywhere—women as well as men—all busily engaged in loading and stacking fish. There was quite a din going on from cranes, engines, lorries and men shouting to each other in English with a rather strange accent.

I strolled over to a nearby crane and stood watching the man working its various control levers. After a while, when there was a short pause in his activities, he looked at me and smiled.

'Off that trawler just in?' he shouted above the noise.

'Yes,' I shouted back.

'Bring in a good catch?'

'I don't really know. You see, I'm only a passenger.'

'Have you come to study, or something, then?' he asked. 'You seem to speak quite good English. Where did you learn it?'

It was a bit difficult to answer both questions at once, so I tackled the first one.

'I've come to join the Royal Air Force,' adding as an afterthought—'I hope.'

I could see that he looked surprised.

'Good for you, sonny, and the best of luck,' he shouted. 'My younger son is training in the Air Force. He is going to be a gunner in a bomber. The other boy is in the Navy. I haven't seen him since just before the war.'

His voice was full of pride.

'By the way,' he went on, 'have you heard the latest? They say that Chamberlain is sending Hitler a diver's suit for his birthday so that he can inspect his navy!' He laughed merrily, and I joined in.

Just then I noticed two men in uniform going on board the *Oli Garda*, together with another in plain clothes. Probably the customs, I thought, and decided I had better get on board again. I said good-bye and hurried back to my cabin.

The customs officers left after a little while, but the man in plain clothes stayed behind to talk to me. He turned out to be a police officer, and showed me his identity badge. He seemed a very charming fellow and I took a liking to him. He appeared greatly interested in my problem, and after having read my two letters, said that the first thing to do was to get in touch with Commander Hawkridge by telephone; he offered to take me to the nearest telephone booth and help me. I was of course very thankful for his kindness, as I would have found this a difficult task to do on my own. So we went ashore, and on the way to the telephone booth—a little way from the docks—I had an opportunity to see some of the town.

Somehow, everything seemed different from what I had expected, especially the fact that there were few signs of the country being at war. The shops were all open, and appeared to be well stocked with goods. The people seemed happy and showed no signs of being at war, and I saw very few men in uniform. I had no clear idea of what to expect, but it was certainly not this.

We passed a fruit stall displaying great quantities of big red apples, oranges, grapes, pears, plums and various other delicacies which we had rarely seen in Iceland during the recent days of depression. And there were bunches of bananas—I hadn't seen bananas for what seemed like years and years, and they were my favourite fruit. How I longed to dig my teeth into a nice big one, and then have another one to follow! I just could not resist the temptation to buy some, and shyly asked my policeman if he thought it was permissible.

'You see, I haven't tasted one for so long,' I added.

He grinned at me and said: 'By all means, sonny, here—let me get you some.'

When he handed me a large bunch of yellow bananas and I asked him how much they cost, he just told me not to mention it. 'And don't argue with a policeman,' he laughingly added. I thanked him, and a few minutes later we were at the telephone booth.

I waited while my escort got through to Commander Hawkridge's office in Hull, and after a few moments he handed me the telephone receiver, saying 'OK, you're through, lad.'

I eagerly grasped the receiver, and asked: 'Is Commander Hawkridge there, please?'

A woman's voice answered, 'No, I am afraid he is away in the country at the moment. I am his secretary, can I help you?'

When I heard this my heart skipped a few beats, and I had a feeling of despair. This was the worst that could happen! The Commander away— and in less than 48 hours the trawler would be setting off for Iceland again, probably taking me with it.

'I am Thorsteinn Jonsson, from Iceland,' I stammered. 'It is very urgent that I get in touch with Commander Hawkridge at once. How soon do you expect him back?'

'Oh, good afternoon, Mr. Jonsson. The Commander has spoken to me about you. He has been expecting you, but he had to go away for two days on important business. I'll try my best to get in touch with him for you, and let him know of your arrival. What is your address now?'

'Oh yes, will you please.' I felt a little more optimistic now. 'You see, my ship is leaving...'. Here the policeman tapped my shoulder and shook a warning finger at me. Of course one was not allowed to talk about ship departures. 'I have very little time, so would you please try your best. My address is... Oh, just a minute, please.'

The policeman slipped me a note of paper, and whispered, 'Use this address.' It was that of the Fleetwood Police Station.

The secretary assured me that she would do all she could, and told me not to worry and just to wait until I heard from her again.

That was not going to be easy without worrying. However, it seemed all I could do, so I resigned myself to it. My policeman took me back to the ship, and said he would call me again next day to see how I was getting on. He told me I would be allowed ashore with the seamen while the ship was in port, and to keep my passport with me wherever I went.

That afternoon I went with some of the ship's crew to do some shopping, as there were so many things they could buy here that were not available in Iceland. In the evening some of the sailors took me to Blackpool, where I had my first introduction to the country's night life. I was much impressed by the huge and beautifully decorated dance-halls, such as the Winter Garden and the Tower, with their attractive, and well-supplied bars, where one could buy practically any drink that came to mind for what seemed like a very reasonable price. Amazingly enough, people did not seem to get drunk in spite of so much liquor being available. What a contrast this was to the much restricted sale of alcohol at home, leading to clandestine boot-legging and illegal sales, and causing a good deal of drunkenness.

During our last day at sea I had noticed that the seamen ate a good deal of salted food, such as salted fish and salted meat. This, they had jokingly explained, was to work up a good thirst for the excellent beer they were about to drink in England. In those days such beer was not to be had in Iceland. They had talked a lot about the beer, and I was looking forward to tasting it, but now, when at last I did, I was disappointed—it tasted too bitter for me.

One of my companions then suggested that I try a 'General Pep', so I boldly went to the bar and asked for it. The barmaid looked at me rather quizzically and said, 'What was that?'

'One General Pep, please,' I repeated, and became aware that I was blushing. People standing around the bar were looking at me with grins on their faces, and it made me a little uncomfortable.

'General Pep?' the barmaid repeated after me. 'Never heard of it. What sort of a drink is that?'

This was an embarrassing situation—I had no idea what sort of a drink it was. I gaped and looked frantically towards my sailor friend, who fortunately saw I was having troubles, and came to my rescue.

'He wants shin-al-pep,' he said.

'Oh, I know what you mean,' replied the barmaid smilingly. 'You want a gin-and-peppermint?'

'Thass right. A shinna pep!' answered my companion triumphantly. Everyone around laughed merrily at his foreign accent, and I felt greatly relieved. This 'General Pep' was the very first drink I bought in England, but the good 'General' did not remain very long at the top of my popularity list. It was not long before plain 'Mr. Beer' dislodged him, and has occupied the top seat ever since. No doubt a whole Amazon river of beer has passed through my digestive tracts since then.

On the way back to the trawler that night I had my first taste of the black-out. The six of us left the 'Winter Garden' dance hall together, but as soon as we entered the street we lost each other in the pitch blackness. Rain was pouring down, and it was so dark that I could not see my own extended hand, and I immediately lost all sense of direction. The only light to be seen was the occasional glow of a cigarette, and sometimes a much-dimmed flashlight would flick on for a second. And yet people seemed to be pushing by me in the street as if they had been accustomed to this darkness all their life.

After much shouting we managed to get together again, for which I was very thankful, as I had absolutely no idea of my whereabouts. Most of the sailors, however, had been here a few times before, and after a while they obtained taxies to take us back to the docks. I felt uneasy all the way as the taxi seemed to have practically no headlights, and it is still a mystery to me how the driver managed to find his way there without running into anything. I was not sorry when, at last, we arrived safely on board the *Oli Garda*.

The next day I spent wandering around Fleetwood, with frequent visits to the police station to see if any news had come from Commander Hawkridge. But no word came, and I grew more and more worried.

The last day of the ship's stay in port arrived. It was due to sail in the afternoon, and if no message came from Commander Hawkridge, I would have to leave with it. As the morning went by, I became more and more restless, and started seriously contemplating the possibility of sneaking ashore and letting the ship go without me. I could then try to make my way to Commander Hawkridge in Hull. But there were a lot of difficulties associated with this. I only had about £9 in English money which would have to last me until I found the Commander. Also, I was very vague about travelling in this country. I might be asked to show some form of identity card before being allowed to buy a ticket for the railway, and then the game would be up. No, there was no doubt that the police would soon find me, and then all sorts of awkward and unpleasant things could happen. I might even be accused of being a spy! It was just the sort of thing a spy would do—sneak ashore unobserved, and hide. Even if nothing worse happened than being caught and sent back to Iceland on the next trawler, it would probably ruin any further attempts to join the RAF.

But then I also thought of the humiliation of returning to Iceland on the same ship, like a beaten dog with his tail between his legs. The realization that I would have to endure the jokes and taunts of my former school-fellows and acquaintances made me decide that whatever happened I would not go back on the *Oli Garda*.

So, with my mind firmly made up, I set about planning my escape from the ship.

There were a lot of people around—both on board and on the dock—and it would have been practically impossible to get my luggage ashore unobserved. I therefore decided to leave it behind, and take with me only what I could put in my pockets. I would wear my mackintosh, and could hide quite a lot of things underneath it.

There were just two more hours until the ship was due to sail, and my luggage was on deck waiting to be taken ashore. I decided that I had better take it down to the cabin again to remove the things I would need. I would then write a note, asking one of the sailors to deliver the remainder to my home on their return to Iceland.

On second thoughts, however, I decided to wait a little longer, just to see if anything would happen. I walked impatiently around the deck, and once or twice went ashore and wandered round the docks so that people got used to seeing me there. This would arouse less suspicion when I eventually left the ship for good. The sailors jokingly asked me if I was beginning to look forward to the return voyage, but most of them showed me sympathy and understood my anxieties. I made one more dash up to the police station, but there was still no news for me there. I kept looking at my watch and time seemed to be flying. On arriving back on board, there was only about half an hour left before sailing, so I took my luggage down to the cabin and started unpacking.

Just then, the captain's voice was heard from above:

'Thorsteinn, are you there?'

'Yes, I'm here,' I replied, hurriedly emptying my stuffed pockets back into the suitcase.

'There is someone here to see you.' I could hear the skipper coming down the companionway, followed by someone else. They entered the cabin, and the stranger, who was wearing a uniform similar to a customs officer, extended me a hand and said: 'Ah, Mr. Jonsson—pleased to meet you. I'm an Immigration Officer, and I have come to give you a permit to enter the United Kingdom. I hear you want to join the RAF.'

I could hardly believe my ears. At last! At last the long awaited moment had arrived. I was to be allowed to go ashore and stay there. I could go to see Commander Hawkridge. And then the RAF, and then... Oh, life was wonderful!

We sat down at the table and the Immigration Officer examined my passport and letters. He then produced a piece of paper, stamped and signed, which gave me permission to remain in the United Kingdom for three months. When I saw this I was a little dismayed—only three months?? The officer told me not to worry about that, and explained that by this time I would probably be in the RAF, or if not, I could apply for an extention of the permit.

I collected my belongings and took them on deck again. Then I went round and said good-bye to my shipmates, who all seemed glad for my sake, and wished me the best of luck, although one or two of them said they still thought I was being a fool. After all the cheerful farewells, I was ready to go, and the ship was ready to cast off. I stood on the dockside with the Immigration Officer, watching her pass slowly through the dock gates—the last bit of Iceland I might see for a long time.

My new escort took me to the police station, where I had to register as an alien. During my frequent visits in the last few days I had got to know the men there quite well. They were a hearty, good-natured bunch, and appeared very pleased at my good news. They told me, however, that as an alien I would have to report to the police every day, morning and night, and it would be necessary to get permission to travel from one place to another. They suggested that my best plan would be to stay in Fleetwood that night, and in the morning they would arrange for me to travel to Hull and see Commander Hawkridge. Having kindly gone to the trouble of booking me a hotel room for the night, they sent a constable along with me to show me the way and help to carry my two suitcases.

I was feeling extremely happy and joyful. Everyone was so kind and helpful to me. Even at the hotel they seemed to treat me as a guest of honour, and in the bar that evening everybody wanted to buy me a drink. When I finally went to bed that night I had no doubt had a drink too many, but what did it matter . . . My dreams were coming true and everything was going to be fine now.

Next morning, arriving at the police station at about nine o'clock, I found a letter from Commander Hawkridge awaiting me, in which he welcomed me to England, and explained that as soon as he got my message he had contacted the Immigration authorities to secure an entry visa for me. He suggested the train I should catch to Hull, and said there would be someone there to meet me.

The police once more gallantly offered their help, and a constable accompanied me to the railway station to assist me in getting the right ticket and train. I remember thinking that I must look like a criminal with a policeman trailing around with me wherever I went. After he had got my ticket, and told me where to catch the train when it came in, I tried to give him two shillings for his trouble, but he wouldn't hear of this. He told me that his younger son was in the RAF and it gave him great pleasure to assist any of the 'boys' whenever he could. He seemed sure I would be accepted by the RAF, and already regarded me as one of the 'boys', which gave me a pleasant feeling of assurance.

True to his word, Commander Hawkridge sent someone to meet me at Hull. I stood on the platform until it was nearly empty, when an elderly man approached me and asked if I were Mr. Jonsson from Iceland, and when I affirmed this, he said that the car was waiting outside the station. It struck me how smoothly everything was going; if this continued all would be well.

Commander Hawkridge's home was in a little town, or village, called Hessle, a few miles outside Hull. It was a large house surrounded by lawns, flower beds and tall trees. The Commander and Mrs Hawkridge received me warmly, and immediately made me feel completely at home. A more charming and warm-hearted couple would be hard to find. That evening I had a long chat with the Commander, and he inspired me with great faith in the future. I was determined to succeed, if only to thank him for his kindness and help.

II 'THIRSTY' AT THE RECRUITING CENTRE

Next morning after a good breakfast, I drove with Commander Hawkridge into Hull. This was to be the great day, the day I had been looking forward to so long, the day that had seemed so unattainable. We were going along to the Recruiting Centre to apply for my entry into the RAF. The day was warm and sunny, but I paid little attention to the weather—I was too excited. What if I were turned down? . . . but I tried not to think of that. And yet, the possibility kept lurking in my mind. Perhaps my English was not good enough . . . or my mathematics were not up to standard, or maybe . . . maybe . . . oh, so many thoughts crept into my mind, and I was beginning to convince myself that I would never pass and should have stayed at home. But then I recalled the Commander's faith in me and his words of encouragement and my confidence returned.

At last we arrived at the Recruiting Centre. The walls outside, and in the entrance hall, were covered with brightly coloured posters depicting soldiers, sailors, airmen, tanks, warships and aeroplanes, and bearing slogans such as 'Join up now', 'Your country needs you', 'Fly with the RAF', etc.

Inside, Commander Hawkridge gave his name to an attendant and asked for a Squadron Leader Rutherford. The attendant went away, but returned almost immediately, saying 'Squadron Leader Rutherford is ready to see you, Sir'.

We were shown into a medium-sized office, and there, rising from a desk to greet us was a cheerful looking young man wearing the uniform of an RAF officer. I noticed he had quite a few rings on his sleeves, although at that time I had no knowledge of the various RAF ranks.

'How do you do, Commander Hawkridge. So this is our friend from

Iceland.' He smiled and shook our hands. 'Please take a seat.'

I began to feel more at ease. Maybe this was not going to be so terrible after all. The Commander and Mr. Rutherford chatted for a while, and then Mr. Rutherford turned to me.

'So, you want to fly, do you? Well, we'll soon make a flier out of you, young man. You're just the type of fellow we're looking for—young, fit and enthusiastic. Of course you will have to pass some severe medical and educational tests, but the Commander here has every confidence in you. Here is a form I want you to fill in and hand to the sergeant that sits at the table in the waiting room. Then, I'm afraid, you'll just have to sit back and wait until you are called upon for your examinations, which could be any time from six weeks to three months. You see, the training schools are all full up at present.'

The form he gave me asked questions about my age, nationality, place of birth, education and religion, and it warned me that that once I had entered the service I would be subject to Air Force law and discipline, and liable to be sent for duty to any part of the world. Mr. Rutherford suggested that I fill in the form straightaway to be handed in before leaving, and after a short time I had answered all the questions. He looked it over and said it was alright, so I took it out into the waiting room.

This was a large oblong room, with a table at one end where the sergeant was sitting. All around the other walls were chairs on which sat civilian-clad men, obviously awaiting their turn to see the recruiting officer.

The sergeant took my form and glanced over it.

'Hmm—what's this? Icelandic?' He looked up at me to see what kind of a creature I was. 'That's certainly unusual.'

He asked me how my name was pronounced, and I spent the next few minutes trying to explain how the name Thorsteinn was pronounced, but with very limited results. (This was something I was destined to repeat frequently in the coming years.) Usually the result sounded like 'Thirsty', or something equally childish—maybe the description was not so far out?— so shortly after entering the service I took to using my second Christian name Elton. Later someone started calling me Tony (like Anton becomes Tony), and that name has stuck with me amongst English-speaking friends ever since.

This was all that was required of me at the recruiting centre, and the Commander and I left and drove back to Hessle. I was feeling in high spirits, now that the first part was over and I was actually enrolled on the waiting list to join the RAF. During the interim period I intended to visit my maternal grandmother in Lincolnshire, and also Mr. John Mitchell, a friend of my father who lived near Cambridge. Mr Mitchell had travelled widely in Iceland, and I remember one time when I was eight years old travelling with him on horse-back. He was one of the group of people who had made it possible for me to join the RAF, and he had been kind enough to invite me to come and stay with him.

In those early days in England quite a few amusing incidents occured due to my incomplete knowledge of the language and customs. For instance, that first evening the Commander had invited some people to his home to meet me. One guest—the commander's son-in-law—was introduced to me as Mr. John England. In Iceland it was unheard-of for a person to possess the name of his country, so I assumed that this was a joke, and brightly replied, 'Oh, how do you do, Mr. England. I am Mr. Thorsteinn Iceland.' This caused a roar of laughter from everyone, and I was at a loss to know whether I had been funny, or merely rude. However when the Commander explained to me that the name really was England, I apologised, probably red in the face with embarrassment, but in the friendly and informal atmosphere the incident was soon passed over.

I also recall another funny case when I was describing to a venerable elder lady, sitting next to me at a dinner table, the restrictions I came under as an alien. I told her that I had to report to the police morning and night, and that I was not allowed to use a bicycle or private car, only public conveniences, and I could not understand why she gave me such a funny look.

Two months passed before the postman brought my calling-up papers. The first two weeks I spent at Hessle, living with Mr and Mrs England. Commander Hawkridge had suggested this, as he and his wife were away a good deal of the time, and he also thought that as his daughter and son-in-law were younger, they would probably be better company for me. I enjoyed myself wandering around the neighbouring countryside, and furthermore my hosts owned horses and took me riding with them. Although I had associated with the ponies of Iceland a good deal, I was a bit overawed the first time I mounted one of these enormous beasts. However, they were well trained horses, and I quickly became friends with them. I also enjoyed exploring Hull and the harbour, as so much of what I viewed was novel to me. However, my inexperience and lack of worldliness soon became apparent. I once went into a barbershop for a haircut, and by the time I escaped out again I had, in addition to the haircut, received a manicure and had my hair washed. I had also been persuaded to buy a bottle of dandruff-medicine, a hair-comb and a packet of condoms!

One day, Mrs. Hawkridge drove me to visit my grandmother in the little village of Grasby in Lincolnshire. I had not been there since I was an eight-year-old lad, but memories of the place, and the delightful days I had spent there, quickly awoke within me. The reunion with my grandmother was joyous, and it was decided that I should spend some of the waiting period with her.

The following three weeks I spent with Mr. Mitchell at Bourne, a charming little place near Cambridge. The weather was glorious all the time, and I wandered along country lanes and fields for miles around, thoroughly enjoying life, but at the same time I started to become impatient —when would the call come? Occasionally I tried to brush up on my maths and trigonometry, but in the heat of those summer days I soon got tired of sitting over stuffy books. I enjoyed great hospitality from Mr. Mitchell, an extremely kind and good-hearted man. He was a widower, and lived with his sister in a large house surrounded by a beautiful garden. He was a widely-travelled man, and it was very interesting to hear him speak of his experiences. He was a great scholar and had been a professor at Cambridge University, but was now retired and his main hobby was his garden, which was faultlessly kept and contained a great variety of flowers, fruits and vegetables. Sometimes he drove me to Cambridge and conducted me around the magnificent old college buildings.

By now critical events were taking place in the outside world. The 'phony war' was over, and Hitler was busy gobbling up most of the continent of Europe, and Britain had landed troops in Iceland. France had capitulated and Britain now stood alone against the might of Nazi Germany. There were many indications that a German invasion was expected; poles were erected in fields to prevent aircraft from landing, all roadsigns were removed and the Home Guard, which consisted mainly of elderly citizens and young lads, trained incessantly, even though their weapons were mainly obsolete old rifles, shotguns and even broomhandles!

I was staying with my grandmother when the long-awaited and fateful summons arrived. The letter informed me that my application for entry into the Royal Air Force had been taken into consideration, and I was requested to appear at the Hull Recruiting Centre on Wednesday, the 26th of June 1940.

III QUIIIIIIICK MARCH!

Nine o'clock on Wednesday morning found me standing in a queue with 50 other hopefuls, at the Recruiting Centre in Hull. They were a varied assortment of men aged between 18 and 25, embracing, it appeared, all types of professions. Like me they were all volunteers, and were talking and joking about the service life they were about to enter. Some of the older men had served in the last war and were now busily engaged in advising the younger ones on how to treat such exalted beings as corporals, sergeants and even sergeant-majors. I rather doubted that this advice was to be taken seriously, but it was all very amusing to listen to.

After a little while the sergeant entered the waiting room, followed by an airman carrying a bundle of papers.

'Quiet, please—no talking there!' rapped out the sergeant, and immediately there was silence.

'You are now all about to be sent to Padgate, a receiving centre in the Midlands, where you will have your medicals and entry exams. Some of you will not be required for immediate service, but those of you who are will be given a few days leave to settle your private affairs. When I call out your names, you will each come up to this table and receive your orders, and then wait outside where you will be collected and taken by buses to the railway station. Now let's see, I need one of you to be in charge of the party ... you'll do, mister,' and he picked out one of the older men; one attired in the conventional garb of a City clerk—black jacket and pin-striped trousers, wearing a bowler hat. I found it difficult to imagine this man wearing the Air Force uniform.

'Your job,' the sergeant continued, 'will be to see that everyone gets on the train and that you all reach your destination together. I'll give you your instructions and travelling warrants when I've dealt with the rest of them.'

He called out our names, and one by one we filed to the table to collect a sealed envelope, which was to be handed in when we arrived at Padgate. These envelopes caused many comments—witty and otherwise—from their recipients ... 'Blimey, the death warrant!' 'My packet of trouble!' and so on.

When he came to one envelope the sergeant looked up and said grinning: 'Here's this blinking funny name again! Where's the Icelander?', and I had to step up to the table and once again endeavour to explain the pronunciation of my name, much to the amusement of the others.

The journey to Padgate went without a hitch, and we arrived there in the afternoon. We had been served with a meal at a railway station, and we were all in good spirits. My first impressions of Padgate were a mixture of admiration and awe—admiration for the size and the neatness of the place, and awe at the endless columns of men, both in uniform and civilian clothes, marching back and forth, and the hustle and bustle everywhere. As far as the eye could see there were rows and rows of wooden barrack huts, each surrounded by its own well-kept flower-bed, with the monotony of the rows broken by large asphalt parade grounds and administrative buildings, canteens and cook-houses.

Immediately on our arrival we were put in the charge of a tough, red-headed sergeant, who wasted no time in making it known that his orders were to be obeyed without complaint. He lined us up in columns, three deep, and called out our names, and once again I had to listen to my name being made into a source of amusement. By now I was beginning to realize that this would continue to happen, and resigned myself to it.

We were then marched off, and we must have appeared a comical sight to any onlooker—all shapes and sizes, all wearing different types of clothes and hats and carrying an odd assortment of baggage. When the sergeant shouted the order 'Quii..ck March' it seemed that everyone started off on a different foot, and at a different time, and the next few minutes were spent in trying to get into step. Naturally, each thought his neighbour was out of step and not himself. My heels suffered quite a few kicks, and so did those of the poor fellow in front of me—so much so that one of his shoes came right off, causing further disorder in our ranks while he recovered it. At last, aided by a good deal of exasperated bellowing from the sergeant, some semblance of order was restored. This chaos was to be repeated frequently during the next couple of days, and we discovered that the corporals and sergeants in charge of us commanded large and colourful vocabularies to describe the wretchedness of civilians and greenhorns.

After a few minutes of this 'marching' we arrived at a large marquee, around which scores of civilian-clad men were sitting and lying on the grass. Here we were to wait until our names were called, and then enter the marquee with our envelopes. Obviously there was going to be a long wait while the earlier arrivals were dealt with, but eventually—about two hours later—our turn came.

When my name was called I entered the tent without concern, as I had found from my companions before me that all that was required of us was to deliver the envelope and answer a few questions about previous occupation, religion, etc. After that I was told, that although I was still a civilian, it would be best for all concerned if I obeyed, without delay, any orders and instructions issued by the officers and NCOs of the camp. I promised to be a good boy!

These formalities over, we were marched to the mess—a huge one-storey building—for our evening meal. There I saw to my dismay a 200-yard long queue of hungry men waiting to be fed, but fortunately however, it was fast-moving, and twenty minutes later I was settled down to a good meal of salad, bread and butter, jam and pudding. After satisfying our appetites we were lined up again and marched to a large colony of bell-tents, which were to be our night quarters. We were shown the ablutions in a nearby hut, and then told we could spend the rest of the evening as we pleased.

There was a choice of the station cinema or one of the large canteens for our evening's relaxation, and I chose the latter. It was a long hall, with some dining tables at one end, as meals could be bought there in the evenings. Centrally there were three counters—one for serving meals, one for chocolates, tobacco, soap and other such commodities, and the third for beer and soft drinks. At the far end of the hall were situated some chairs and tables for those who were drinking, and also a piano which someone was playing, and a group of men standing around it singing.

That evening in my tent I summed up the impressions of my first day in the RAF—or rather RAF surroundings, as I was still a civilian. So far it had not been too difficult, except that the queues, and all the hanging around waiting, had been rather depressing. However, this was only to be expected when one considered that hundreds—or rather thousands—of civilians came here every day to be turned into budding airmen. A tremendous amount of organising must be necessary to accomplish this.

IV   SIXTEEN TIMES EIGHTY-FIVE

Next morning after breakfast we faced our moment of destiny. We were taken to a large building where the selection board was housed. This board consisted of a group of officers who were to evaluate each applicant's educational standard, intelligence, ability and temperament, and decide in which branch of the Royal Air Force he would best qualify to serve his Majesty. Following that we would be thoroughly examined from top to toe by an army of doctors to decide if we were physically fit for such service.

We sat down on chairs and benches in a large hall, and now a nerve racking wait commenced. The men that were about to interrogate me had my future in their hands and could decide whether my dreams of becoming a pilot became true or not. What was this darned selection board like? I turned this over in my mind and envisaged a number of stern-looking senior officers sitting on a dais in a semicircle above me, staring at me with disapproval for showing lack of knowledge and hesitation when trying to answer their questions. Then, when they had reduced me to a total nervous wreck, they would have a little discussion between themselves before the director, a large bald-headed man with large horn-rimmed glasses, would pass me a slip of paper, which I would hardly dare to look at. It would be so terribly embarrassing to end up in some lowly job on the ground after having told everyone back home in Iceland that I was going to become a pilot. Now it was too late to be sorry, but I was beginning to regret that I had not spent more time revising trigonometry. Or geography; I wasn't very strong in that department. Or...

The names of my fellow sufferers were called up one after the other, and the person addressed would disappear through a door in the wall facing us. He would remain in there for ten minutes or longer, but to the rest of us waiting it seemed like an eternity. When he eventually re-emerged he would hold a slip of paper in his hand and his face would either show joy or dejection. We looked at him and waited for him to tell us what position he had been given. Some, looking pleased, would say: 'pilot', but it was much more common to see a look of disappointment and hear the words 'gunner', 'radio-operator', 'mechanic' or one or other of the many ground trades which form a part of an air force. Then the person in question would disappear down a long corridor that led to the medical department.

While sitting there waiting we let our eyes wander or stared at the ceiling, each one deep in his own thoughts. Some tried to start conversations but they quickly petered out, and silence remained. This was much more of a strain than sitting for school exams at home, although they could at times test one's nerves. It was obvious that many of my companions were just as nervous as I was, which was not surprising, as the majority wanted to become pilots, but if the rejection rate amongst those who had been ahead of us was anything to go by, the prospects of reaching that goal were not very great. I was beginning to convince myself that the situation was hopeless... but? Hadn't Mr. Rutherford said that I was just the sort of character they were looking for: young and enthusiastic? Could it be that I might be considered too young? No, of course not—the limit was eighteen and within four months I would be nineteen. And I certainly did not lack enthusiasm. On the physical side I should have no worries. I was over medium height, in good form, had good eyesight and excellent health. No, there was nothing to worry about in that department. And yet...? I had heard stories about candidates having to blow a column of quicksilver in a tube up to a certain height, and to keep it there for a whole minute, while measurements were made of their heart-beat and blood-pressure. Perhaps I had been smoking too much lately. Also there was supposed to be some sort of a balance test when one was blind-folded and made to stand on one foot for a certain length of time. Another test reputedly consisted of repeating words that were whispered some distance away, and owing to my insufficient knowledge of English I might misunderstand the words and give the wrong replies. And what if this also caused me problems in front of the selection board?

Now my imagination was running wild, and that would never do. I therefore started talking to the fellow by my side. We had chatted together before, and I rather liked him. As it turned out we were to become roommates and great pals during the next six months. His name was Ronnie Batten and he came from Scotland. Like me, he had hopes of becoming a pilot, and we began comparing our knowledge of the subjects in which we were likely to be questioned. To my dismay I discovered how many concepts and technical phrases were missing from my knowledge of English.

At last my name was called. I jumped up and walked to the door, feeling sure that everyone could see I was trembling. When I entered the room I was surprised to see how different it was from what I had imagined. It was not a hall, but just a rather small room, furnished with two tables—one at each end—and a few chairs. Sitting at one of the tables was an airman shuffling some papers. At the other sat two officers, one of them an elderly and kindly looking gentleman with many rings on his uniform sleeve, and a younger one who was obviously of lower rank. So this was the terrifying selection board that I had dreaded so much.

As I stood hesitating in the doorway the elder officer looked up from some papers he was studying, smiled to me and said: 'Please come in Mr. Jonsson and take a seat.' He pointed to a chair in front of his table, and I was glad to sit down, as I was afraid that he might see how hard I was shaking and immediately judge me to be too much of a nervous type to become a pilot.

I tried to assume an air of nonchalance while the officers studied papers, which I could see comprised the various forms I had filled in, but I was sure that the drumbeat within my chest could be heard by all.

After a little while, the senior officer looked up again.

'Well, Mr. Jonsson, I see that you come from Iceland, and you wish to become a pilot in our Air Force.' His kindly face and friendly way of speaking immediately put me more at ease. 'Are there many Icelanders coming across to join our Forces?'

'No, I—I don't think so,' I half stammered. 'You see, although some might want to, the British authorities make it too difficult for them.'

'Oh, is that so. How did you manage it then?'

'Well, it was only through the help of some of my father's friends in this country—sir.' The word 'sir' I added rather tentatively, as I was not accustomed to this mode of address, there being no equivalent to it in my own country.

'I see. Very interesting. What is your father's occupation?'

'He is a bookseller and official translator in Iceland, sir. My mother was English, but she died four years ago,' I added.

'So that accounts for your command of the English language. Will you tell us something of your educational system in Iceland. What sort of schools do you have there?'

I tried to explain this as best I could, and told him about the schools I had been to, and also about our University. He took a great interest in all this, asking me many questions about our schools and praising our system. I felt as if I were speaking to a kindly old teacher, and my nervousness was rapidly vanishing under his reassuring manner.

'And now we are going to ask you some questions on general knowledge,' he said. 'Do you speak any languages other than English and Icelandic?'

'Yes, I speak Danish fairly well, and understand Norwegian and Swedish well enough to get along, and also a little German.' I had just started French when I left college to come here. I felt quite proud of being able to reel off all this linguistic ability, although admittedly my command of these languages was not quite as firm as I may have insinuated. I noticed that both officers were making notes on pads, but I couldn't see what they were writing.

'Quite good. Now, how far have you reached in mathematics? Have you studied Trigonometry?'

On my affirmative, he asked me some fairly simple questions about tangents, sines and cosines, which I answered without much trouble. This was followed by an algebra problem to work out with paper and pencil, and also some fairly complicated fractions and logarithms. These I managed to complete after one or two small mistakes, due more to hurrying too much, rather than ignorance. I was then asked the square roots and powers of various figures, and given a small problem to solve.

'Can you calculate mentally what 16 times 85 is?', the officer asked suddenly. After a few hurried mental exercises I announced triumphantly: 'One thousand, three hundred and sixty, sir!'

'Quite right. Now, can you tell me what time it would be in Singapore if it were eight a.m. in London? The longitude of Singapore is 105 degrees east.'

I thought for a moment, and then replied: 'Three p.m., sir.'

'Yes, and how do you arrive at that conclusion?'

I explained that for every 15 degrees of longitude east from Greenwich one hour was added. He appeared satisfied with this, and next asked me what countries touched the Mediterranean. I took a mental voyage around the Med, starting at Gibraltar and named the countries as I sailed by them, and I managed to do this without stranding.

This had been quite easy so far—if only it could continue.

I was given a few more geographical questions, and, with the exception of one, managed to answer them all. The officer then asked me to what extent I had studied chemistry and physics, but did not question me on these subjects. After inquiring what sports and games I played, the two officers compared their note-pads, and the senior took a piece of paper and wrote something on it.

'Well, Mr. Jonsson, that is all. Will you please take this along the passage to the left where you go for your medical, and give it to the orderly sitting at the table there.' Then he smiled and added: 'The best of luck.'

I hardly dared to look at the piece of paper he handed me. But when I did, the words: 'Pilot/Observer', seemed to jump up at me and I let out my breath in a sigh of relief, feeling strangely weak at the knees. I had drawn the top prize in the lottery. I held in my hands the passport to my dreamed-of future. I would become a pilot!

Then suddenly it seemed as if a cloud had passed before the sun. The words 'Pilot/Observer' stared me in the face. What was the significance of the word 'Observer'? Did it mean that I might be trained as an observer—which in the modern RAF meant navigator—instead of training as a pilot? Perhaps they already had too many pilots, and I would have to become an observer. But I didn't want that. I would much rather be a gunner if I couldn't be a pilot.

'Will I... does this mean that I may be trained as an observer and not a pilot?' I stammered.

The officers grinned. 'No, it only means that you are suitable to be trained as both,' said the senior of the two. 'Primarily you will be considered as a pilot under training, but should you for some reason fail in your flying, you could be trained as an observer.'

'Oh, I see!' I exclaimed, greatly relieved. With the knowledge that one day I would fly, I walked out of the room with my head held high.

The medical examination proved to be fully as severe as the rumours had predicted. In spite of having spent much time practising, I lost my balance at the first attempt, and feared that I had failed the test. However, the doctor just grinned and told me to try again. Apart from this, all went well. At the end of it, the chief medical officer looked up from his desk and said: 'There's nothing wrong with you, lad. You may get dressed.'

V   SHURRUP THERE!

Later that afternoon we were told that the training schools were full up, and given the choice of returning to civil life pending recall, or joining up immediately and serving as General Duty hands until the schools were ready to take us. Having no other occupation to return to, I chose the latter, and was pleased to find that my newly-made acquaintance, Ronnie Batten, did the same.

Those of us who opted for immediate service were taken along to a hall to be sworn into the Air Force. There, an officer lectured us on discipline, and the rules and regulations of service life, and emphasised that as soon as we had taken the oath we would be subject to military laws, and warned us of the various punishments for breaking these laws—the greatest crimes being treason and desertion, both punishable by death. We were then each given a Bible to hold whilst we repeated, after a padre, the oath of allegiance, swearing to serve His Majesty and his government faithfully during the present emergency, and to obey unquestioningly those of superior rank to ourselves.

I was no longer a free man. No longer free to go as I pleased or do as I pleased—now I had to do as I was told. I was no longer Mr. Jonsson, but just a name and number and bore the rank of AC2 (Aircraftman 2nd class), the lowest rank in the Air Force.

Next we were taken to the stores to draw our uniforms and equipment, which consisted of a complete set of clothing from forage-cap and overcoat to boots, two sets of underwear and shirts, a gas mask. Our quarters were changed from tents to barracks—long, one-roomed huts, with thirty of us in each hut. Our beds were hard, and a lot of good-natured grumbling went on during that first night, but we all survived, and next morning were ready to start our new life.

And now began a relentless and rather monotonous period of training which was meant to teach us discipline and military bearing, and improve our physical fitness. We were driven out of bed every morning at 6.30, by merciless corporals, to make the beds and clean out the hut. Everything had to be spotlessly clean—not a speck of dust was allowed to be seen any-where. The beds had to be exactly placed and lined up in neat rows, with all the blankets folded in the same way, our kit laid out in the regulation manner on the shelves above, and the floor swept and polished so thoroughly that it resembled a mirror.

After breakfast at 7.30 the day of hard work began—physical training, drill, lectures and sports, broken by an interval of an hour and a half for lunch. After five we were free to do as we pleased within the camp, but a good deal of our spare time was spent on 'housework', such as polishing uniform buttons and the brass on our webbing equipment, shining shoes, darning socks, and generally keeping one's kit in order for the frequent inspections.

This 'breaking in' period is the most trying part of every serviceman's career—the change from the comforts of civilian life to the rigorous and intensified initial military training. Great emphasis was placed on PT and foot-drill, and the first two days left us complete physical wrecks—our bodies ached so much that we could hardly move. One of my roommates, lying exhausted on his bed after the second day's work, summed up our state perfectly by exclaiming: 'I feel exactly like a rusty old car must feel. I can almost hear my joints squeak when I muster up enough energy to move. I guess nothing short of a good soaking in warm oil will ever loosen me up again.'

However, the oil proved unnecessary. Within a week we were feeling fitter than ever before.

Ronnie Batten and I stayed together as much as possible, and a trio was made by Ian MacLean—another Scotsman—who often caused us much laughter by frequently doing things wrong merely by striving too hard to do them right! But he took this all calmly as he had a keen sense of humour, and was a warm, sincere lad, as indeed Ronnie was too. Ian had also applied for training as a pilot, and I counted myself lucky to have gained two such good friends so early in my military career, when so much new was to be learned. Ronnie had done a good deal of rifle- and foot-drill as a cadet during his school days, and was a useful mine of information on the subject, often coming to our aid.

The rest of our roommates were destined for other posts within the service, and were a diverse crowd from all walks of life, and of varied standards of intelligence. But the qualities which set their stamp on the group as a whole were an ever-ready sense of humour and spirit of companionship, and indeed, I was to find these the distinctive characteristics of most of my comrades throughout my service career. As is always the case when a group of men are together, we had in our midst our own prominent comedians, and much amusement was derived from listening to their entertaining back-chat in our huts after 'lights out'. At this stage of our training we were not allowed off camp, so our spare time in the evenings was mostly spent in the canteen or camp cinema.

The part of our training which I enjoyed most were our visits to the rifle range. I had fancied myself as a good shot, but found I was nowhere near Ronnie's standard. He was outstandingly good.

During the middle of the second week it was announced that the Station Commander was to make an inspection of our colony of six huts, known as a Flight. Each hut was called a Squad. We were given a whole morning to prepare our huts for the visit, and the occupants of each hut were to compete with the others for the cleanest and neatest quarters—the winners to have a pass for going off camp the following Saturday evening. Although we had only been on the station for ten days, the outside world already seemed very remote, so we got down to scrubbing and polishing with great vigour and a determination to win the competition.

Everything was cleaned and tidied, both inside and outside, even to the extent of mowing the grass around our hut, re-organizing the flower beds, laying new pavement, and forming the number of our hut—152—with coloured pebbles on a patch of ground outside our front entrance. When all this was completed we viewed our room from the doorway. No-one was allowed to walk on the floor. We certainly saw a picture of perfection; the whole room was shining like a crystal palace; the rows of beds on each side—their exact position had been measured to a fraction of an inch—were reflected on the floor like a landscape in a calm pond. We were certainly proud of our handiwork, and started planning what we would do on our Saturday evening leave.

The inspection was to take place in the afternoon while we were doing our usual drill, and we would not know the results of the competition until during the last period. The time seemed to drag on slower than ever before. At last our flight sergeant appeared on the parade ground where we were being drilled, each squad by its own corporal. We were all lined up and stood to attention while the sergeant strolled back and forth in front of us, grinning at our suspense.

'Well, I've got the news I guess you are all waiting for,' he said at last. 'The CO has finished his inspection and decided the occupants of hut...' Here he paused teasingly, while we were on tenterhooks. 'Hut number 153—the winners.'

We could hardly believe our ears! We had been beaten by the hut next door.

'However,' continued the sergeant, 'the CO wished me to tell you that the huts were all very good, and that he was extremely pleased with your efforts. Alright, corporals, carry on.'

'So, the CO was pleased with our efforts,' muttered one of my companions between clenched teeth. 'A fine lot of good that'll do us, I must say!'

'Stop that nattering!' yelled our corporal. 'You're supposed to be standing to attention, but you're behaving like a bunch of girl-guides. The next man I catch talking will run around the parade ground five times.'

A few of us grinned at this. It was a hot day, and the parade ground a large one. No-one felt like doing any running.

'And wipe those grins off your dials!' he shouted, 'or else I'll come and do it for you.'

Our corporal was certainly our lord and master, to be taken most seriously. On the whole, our instructors were very strict disciplinarians, and at times they seemed inhuman to us. More than once I found myself cursing them and longingly looking forward to the time when I would become a sergeant myself, or even an officer, and could get my own back on these accursed corporals! I realized, of course, that it was their job to be strict, and most of them were by heart kindly persons. It must have been a difficult and trying undertaking to receive one group of thick-headed recruits after another and turn them into fully drilled and disciplined servicemen, but somehow they managed it. After the first week—feeling battered and bruised from our own and our companions' rifle-butts—most of us knew our left from our right, and at the end of our three weeks training, we considered ourselves to be pretty good. And in fact the transformation was remarkable, and all credit must go to our untiring and zealous corporals. Instead of the scruffy, straggling bunch of civilians we had been three weeks before, we were now smart and well disciplined squads of airmen who proudly showed off their knowledge of foot- and rifle-drill.

Our great moment came at the end of the three weeks, when there was a big passing-out parade and march-past, headed by a military band. The evening before was spent in preparations—polishing buttons, shining boots, whitening webbing and backpacks, cleaning and oiling rifles and generally sprucing ourselves up for the big event. Everything had to be in perfect shape.

The parade certainly was most impressive. Two flights—360 of us—were marched onto the large parade ground, and lined up in squads, all carrying full packs and rifles. It was a great strain and test of endurance. The day was hot, with the sun beating mercilessly down on us and it became increasingly difficult to stand completely still. Our packs and rifles seemed to grow heavier and heavier.

After a long wait the Commanding Officer arrived on the parade ground and, following much ceremonial presenting of arms and other drill movements—which came as a relief after standing motionless for so long—our ranks were opened up for inspection. Once again came a long period of standing to attention while the CO walked slowly up and down the lines, stopping once in a while in front of some unfortunate airman to point out some minor defect in appearance. Such an occurrence was dreaded by all—to be singled out by the CO was appalling. The NCO in charge would consider it a reflection upon his flight, and the corporal upon his squad, and it almost certainly meant fatigue duties for the rest of the day.

The strain of the inspection became steadily worse, and the packs began to feel as if they were filled with lead. Suddenly there was a slight commotion in one of the ranks behind ours. No-one dared to look round to see what had happened, but the whisper soon reached us that someone had fainted and been carried off. And it was no wonder in that heat. A few minutes later another airman fainted, this time in front of us, and he too was carried away, but shortly recovered and returned to his position in the line.

'Passing-out parade, indeed' someone whispered out of the corner of his mouth, 'how rightly named!'

At last the inspection was over. A few more drill movements took place before we were marched in a long column, with the band leading, past the saluting-base and once round the camp. What a relief it was to loosen up and move again.

Each squad was then marched to its own hut and dismissed. Once inside, we dropped our packs and rifles and flung ourselves on our beds to relax and rejoice. This was the end of our three weeks course (or hard labour, as we preferred to call it) at Padgate. We were now versed in the rudiments of military lore and behaviour, and next day we would be posted to various aerodromes and RAF establishments around the country to serve as General-Duty hands until the training establishments were ready to accept us.

That evening was our first off camp. We had nearly forgotten what the world of civilians looked like. Most of my squad-mates were going to pay a visit to the photographers, so they could send photos home to their mothers, wives and sweethearts, to show them what fine-looking men they were in their uniforms. We already had a feeling of importance, and enjoyed strutting around the streets of the little town of Warrington, showing off, and fondly imagining ourselves being admired by every passer-by. It never entered our swollen heads that the good citizens of this town were long since fed-up with the multitudes of lads in blue.

VI   LOOPS AND ROLLS

Ronnie and I, along with a few other budding pilots were posted to Debden aerodrome in Essex, not far north-east of London, where we were to carry out general duties until such a time as the flying schools were able to accept us.

Debden was a Fighter Command station in 11 Group, and was the home base of three front-line fighter squadrons (later I was to spend several months there as a pilot with my own squadron), and I was thrilled about going there as it meant that I would be in close touch with flying and—most important—real fighter planes. I was even childish enough to have hopes of being taken up for a flight, until Ronnie, who was not such a dreamer, dashed those hopes by pointing out that fighter planes only had one seat.

While we waited for the transport to fetch us at Saffron Walden railway station, we watched the planes flying around and noticed that they were Hawker Hurricanes. At that time they were the main fighter-planes of the RAF, and being on an aerodrome so close to them came only second in my mind to being a pilot and flying them myself.

On our first evening Ronnie and I wandered over to a hangar where work was being done on several Hurricanes. After having carefully observed that no-one was close, we walked over to a Hurricane that stood outside the hangar, to have a closer look. It appeared to be brand new, and oh how slender and streamlined it looked. I was captivated by being in such close proximity to this beautiful aircraft, and furthermore I was able to touch it!

Suddenly we saw a mechanic clad in overalls approaching and we scurried away. However, he had seen us and laughingly called to us that we were welcome to come back and have a closer look. We explained our curiosity by telling him that we had hopes of becoming pilots and were awaiting vacancies at the flying schools. The mechanic kindly conducted us around the aircraft explaining various items. He pointed out four holes on the leading edge of each wing and told us they were the muzzles of the Browning machine-guns. They were now covered with tape to keep rain and dust out. He then showed us the firing button on the control column— or the stick as he knowingly called it—and how the safety guard worked. He told us that the day before, one of the pilots had forgotten to place it on SAFE, and a mechanic who was running up the engine had inadvertently pressed the firing button. This of course resulted in one hell of a racket with bullets from the eight machine-guns slamming into the hangar wall. Fortunately the guns were pointing high enough up to miss hitting anyone, but they certainly made an awful lot of holes in the wall.

The mechanic allowed us to sit in the cockpit, and whilst sitting there I had a feeling of ecstasy—I imagined myself flying this dream machine. It must be said, however, that dreams can be fickle. At that moment I felt this aeroplane must surely be the pinnacle of creation—no other aircraft could touch it—yet a few months later I was greatly disappointed when I was posted to a squadron equipped with it! The mechanic, our new friend, pointed out the various controls, instruments, switches and buttons, and to us it seemed absolutely amazing that anyone should be able to keep track of all this, fly the aeroplane and at the same time fight for life or death.

'Here comes Dickie Lee to flight-test this plane,' the mechanic suddenly said. We hurried away from the Hurricane when we saw an officer wearing a flying helmet and carrying a parachute approaching. He nodded to us and after conferring with the mechanic for a while he climbed into the cockpit and fastened his straps. He started the engine and when he ran it up the noise was deafening and one had the feeling that so much strain must surely tear it to pieces. The storm that it created was of the same magnitude as its namesake.

The pilot gave signs that the mechanic should remove the chocks from in front of the wheels, waved to us and taxied briskly to the airfield boundary. After a short delay he moved off with a din, going faster and faster until the aircraft lifted off the ground. I watched with fascination as it climbed steeply in a curving arc until it disappeared into the clouds.

'He's our greatest aerobatics pilot,' the mechanic said. 'You should see him when he is in the right mood. He flies upside down and does rolls and loops and all sorts of manoeuvres so close to the ground that at times it is amazing that he avoids hitting it. The other day he won a bet by flying upside down through this hangar, yes, in through one end and out the other. You should have seen that!' We suspected that our friend might be exaggerating a little, but we listened to him with fascination.

After a short while we heard the noise from an aeroplane, and looking up we caught sight of the Hurricane. It had dived out of the clouds and was heading directly for us at high speed. Lower and lower it came until we felt it must hit the ground in front of us, and Ronnie and I instinctively started to retreat. At the last moment it pulled out of the dive and flew over our heads with an awful din that shook the earth. It then pulled up as if to do a loop, but at the top, when upside down, it rolled over, lowered the wheels and in a graceful descending arc landed as light as a feather just in front of us. Yes, this airman certainly knew how to fly, and in my eyes he was nearly a demigod.

Our stay at Debden was both enjoyable and effortless after the grind of Padgate. The day's routine started with a flag-raising parade at 8.30 followed by a roll-call, so getting up at 7.30 gave us plenty of time to get dressed, shave, make our beds and have breakfast. We quickly learned to complete these morning chores in even less time.

After the parade we general-duty lads were allotted our jobs, such as cleaning the airmen's canteen, gardening, transporting coal, peeling potatoes, running errands, collecting garbage and numerous other of these rather tedious, but necessary, activities. By about five o'clock these duties were completed and we were free to do as we pleased. We could leave camp if we wished to, but had to be back inside again by 10.30.

The month of June 1940 was drawing to a close, and the war outlook for Britain was far from encouraging. Hitler had conquered France and now controlled the shores of Europe from northern Norway to Spain. Although Britain, by the grace of God, had managed to get the greater part of its soldiers back across the Channel from Dunkirk most of the weapons had been left behind. The Germans, armed to the teeth, occupied the French coast, and it escaped no one that they were preparing to invade Britain.

Occasionally we would see the newly-formed Home Guard training, and although they showed grit and determination, their odd collection of weapons was a pitiful sight. But rarely, if ever, did I see signs of fear, or hear talk of defeat, among the general public or my companions in the armed forces, and it can be truthfully said that we gave the situation little thought. The period I spent at Debden could be called the 'calm before the storm'. The Battle of France was over and the Battle of Britain had not yet commenced.

Our three fighter squadrons, as most other fighter squadrons in the south-east of England, had suffered many casualties during the last few weeks, and now much of the time was spent in training replacements. Every now and then the squadrons were sent to protect convoys sailing in the Channel. The Germans were now attacking these in ever greater force, obviously with the intention of testing the strength of Britain's Fighter Command. We at Debden naturally became aware that at times not all our aircraft returned, nor did we miss our pilots' jubilations when they performed the so-called victory roll over the aerodrome on return.

One day there was a bad accident close by. I did not see it happen but was on the scene shortly afterwards, at a small coppice near the airfield boundary. It was an ugly sight. Bits of Hurricane were strewn over a large area, even up in the trees. Amazingly no fire had broken out as is most common when aircraft crash. Later I heard what had happened. A young man in the ground staff had harboured a burning desire to become a pilot, but had been turned down due to some slight physical shortcoming. He had done some flying on small aircraft before the war, and had repeatedly applied for flying training without success. Then the time came, when he was performing some job in connection with a Hurricane, that he decided that he would prove to his superiors that he really could fly. However, he did not get very far because the engine cut just after take-off, and the aircraft dived into the woods with the aforementioned results. The fuel tanks had been empty. The poor fellow did not live long enough to be court-marshalled.

Our stay at Debden had lasted for just over a month when the long-awaited signal came: 'Be ready to leave at 8 am tomorrow!'

VII   DON'T BREAK IT!

This time we were posted to Babbacombe, a small seaside town close to Torquay in the south-west of England. The establishment that the Air Force ran there was known as an ITW (Initial Training Wing). On arrival we were greatly disappointed to discover that flying training did not commence there as we had hoped, but rather it appeared to be a continuation of the drudgery of Padgate; physical training, running and drilling. Actually we also had to attend lectures, usually held in one of the town's cinemas, the subjects of the lectures usually being something boring such as patriotism, unity and esprit de corps. We had a very limited interest in all this 'nonsense', at least at this stage. We wanted to hear about flying and aeroplanes. There was a heat-wave during this period, and we had the greatest of difficulties keeping our eyes open in the stifling heat during these dull discourses. Once I was awoken by a poke in the ribs by the person sitting next to me—I had been snoring loudly. I looked around and saw that a large number of my fellow sufferers were journeying open mouthed in the 'Land of Nod'.

The drilling was done on a wide sea-front road, and we aspiring pilots considered all this marching and 'square-bashing' not only boring but absolutely futile. What possible use could it be to a pilot to be able to do left and right turns with a rifle on his shoulder? We were told that it taught us discipline and military bearing, but we considered this absurd, and had a good descriptive name for it.

Once, however, a humorous incident took place during one of these periods, that enlivened our existence. Because of the heat we had been allowed to take off our tunics and lay them folded on top of our gas masks along the wall of a house. Sixty of us were standing there stiffly to attention in three rows, listening to the corporal shouting at us for our incompetence, when suddenly a bitch appeared from around a corner and strolled past our belongings, followed by a file of dogs. The corporal, who had his back to the wall, was flabbergasted by our insolence when we started roaring with laughter in the middle of his diatribe. Our laughter was aroused by the antics of the dogs. The first one following the bitch walked to one of the tunics, sniffed it, lifted a hind leg and let go a jet of urine. This was repeated by all the other dogs that followed. When at last the corporal looked over his shoulder and saw what was happening he also burst into laughter. Now everyone was roaring with laughter except the poor fellow who owned the tunic and gas-mask.

But the distance between mirth and sorrow is not always great. The Battle of Britain was now underway, although we were too far to the west to be directly aware of the struggle. However, one morning two Messerschmitt fighters swept in off the sea and fired on a group of airmen drilling on the sea-front. The attack was short but left many dead and wounded airmen lying on the street. My group was lucky enough to be on a cross-country run at the time, thereby avoiding the attack.

This incident led the authorities to decide that the establishment was too near to the battle area and we were quickly moved to Aberystwyth on the west coast of Wales. Aberystwyth was a pretty and peaceful little university city, which we instantly took a liking to. And furthermore, there was now a sharp decrease in the 'senseless' drilling, this being replaced with classroom courses on subjects that aspiring pilots were much more interested in, such as theory of flight (airmanship), navigation, signals, Morse-code, armaments and other useful items. The course finished with final examinations towards the end of August 1940, and now the time for actually learning to fly drew closer.

As the flying schools in Britain were overcrowded, the RAF was establishing schools in Canada, and we were now told that most of our group would be sent there for flying training. I was delighted, as it offered prospects of seeing more of the world. Before departing we were sent off on a short leave, and now fate took a hand. I had only spent a few days at Grasby with my grandmother when I was taken ill with an attack of Yellow Jaundice and had to enter a hospital, where I lingered for a fortnight, during which time my companions sailed for Canada. I was naturally downcast over this, but after a further two weeks of recoupment, the eagerly awaited telegram arrived: I was to report to No. 7 EFTS (Elementary Flying Training School) at Desford on October 11th 1940.

Desford was a small grass airfield not far from the city of Leicester in the Midlands. A small Aero-Club had used it before the war, but now it had been taken over by the RAF. Now, once again, I was a member of a course; this time a course of thirty airmen who were to learn to fly, or failing that, to be 'washed out' and posted to some other branch in the RAF. Being 'Washed Out' (the current slang for failing pilot training) was quite a common occurrence, and perhaps this was not surprising when one considers what a mixed bag of candidates we were. It was deemed good if more than 60% of each course continued for further flying training.

The atmosphere here was very different from the previous training establishments; no drilling or strenuous physical training, and no bad-tempered corporals or sergeants shouting at us. Here there were only flying instructors whom we greatly respected and addressed as Sir, even though some of them were not actually officers. And here we climbed up two steps in rank and became LACs (Leading Aircraftmen) and our pay jumped from two shillings a day to a lordly three!

On arrival we were taken to the store and issued with our flying gear. This consisted of a leather flying helmet, goggles, a woollen sweater, a flying suit (overalls) with a fur collar, silk gloves and leather gauntlets, a silk scarf, thick woollen stockings and fur-lined flying boots. The aircraft that we were to fly were DH Tiger Moths, biplanes with open cockpits, so it was just as well to be warmly dressed, especially now that winter was settling in. Furthermore, each pupil was issued with his own parachute.

As there were no living quarters on the aerodrome we were billeted in private homes in the neighbourhood, which we felt was a pleasant change from the standard airmen's barracks. I joined a middle-aged couple who owned a pretty bungalow on the outskirts of Leicester. They were extremely kind-hearted and made me feel very much at home. To enable me to get to and from the field they lent me their son's bicycle as he was away in the Navy.

Our course was split into two groups which took turns flying one half of each day and doing classroom work the other half. However, the weather was frequently unsuitable for flying and the time would then be used for sports, or we were released so we could go into town for a cinema show or other recreations. By now the Germans had started bombing towns and cities all over Britain, under the cover of darkness, and Leicester had already received its share—bomb damage was to be seen in various parts of the city—but the citizens appeared to take this in their stride and life continued normally; shops, cinemas and pubs were 'open as usual'. Our finances did not allow us to frequent the pubs to any extent, but of course we did allow ourselves the occasional pint of beer.

Each flying instructor had 3-4 pupils. As was to be expected these instructors varied greatly. Some were already too old to take an active part in the air war, but felt they were doing 'their bit' and were content. They were usually the best instructors. Others had already participated in the conflict, including the Battle of Britain, and were now deemed to be resting. It was obvious, however, that most of them were fed up with the routine, and the lack of excitement that was part of instructing, and were impatient to get back into action with their squadrons. They were excellent pilots but had little stomach for the job in hand. My first instructor, Flight Lieutenant Bamber, belonged to the latter group. He had been in action right from the start of the war. That he was a first-class pilot was never in doubt; the ribbons under his pilots' wings testified that he had been decorated for valour. He could not really be accused of apathy but, still, it was obvious that his heart was not in the job and he was pining to get back 'into action'.

And now the long-awaited moment was on hand—I was about to go on my first flight. This was the moment I had been fantasising about since the early days of my youth, and which I had been awaiting with ever-increasing impatience during these last few months. It so happened that Bamber picked me to be first of his three pupils, and I hurriedly donned my flying suit (I had already practised this many times) and my parachute, which Bamber then carefully inspected to make sure the straps were correctly set.

Then I was invited to climb into the rear cockpit of the Tiger Moth where I was tightly strapped in.

Bamber explained to me the controls and the instruments, which were of course very few and simple compared with latter-day aircraft. There was no radio, and communication between the two cockpits was via so-called Gosport tubes. Rubber hoses led from the ear pads of the flying-helmets, rather like a doctor's stethoscope, and were plugged into a receptacle on the instrument panel, where there was also a funnel for speaking into. This system worked remarkably well and the instructor's voice came through clearly in spite of the noise of the wind and the roar of the engine when the aircraft was aloft. Bamber got into the forward cockpit, and after having confirmed that communications between us were in order, he signalled to a mechanic to swing the propeller, and the engine jumped to life. As this was the first flight of the day he let the engine idle for a while to warm up. He then increased the power and tested the magnetos, following which he gave signs to have the wheel-chocks removed.

The aircraft started moving as soon as he increased the power again. These Tiger Moths had no brakes, and instead of a tailwheel they had a tail-skid which was dragged along the ground. The rudder was used to control direction on the ground, and as the engine in the nose of the aircraft rather impeded forward vision, it was necessary to jink from side to side whilst moving on the ground. All this Bamber explained to me as he taxied to the take-off position at the airfield boundary. There he turned the aircraft into the wind and increased power until the engine was screaming. I was thrust against the seat-back and suddenly we were rushing along at ever-increasing speed and I became aware that the ground was receding below us. Unfortunately I do not have the intuition nor the command of words to describe the feeling of ecstasy that overtook me at that moment. Up, up we climbed, higher and higher and the trees and the houses and the roads and the cars below got smaller and smaller. Then the horizon started to tilt even though we were sitting upright in our seats. This was a clear sunny day, with just a few scattered clouds that looked like wads of cotton-wool. The view was perfect, as when standing upon a high mountain peak back home in Iceland on a clear day. There was, however, an enormous difference. From the mountain top the horizon all around was rock-steady, but here it was continually wandering; sometimes below and sometimes tilted above, but forever on the move. The landscape below us was like a multi-coloured chess board, and smoky haze lay over the towns. We were hanging in the air, free as the birds and to me the feeling this produced was indescribable. After a while I began to long for more—to feel this freedom even more strongly. I dug up the courage to request Bamber to increase the manoeuvres—even to perform a few aerobatics.

I could hear the surprise in his voice when he said: 'What's that laddie? Already on your first flight! Well, you asked for it, and you shall have it.'

Suddenly the horizon was far above us as he shoved the nose of the aircraft down, but gradually it started to sink again as I was pushed down into the seat with great force, and the nose rose slowly into the air again until the earth was above us and the sky below—we were in a loop. This was followed by one manoeuvre after another, and I found myself either hanging upside down in my straps or pressed down into the seat. I do not doubt that Bamber, the fighter pilot, was enjoying this relief from the dull routine of teaching the rudiments of flying. After a while he teasingly asked if I hadn't had enough, and my answer was to the effect that I could never have enough. He laughed and said: 'OK we'll repeat this some other time, laddie.'

A short time later he landed lightly on the grass, and my first flight was over. I was overjoyed, even though I still had not touched the controls—I had flown around the skies and enjoyed it more than words can say. I had discovered a new world.

Before going on this flight I had been worried by the thought that I might have an aversion to heights. All my life I have experienced vertigo when standing on the edge of high cliffs, or similar structures, and looked down. This could be so intense that I felt the sensation of being pulled over the edge. To my great relief I had now discovered that I had no such sensations when in an aeroplane.

Now a period of traditional flight instruction commenced, which I will not try to describe in detail. After a few days Bamber left and a middle-aged gentleman, Flying Officer Horsfall, took his place. He was a kindly person and an excellent flying instructor. He always had plenty of time and care for us, his pupils, and was very painstaking. He never quit on any subject or project until he felt we had mastered it to his complete satisfaction. The Tiger Moth was a good aeroplane for the job; simple and fairly easy to control, but a fair amount of concentration was needed to fly it correctly. Well do I remember the tone of admonition in the instructor's voice when, with great patience, he uttered into the speaking tube: 'I asked you to make a 90 degree turn to the right, not a change of direction.'

It was not long before empty spaces began to appear in our ranks. Pupils were mercilessly failed if they showed the slightest signs of discomfort, apathy or lack of talent. In addition we had two fatal accidents amongst the members of our course. In the one case the pupil taxied his plane into another stationary one and this resulted in a fire in which he perished. In the other case the pupil landed his Tiger Moth a little short so that the wheels ran into a shallow ditch causing the aircraft to somersault. The pupil hung there in his safety-straps, upside down, about five feet from the ground, and nothing worse should have happened to him, but through thoughtlessness, or due to panic, he undid his straps and fell on his head and broke his neck.

It was naturally a matter of ambition and even pride to be sent up without an instructor (or go solo, as it was called) within the shortest time possible, and it irritated me that I was the last of Horsfall's three pupils to achieve this.

There is an amusing story about a pupil who was making excellent progress in all aspects of his flying training, but his instructor simply could not persuade him to go solo. The instructor was certain that this pupil had the necessary ability, so one day he decided to take action. When they had reached a good height he unscrewed his stick (control column), held it aloft so that the pupil could see it and then threw it overboard whilst saying into the speaking tube: 'Ok sonny, now you're in control, you'd better get us down.' It so happened that, unknown to the instructor, the pupil had received warning of what was going to happen, and came prepared. He flew the aeroplane over the airfield, drew up a spare stick, which he had brought along, tapped the instructor on the shoulder with it so he would see it, and then threw it overboard. The instructor now thought that the aircraft was without controls and wasted no time in bailing out, and floating down onto the airfield. He had to suffer the humiliation of watching his pupil make a faultless landing and taxying up to him to offer him a ride to the dispersal!

Fortunately my case was not quite as involved as that and eventually, after about ten hours dual instruction I was sent aloft with the Chief Flying Instructor for a test. After landing I heard him say into the speaking tube: 'Right, I am now going to stand here on the ground and watch you land.' Having said that he climbed out of the cockpit, patted me on the shoulder, winked at me and shouted as he jumped down off the wing: 'Don't break it!'

I had been apprehensive about flying alone for the first time, but now I felt no fear. I took off, flew a circuit around the field and landed—without breaking anything. Now at last I felt I was a pilot—I could take to the air and land again without help. That evening I celebrated with at least one more beer than I could really afford.

But now I had also reached the most dangerous period in the life of a budding pilot; the period when most accidents take place; the period when the student is filled with false self-assurance—the belief that he knows it all and is able to cope with any situation. Some have family or friends within flying distance, and the novice feels he must demonstrate to them what a skilful pilot he has become. These demonstrations usually take the form of dives and steep turns at low altitude, often ending in disaster. Most of us had girl-friends in the neighbourhood who naturally must be subjected to the pleasure of seeing their intrepid airmen doing their stunts.

Joyce lived in a Leicester suburb, and one Sunday morning I decided to give her reason to admire me for my flying skills. I circled a few times low over the house to give the whole family time to get outdoors to watch the great flying-warrior. I then went into a steep dive down towards the house, but at the last moment I realised that I had failed to take into account that there was a large chestnut tree just beyond it, right on my line of flight, and it was only with the greatest exertions that I managed to avoid crashing into it. This really shook me thoroughly, and with my heart beating wildly I hurried away. When I, 'the great stunt-flier', had finally got my nerves sorted out, I landed and taxied to the dispersal.

As I jumped onto the ground I noticed to my mortification that a small branch with red and yellow leaves was clinging to the undercarriage structure. I furtively tried to remove it, but ran out of luck. One of the instructors saw it and I was immediately summoned to the Chief Flying Instructor's office. He gave me a thorough telling off and said he could not care less whether I threw away my contemptible life, but on the other hand he had great concern for the aircraft, as it was the property of His Majesty. If I was ever caught doing such a stupid thing again I would immediately be court-martialled and kicked out of the RAF in disgrace. I staggered away with a feeling that I was fortunate to be allowed to continue my flying training.

Around about this time a tragic incidence took place. George, one of my companions, lived in the same suburb as I, with about 10 minutes walking distance between the two houses. Usually we did our homework together in my digs, as my room was slightly larger than George's. However, one evening the married couple George was billeted with wished to go to the cinema and asked George if he would mind baby-sitting for them. This request was readily granted and we did our studying at his place. That evening we became aware of a steady stream of German bombers passing overhead, but this time the attack was directed against the neighbouring city of Coventry. Occasionally, though, a bomb would fall in our vicinity, but we were getting used to such happenings and didn't take very much notice of them. Later that evening, when I cycled home all I found, where the bungalow had stood, was a bomb-crater. My Guardian angel was already on the job. I wonder if he realized what a busy time lay ahead.

Now the course was drawing to a close and we sat our final exams, followed by a final flight test conducted by the Chief Flying Instructor. A further two unfortunate pupils fell by the wayside, so in the end only sixteen of us were left of the thirty young men who started the course full of optimism and high hopes. We, the lucky ones, would continue our training in establishments that were called SFTSs (Service Flying Training Schools) and would be given the choice of becoming bomber pilots, fighter pilots or Coastal Command pilots. Naturally individuals varied in the type of flying they preferred. Some had little taste for aerobatics and violent manoeuvres that were inherent to flying fighter planes, and they naturally chose the more sedate type of flying associated with bombers or anti-submarine aircraft. However the greatest lustre, or glamour, was attached to flying fighter planes, especially after the glorious achievements of the pilots fighting the Battle of Britain, which had just recently concluded. To be a master of one's own destiny; to be alone in a little fighter plane dashing about the skies chasing the enemy and shooting him down—well, that was what most of us wanted. It was therefore not surprising that the majority of us applied for fighters. From my point of view nothing else mattered. I had a very limited desire to fly for hours on end over the oceans looking for submarines, and even less enthusiasm for flying bombing missions.

We all eagerly awaited the decisions of our superiors. When finally the list was pinned on the board I could hardly contain my joy. Under the column headed FIGHTERS, there were only two names: T Jonsson and M Pearson. The disappointment of many of my companions was obvious but I floated in the air high above the clouds. I had reached the second stage in my resolution to become a fighter pilot.

VIII   THE TREES GROW TALL IN SCOTLAND

On a sunny Sunday morning I stood beside my kitbag on a railway station platform in the little town of Montrose on the east coast of Scotland, and stared with fascination into the clear blue sky. I was intently watching the aeroplanes that were flying around. They were of the type known as the Miles Master, the type I would be flying during this next stage of my training. I was greatly excited with the prospect, and infatuated with this aircraft—it was so close to being a fighter—a low-wing monoplane with a closed cockpit, a powerful engine that could propel it forward at high speed, and furthermore, it had a retractable undercarriage. Whilst my companions continued to descend from the train I watched closely one of the planes a short distance away doing aerobatics at an altitude of about four to five thousand feet. Oh, how beautiful it was—so streamlined and graceful—as the pilot did his stunts there up in the sunny sky—rolled, dived, looped, stood on end, flew upside down, dived again and started pulling up into a loop when... No, my God! I can't believe it! I watch in horror as a wing breaks off and the aircraft starts to spins downward with the wing following like a falling leaf. There is the thump of an explosion, followed by a pall of black smoke that rises above rooftops.

That was my introduction to the Miles Master.

The grass-covered airfield was on the coast a short distance north of the town and in addition to the flying-school's aircraft there were four Spitfires stationed there for defence purposes. It would occasionally happen on cloudy days, when the clouds over the field reached out to sea, that raiders based in Norway paid uninvited visits. They crept up to the coast low enough to avoid detection by radar, dropped their bombs and scurried up into the clouds for their get-away. Due to lack of warning the Spitfires were usually still on the ground when the bombers appeared. The bombers could, however, never be sure of this, so they dropped their bombs hurriedly and rather haphazardly, rarely doing much damage as the bombs mainly fell in the fields beyond the aerodrome. The crew of one raider, however, managed to do more damage then they could have dreamed of. Three bombs were released, the first two fell harmlessly onto open fields but the third fell further inland and landed on a large whisky distillery. A fire broke out that lasted for three days and nights. We later learned that 600,000 gallons of Scotland's most valuable export commodity went up in flames (and down the drain, as there were reports of whisky running in the gutters). And this was at the time when in the various mess bars whisky was rationed to one dram per person! Hitler would no doubt have awarded the Iron Cross to this 'valiant' crew if he had known about this 'most successful' bombing raid.

Little flying was done in the first week after our arrival as all the Miles Masters were withdrawn from service and thoroughly inspected, due to the tragic incident that I had witnessed on my arrival. However, training gradually got back to normal—classrooms half the day and flying the other half. The day began with the pupils being marched onto the parade ground for the flag-raising ceremony. On Sundays the CO formally inspected our ranks, after which we were marched off to church, (this was called Church Parade).

I quickly took to the Miles Master, and soloed within a short time. Now we were taught to fly by instruments (usually called blind-flying), both on the ground in a sort of simulator, called the Link Trainer, and also in the air when the pupil's view was curtailed with a screen so he could only see the instrument panel. We also started night-flying and I had no difficulties in getting to grips with that. Not all the pupils were so fortunate in this respect—one of my companions was killed and another was seriously injured.

The former lost his nerve during his first night-solo. After making a few unsuccessful attempts to land he started circling the field, probably for the purpose of calming his nerves and gathering courage for a further attempt. In those days the training aircraft did not carry radios, so unfortunately the instructor down on the ground was unable to get in touch with his pupil to give him encouragement and advice. We stood around in small groups and watched the aircraft's navigation lights circling round and around and no doubt we all felt compassion for our companion and sent up silent prayers for him. At last he got around to making his final attempt to land. The approach looked good but unfortunately he levelled out for landing too soon. Many voices could be heard shouting: 'Not yet, you fool! Come down lower! Go around again!' and other such advice. But all this was of no avail; the aircraft fell to the ground with a thud and bounced into the air again. The pilot added power to the engine with the obvious intention of going round again. We bystanders let out sighs of relief, but suddenly the tragedy occurred. The aircraft rose too steeply, stalled and plunged into the ground. Fire broke out immediately but the fire engine was on hand and quickly doused the flames. The pilot showed signs of life when pulled out of the wreck, but died in hospital a few hours later. Fortunately this was the only fatal accident to members of this course, and life carried on normally without any other major incident.

The school had at its disposal an old Mark I Hurricane which each pupil got a flight in before the end of the course. Although this was already by now an ancient type, with a two-bladed wooden propeller, we could feel that we had our hands on a real fighter aircraft. It was faster than the Master, as its engine was considerably more powerful, and it was also more agile.

There is no denying that there are many flaws in my personality, and amongst them are those that can be classified as negligence, carelessness, indifference and lack of discipline. These traits now began to take a hand in the running of my life, as they had done on occasions before.

At the end of our elementary training at Desford we pupils were divided into two categories: officer and NCO material. The former were identified by a white flash in their forage-caps, and for some incomprehensible reason I found myself in that group. I do not know why the distinction was made at this stage of our career, but most likely it was expected of us aspiring officers to behave in a more disciplined and refined manner than the others. This did not happen in my case, however, as I committed various breaches of discipline which delayed my promotion to commissioned rank for quite a while, and I shall now recount some of them.

At the end of each day's work we pupils were allowed off camp, but had to check back in at the guard room no later than ten o'clock. The aerodrome was enclosed with a high wire-net fence topped with barbed wire, so the main gate by the guard room was supposed to be the only means of access. Between the airfield and town there lay a golf course, and in the boundary fence by the golf course I discovered a small tear large enough to crawl through. At that time I was dating a pretty young girl called Doris Alexander, whose father was the steward of the golf club, and on occasions I would crawl through the fence under cover of darkness to meet Doris and stroll around the golf course with her. Such was my first introduction to a golf course, but many years later when I started playing the noble game of golf I put such venues to entirely different uses! One evening when I was out with Doris it started to rain, so we took the risk of going into a pub for a beer. But luck wasn't with me—one of the station's officers came in, and that was that. Next morning I was summoned to the CO's office where I received a severe reprimand and was confined to camp for two weeks.

Another of my misdeeds would come in the same category as the incident that happened at Desford. I had been ordered to take a Master up to above ten thousand feet to practice aerobatics. This I carried out conscientiously for a while, but then I suddenly found myself in the grips of an over-powering desire to do some low-flying in the enchanting Scottish Highlands on such a beautiful day, and I gave in to temptation. After having thoroughly enjoyed myself for a while flying low up and down the beautiful mountain sides and along enchanting valleys, I turned home full of joy. My instructor, Flying Officer Dibnah, strolled over to me as I was climbing out of the cockpit.

'Well, Jonsson, how did the aerobatics go?'

'Oh, quite well, sir' I answered innocently.

'And no doubt you stayed well above ten thousand feet?'

I felt a bit uneasy. 'Yeees—most of the time,' I answered, but now I had a nasty feeling that something was wrong.

'Well, well it's amazing how tall the trees here in Scotland can grow. Come and have a look at this,' he said as he strolled round to the front of the machine. I followed him, and to my mortification I saw a little tree branch stuck into the oil cooler. I had to pay for my little bit of fun. After school during the next few days I was given the pleasure of peeling potatoes, washing dishes, disposing of garbage and other such delightful jobs.

But probably my greatest sin was to oversleep on a Sunday morning. I had been knocking back drinks until very late the night before and had problems waking up. The occasion for the booze-up was valid enough— earlier during the day my closest pal had been informed that he was unsuitable for further flying training—he had been 'washed out'—and we had employed the aid of Bacchus to help us drown his sorrows. My barrack-mates made repeated attempts to get me out of bed next morning, and I had got as far as placing my feet on the floor by the time they went to breakfast, but was fast asleep again when they returned. Whilst I at last got around to dressing the others prepared for the Sunday parade by polishing their buttons and shoes. I had not even started on this when the call came and we had to rush out to the parade ground and 'fall in'. The flag was saluted and this was followed by the station commander's weekly inspection of our ranks. As we stood there to attention waiting for the CO to pass by I lowered my eyes and caught sight of my dull looking shoes; they were strikingly noticeable in between the highly polished shoes on either side. Furthermore, I was acutely aware of the fact that I had not shaved and that my tunic buttons were badly in need of a polish. I was therefore not very surprised when the station commander stopped in front of me, looked me up and down with contempt and said to the NCO that followed him: 'Corporal, write down this airman's name'.

With that any hopes I had entertained of becoming an officer were scattered to the four corners of the earth, at least for the time being. This was confirmed at the ceremonial parade, a short while later, when we officially graduated as pilots, and were handed our wings, to be born with great pride on our left breast. As our names were called out we were addressed either as Pilot Officer or Sergeant. I admittedly found it rather degrading, that amongst all those wearing the white cap badge, I was the only one to be addressed as Sergeant, but I had only myself to blame. By my unruly behaviour I had managed to provoke the Commanding Officer into disfavour, and I am sure I detected a look of sarcasm and an emphasis on the word Sergeant when he handed me the wings. I had for some time realized where I was heading in this matter and had come to terms with it. The main thing was that I had now received my 'pilot's wings', and the time was rapidly approaching when I would join a squadron as a fully qualified fighter pilot. Furthermore, I felt that becoming a mere sergeant was still a great jump upwards, both in rank and in pay. This rose from three to fourteen shillings a day.

When I look back I am inclined to think that this outcome was in fact rather to my advantage, although by saying that I run the risk of someone shouting sour grapes. By starting my career as a pilot in the lower ranks, and later receiving my commission, I came into much closer touch with the heart and soul of the RAF, and in fact when it came down to the serious business of aerial warfare the sergeant pilots were given no less opportunities than the officer pilots, within each squadron, to assert leadership in the air. It was the overall experience and ability of the individual that counted, not rank. It was not uncommon, as will become apparent later in this narrative, that sergeant pilots led squadrons into action, and certainly quite common that they led lesser formations or sections, although officers naturally headed squadrons, and their flights, on the ground.

Sergeants had their own messes, like the officers, and in fact there was very little difference between the two. On the other hand the sergeants' mess was usually the more lively, as its members did not have to be concerned with the presence of senior, or high ranking, officers as was often the case in the officers' mess.

In addition to dining halls these messes had spacious lounges with armchairs and coffee tables where all the main newspapers and magazines were to be found. They also contained card- and chess-playing tables, dartboards, a piano and a radio set. A cosy bar was to be found in the hall, and there was also a billiard room with one or two full-sized snooker tables and sometimes a ping-pong table. Mess stewards in white jackets were on hand to attend to members' needs.

Airmen (and airwomen, or WAAFs as they were called) of lower rank had messes that were nearly exclusively dining halls, so their main place of recreation was the NAAFI canteen, which I have already mentioned. Also there were cinema halls open to all station personnel. All the main aerodromes had adequate facilities for sporting activities such as a gymnasium, squash and tennis courts and football fields, to mention a few.

Following the graduation ceremony we newly baked sergeants sewed our stripes and wings onto our uniform tunics and marched proudly off into town to give the good citizens a chance to admire us. This the 'poor' officers could not do as they had to wait for tailors to make their new uniforms.

IX   HE'S PROBABLY LOST HIS NERVE

After a period of leave, which I spent visiting the Hawkridge family and my grandmother, the final phase of my training commenced. At the next establishment, which bore the name OTU (Operational Training Unit), the main emphasis was on training the pilot for the type of operational flying he was about to enter into; in my case as a member of a fighter squadron. At the completion of this course we were considered fully qualified to join a squadron, although training would naturally continue constantly after that. Now we were to be taught fighter tactics, both offensive and defensive, and the use of the fighter plane's armaments. Also a great emphasis would be laid on practising formation flying.

The school was based at Heston aerodrome in the western suburbs of London, and its aircraft were Spitfires of the oldest types, Marks I and II, and I eagerly awaited the chance to fly this famous aeroplane. As the Spitfire has only one seat there was naturally no question of going aloft with an instructor for the first flight, so we spent a considerable time sitting in the cockpit to get acquainted with the various instruments and controls, before taking off. It had caught my attention that the fellows that flew before me seemed to have problems controlling the aircraft immediately after becoming airborne, and gave the impression that they were playing leap-frog for the first 10-15 seconds.

The explanation of this phenomenon was, that in the oldest type of Spitfire, the Mark I, the pilot had to reach for a long handle, low down in the right-hand corner of the cockpit and jerk it up and down to pump up the undercarriage, and there was a tendency to move the other hand, holding the control column, in unison. We, who still had not flown, smirked arrogantly at the clumsiness of our comrades, and I was determined not to let this happen to me. To my mortification, however, that is just what did happen; the control column was so light and sensitive in comparison with the Miles Master, that the jerking automatically took place before I realised what was happening. The later marks of Spitfires were fitted with a bottle of compressed air for operating the undercarriage (and flaps) and then it became necessary only to press a switch.

After the wheels were up I turned my attention to the business of flying. The machine climbed so rapidly, that before I knew it I had reached three thousand feet, the altitude assigned to me whilst I flew around getting familiar with the aeroplane. Now my dreams were rapidly being fulfilled— I was flying the aircraft I had yearned for more than anything else. The adrenaline flowed into my veins and I was wild with joy. I started doing steep turns in both directions and got the feeling that this delightful machine was reading my mind and anticipating my every move, as if I myself was an integral part of it, and therefore flying myself. Oh, how spirited it was, yet light on the reins like an outstanding thoroughbred. I looked out onto the delicate, curving wing—a more beautiful aeroplane was surely not to be found anywhere in the world. I longed to throw it around the sky in wild abandon, but I was forbidden to do so on this first flight, so I had better get down to the assigned task, which was to practice landings and take-offs.

Now let's see, where was I? I could not see the aerodrome anywhere, but below me was a railway line running east-west and in the distance I could just make out the barrage-balloons over London, so Heston must lie somewhere in that direction. Shortly I caught sight of the large gasometers located near the airfield, and this solved the problem as the visibility was unusually good that day. I now descended to circuit height at the airfield, and as I was equipped with R/T (receiver/

transmitter) I requested permission to land, which was immediately granted.

I now commenced the approach, and as the large engine impairs the forward view below, it is advisable to approach the landing spot in a descending curve. This presented no problem, but due to the streamlined slenderness of the aircraft, I had, before I knew, built up too much speed in the descent, and had to abandon the landing.

I now took on the task again and this time I lowered the flaps much sooner than before, but even then my speed was too great when I levelled out above the ground, and the aircraft floated across half the field before touching down. It became obvious that I would not be able to stop in time so there was nothing left to do but to add power to the engine and go around again.

I was now beginning to feel slightly harassed. It would be a fine mess if I were to crash a Spitfire on my first flight. I now set out on my third attempt and this time I managed to have better control over the speed. Half way through the approach I lowered the flaps but then a horn started emitting a loud noise that made me feel confused, and it took a while before I realised that this was a warning that the undercarriage had not been lowered. At the same time red warning flares arose into the sky from the control tower. I had forgotten my wheels and was about to make a belly landing—one of the most shameful things that can happen to a pilot. Now it was too late to pump the wheels down and maintain control of the approach at the same time, so I had to abandon the landing once more. I was now starting to perspire, but on the fourth attempt I managed to get down without further disgrace. The touchdown, however, was terrible. The aircraft hit the ground a little too soon, bounced back into the air and continued to leap-frog across the field. I nearly dropped it down onto one wing but finally managed to assert control.

I was not feeling very cocky, to say the least, when I taxied into the parking area. I felt sure that many eyes had been watching my fiasco and that I would be mocked unstintingly. When I climbed out of the cockpit, shaken and perspiring, I noticed that one of the instructors, who stood a slight distance away, grinned at me, shook his head and walked away without saying a word. He'd probably seen something similar a few times before!

One of my comrades told me that a group of instructors and pupils had been watching my performance and some of the instructors had become uneasy. One was heard to mutter: 'He's probably lost his nerve.'

I am happy to say that after this I never had any great difficulties controlling this lively mount, and we soon became the best of pals.

*

X   THAT DAMNED BRIDGE

All of us managed to escape breaking anything on this first flight, and the routine curriculum now got under way. On my second or third flight I experienced a little 'adventure'. Due to poor visibility in a smoke-haze I lost my bearings and descended to a low altitude to try to identify landmarks. Suddenly, to my terror, I discovered that I was flying around in amongst the barrage balloons. This shook me thoroughly as hitting one of the cables was practically a death warrant. There was only one thing to do: push the throttle forward and pull the stick back and climb vertically in the hopes of getting safely out of the 'jungle'.

Shortly after this the authorities took the sensible decision to relocate the OTU, as Heston was a most unsuitable airfield for this type of activity. It was to a large extent surrounded by houses and factories and, due to the closeness to London, visibility was generally rather poor. We frequently had great difficulties finding the aerodrome, and as our R/Ts were obsolete, and usually u/s (unserviceable), they were not to be relied on for assistance.

The airfield chosen to replace it was named Llandow, and was situated in the beautiful countryside of South Wales, not far from Cardiff. It was surrounded with fields and woods, and here the air was usually as clear as the mountain air back home in Iceland. We worked with zeal performing whatever exercises were put before us, including firing the aircraft's guns, either at a target situated on a lonely beach or at a drogue towed on a long cable behind another aircraft.

I think it is now appropriate to explain to the reader a little about the armament of the fighter aircraft of those days. This usually consisted of a number of fixed machine-guns firing forward. These guns were most frequently embedded in the wings (the earliest marks of Spitfires had eight, four in each wing) and were aligned in such a way that when fired the bullets from all guns met in a tight pattern about 250 yards ahead. The aircraft itself was aimed at the target, not each individual gun. The trigger, which incidentally was a button, was located at the top of the control column, and was pressed with the thumb. There was a safety guard over the button that had to be removed before the guns could be fired.

For the purpose of aiming the aircraft onto the target a device called a reflector sight was employed. When switched on it cast an orange-coloured sighting-ring with cross-lines onto the windscreen in front of the pilot. If the target was stationary, or straight ahead and moving in the same direction, it was sufficient to keep the centre-dot of the sight on target. If, however, the target was moving, and being approached from the side, the aiming point had to be ahead of the target so that it and the bullets met. This was called deflection shooting and proved to be one of the most difficult tasks facing the fighter pilot. He had to take into consideration the speed of the target, his own speed and the degree of angle between the two, and only the most skilful fighter pilots ever fully mastered it. I personally never became adept and sprayed a large number of bullets into the sky with very limited results. Fortunately our opponents faced the same problems, as otherwise I would not be here now to tell the story.

In addition to marksmanship, we practised formation flying, as the ability to fly in a formation with other aircraft is very important in a fighter squadron. We also constantly practised aerial combat, or 'dog-fighting' as it was called. Our aircraft were equipped with cine-cameras which started up whenever the firing button was pressed, and the film would consequently show whether the bullets would have hit their target or not. Needless to say, our guns were not loaded for these exercises.

On the whole we led an idyllic life in the sunshine of southern Wales those early summer days of 1941, although two shadows were cast on them. One of the shadows was caused by a fatal accident to two of our comrades. Our group was relatively small and consequently a fairly close comradeship was formed, and we sensed an acute loss when such a gap was made in our ranks. We were not yet hardened to such blows, as we later became when we joined the fray, and the loss of friends was a common occurrence.

This tragic incident happened on a sun-drenched day towards the end of our course. A few of us lay around on a grassy patch outside the dispersal hut, chewing on straws and chatting while we awaited our turn to fly. We looked up into the sky and watched two Spitfires dog-fighting at about 5-6000 feet above us, and jokingly wagered on which one would 'shoot the other down'. Then suddenly this was no longer fun. To our horror we watched the two planes collide. One of them instantly burst into flames and plunged vertically to the ground. A wing broke off the other one and it started spinning wildly, and we could see that the pilot was baling out, but his parachute got entangled with the tailplane and he got dragged to his death. This had a paralysing effect on us, and certainly none of us enjoyed the flying for the rest of that day.

The other shadow was of a very different kind and could be classified as tragicomic, but it affected me like a nightmare for quite some time. It so happened that our airfield was not very far from the river Severn, over which there was a railway bridge constructed of many tall, narrow arches. The rumour got around that some daredevil had flown a Spitfire through one of the arches, but our instructors made it abundantly clear that such madness was strictly forbidden, and that we should not even dream of trying it. I was personally most satisfied with this order, but then a fool of a daredevil in our group sneakily went and proved that it could be done. Then, of course his bosom pal had to prove that he was no lesser a man, and pretty soon it had reached the stage when no-one could hold his head high until he had proved his courage. Of course the suspicion crept in that one or two false claims might have been made, but there was no getting away from it—I simply must pass this test to obtain peace of mind. Many times I flew towards that darned bridge to get the irritating deed over with, but each time I approached it the arches seemed too narrow, and I lost my nerve. One day I only just escaped being involved in a nasty accident. I approached the arches, but abandoned at the last moment and pulled up over the bridge, and wooosh!—I just missed a Spitfire going in the opposite direction. Another pilot had approached the bridge from the other side, and our saving grace was that we had not chosen the same arch.

Of course, this feat could only be done on a relatively calm day, so I was always relieved whenever there was too much wind to make the attempt. However, that was just an excuse for putting off something that had to be done sooner or later. Now it was reaching the stage when so many of my comrades claimed to be 'bridgemen' that I could not delay it any longer without loosing face. Oh, what a relief it was when at last I got it over with. The arch I chose seemed too narrow up to the very last moment of approach, but I scraped up the courage, and suddenly I was through!

I may add that we heard later that someone tried to go through in a Fairey Battle, an aircraft with a considerably greater wing span than the Spitfire. The attempt ended with both wings being left behind at the bridge and the fuselage skipping on the surface of the water and landing on the bank. Amazingly enough the pilot escaped without serious bodily injuries. Shortly after this the authorities had steel wires stretched across the arches, thereby relieving our heirs of this 'headache'.

Soon the course drew to a close and there was no denying that we greenhorns were now tempted to look upon ourselves as highly qualified fighter pilots and confident that our prospective opponents had better start saying their prayers. Of course most of us were to discover the hard way how much there was still to be learned, and not many of us were fortunate enough to live to see peacetime again.

The Battle of Britain had been over for some time now and the boys in the light blue uniforms were idolised by the country's citizens. On the other hand all seemed to be going badly for the poor Army—it kept on losing battles in North Africa, Greece and Crete—and the Navy was in a tight spot. Only the Air Force seemed to be standing up to Hitler. Bomber Command was steadily growing and attacked Germany with increasing weight during the hours of darkness, whilst during daylight Fighter

Command escorted bombers into the occupied countries across the Channel. Although these attacks were directed against factories and other military targets, there is no doubt that another purpose was to force the Germans to maintain strong fighter units in the West, which otherwise would have been used against the Soviets which had recently been attacked by Hitler's hordes. The RAF sent large numbers of fighters on these expeditions and substantial aerial battles were fought over France almost daily. It has now been established that the loss of men and machines was fairly evenly divided on both sides, the RAF probably suffering greater losses than the Luftwaffe, but at the time the RAF considered itself to have the advantage.

We, the newly fledged fighter pilots were naturally full of self-confidence and could hardly wait to leap into action. We also had a firm belief that the newest marks of Spitfires were superior to the German Messerschmitts, but this was based more on wishful thinking than facts, at least at that time. The Daimler-Benz engines of the Messerschmitts were by then turbine driven, which meant that above 20,000 feet they were marginally faster, but on the other hand the Spitfires were always more agile, and could out-turn their opponents. The Spitfire's Rolls-Royce Merlin engine continued to be improved, but it was not until early 1943 that a version embodying a two-stage blower was fitted to the Spitfire Mk IX, which then gave it a superior performance at all altitudes. The Germans did not sit back idly and watch, but continued to increase the horsepower of D-B engines, and both sides continued this leapfrogging, until the end of the war, each gaining the advantage in turn. Furthermore, new types of fighter planes came into production, such as the German Focke-Wulf 190 and Me 262, and the Allied Typhoon, Tempest and Mustang, just to mention a few. There will be further references to these later.

The end of the course did not lead to any official festivities, but we newly graduated fighter pilots carried out a 'fighter sweep' against the local pubs, and their landlords were no doubt very relieved when we finally withdrew. We returned to base without loss. Now we faced distribution to the 'eagerly awaiting fighter squadrons' that were to enjoy the good fortune of being reinforced with the model fighter pilots that we no doubt were.

XI AT THE END OF THE WORLD

During the ensuing days lists appeared on the notice board bearing the names of pilots and where they were to proceed to, and eventually my name appeared:

Sergeant T E Jonsson
Sergeant M Simonsen, 17 Squadron; Elgin, Scotland.

Simonsen, or Simy as he was usually called, was a tall, blond Canadian of
Danish descent. We had become acquainted during the foregoing weeks
but now we rapidly became close friends.

17 Squadron, equipped with Hurricanes, was already famous and had
been in the forward battle line right from the start of the war. I had already
enjoyed a brief acquaintance with the squadron at Debden, but now it had
been moved to Scotland for a deserved period of rest and recoupment. Two
things however, greatly frustrated Simy and me. Firstly, we had been
trained on Spitfires; we were now inclined to look down on the Hurricane
as an inferior fighter plane, but more serious was the fact that we were to be
stationed up in the northern part of Scotland, a great distance away from
where all the action was taking place. Whilst our lucky comrades, who had
been posted to squadrons in the south of England, were already chalking up
successes, and making names for themselves, we would be languishing in
the heather and bogs of northern Scotland. In fact we were 'pissed off',
using the common slang of the time.

After a long and arduous railway journey over the length of Britain, in
overcrowded trains, tired and irritated, we finally reached the airfield, near
the town of Elgin on the north coast of Scotland. The adjutant allocated us
rooms in a barrack and then took us to meet our CO, Squadron Leader
Stone.[1] He was a tall, slender man of about 25 with a congenial manner. He
shook our hands after we had saluted him, bade us welcome and expressed
hopes that we would quickly adapt to the squadron and feel at home. In that
respect he was in for a disappointment, as we shall later see. He placed us in
'A' Flight, and told us to turn up at nine o'clock next morning.

A fighter squadron was an independent unit that operated twelve
aircraft, and had a few spare ones at its disposal. The squadron's pilots
usually numbered around twenty, divided into two flights, A and B, led by
flight commanders. In addition to the pilots each squadron had the
following personnel:

An Adjutant with a staff of 3-4 under his command, led by a corporal or
sergeant. An Intelligence Officer, whose main function was to collect and
distribute information, and who was colloquially called 'Spy'. A Medical
Officer, assisted by 2-3 orderlies. An Armament Officer, commanding 10-
15 armourers who tended to the aircraft's guns and any other armaments
they might carry, and finally an Engineering Officer, who had under his
command two flight sergeants (usually called 'Chiefies'), one for each
flight, who in turn supervised the squadron's mechanics. For each aircraft

---

[1] S/Ldr OAC 'Bunny' Stone, DFC and Bar.

there were two mechanics, one called a fitter to take care of the engine and one called a rigger to tend the rest of the aircraft. In addition to these, a group of mechanics worked in the hangars on major overhauls and repairs.

Most Fighter Command aerodromes accommodated three squadrons which formed a Wing, led by a Wing Commander. Each squadron was allotted a certain area on the airfield called a Dispersal Point where it had its 'home' in a Dispersal Hut, and here the pilots spent their time when they were on standby or readiness or otherwise awaiting to fly. At one end of the hut there was an office for the CO and his two Flight Commanders, and in front of that stood a table with a telephone at which a watch-keeper sat to receive and pass on instructions from the control centre. On the wall behind him there was a blackboard on which were entered the names of the pilots on duty and their positions in the squadron formation. Scattered around the room were armchairs for the pilots to relax in. There were also tables for card and chess games, dart boards, shove-ha'penny boards, books and magazines, a radio and a gramophone, to help to while away the waiting time. Apart from a few 'girlie-pictures', the walls were mainly covered with silhouettes of aircraft seen from various angles, as great emphasis was put on the pilots' ability to recognise all the current aircraft. On days when the weather was good the pilots would usually relax outside in the sun in deck chairs or lying on the grass.

On the stations there were also various other common establishments, such as messes, canteens, dining halls, barracks, headquarters, hangars, transport section, parachute section, sick bay, gymnasium, laundry, chapel, control tower, guard room and various others. All this was under the management of a Station Commander who usually held the rank of Group Captain.

The above description applies to the standard Fighter Stations as they were in Britain at the beginning of the war, but as the Air Force expanded, and especially after the arrival of the Americans, temporary airfields sprouted like mushrooms all over the country. These, naturally, had to be provided with most of the establishments mentioned, but they were characterised by buildings and barracks (usually Nissan huts) of lower quality.

Simy and I turned up at the dispersal hut at the appointed time and met our Flight Commander who welcomed us cordially and introduced us to the other pilots present. We got the impression that they were rather a lack-lustre and indifferent bunch, and it was soon to become even more manifest that this was a distinctive feature of the atmosphere within the squadron at that time. Most of the squadron's experienced pilots who had survived the aerial battles of the previous months were now 'resting'; that is to say they were employed at OTUs training new pilots. This left the squadron with a bunch of less experienced pilots who seemed to have a very limited enthusiasm for the rather uneventful role the squadron was now playing, escorting convoys off the coast, and standing readiness watches awaiting enemy bombers that no longer showed up in these remote areas.

'Well, lads,' the Flight Commander said, 'as you did your training on Spitfires you'd better start to get acquainted with our delightful Hurricanes. Take up those two kites standing outside there, YB-S and YB-T, and fly them until you feel fully familiar with them.'

What a difference a year had made. Twelve months ago at Debden I had stared with fascination at the Hurricanes of this squadron and admired their grace, and I had yearned for the day when I would step into the cockpit of one of them and fly it. Now I looked at it with displeasure. Oh, how ungainly it looked in comparison with the graceful Spitfire.

I studied the handling manual for the aircraft for a while. I had in fact flown a short flight in a Hurricane before—at the SFTS at Montrose—but that had been an obsolete Mark I. This was a Mark II, the newest, and greatly improved model. When I had studied the manual, I started the Merlin engine, which was a more powerful version than the ones in the OTU's Spitfires. I found that the aircraft handled nicely during take-off, followed with a surprisingly good rate of climb, and I immediately liked the feel of it. The controls were light to the touch and performing aerobatics was a pleasure. Actually, the elevators felt slightly heavier than the Spit's but on the other hand the ailerons were lighter. The speed in level flight appeared to be fractionally less than the Mark II Spitfire's, but now it would be interesting to find out how fast it could go in a power-dive.

I climbed up to 30,000 feet, rolled over and shoved the nose down into a dive with the throttle forward. I watched as the needle of the airspeed indicator gradually moved clockwise, passing the numerals 300, 400 and 500, which was the highest value on the dial. By now the engine was roaring and the wind screaming as it passed the canopy, and I felt it was time to pull the throttle back and start slowing down, but just at that moment it seemed like an explosion occurred in the cockpit as one of the canopy-panes blew out and my head got sucked into the hole it left behind. I managed to free my head and started pulling at the control column to come out of the dive. To my surprise, and a little later to my horror, I discovered that I could not move the stick. I pulled with all my might but nothing happened and the aircraft continued diving vertically towards the ground at high speed. The hands of the altimeter were unwinding fast and I saw that I was already passing 10,000 feet. Now I was becoming seriously alarmed. I undid my safety straps, put both feet on the instrument panel in front of me, wound both hands around the control column and heaved with all the strength that I could muster. And, thank God, the nose started slowly inching away from the vertical. Now the sweat was pouring off me as I continued to pull with all my might, and suddenly it seemed as if something gave in and the nose started to rise rapidly. I got pressed down into the seat with tremendous force and the blood drained from my head—all became black and I lost consciousness. When I came-to again the aircraft was climbing vertically and very close to stalling. Although I was giddy I managed to regain control and get the aircraft flying level again. I looked at the altimeter and it showed 5000 feet. I shall never know how close to the mountains of Scotland I was when I passed out, but it cannot have been very far.

When I taxied to the parking stand people gathered around to stare at the aircraft. In addition to the pane in the canopy an access panel to the radio compartment had blown off, but what mostly caught people's attention were the wrinkles on the upper surface of the wings. Measurements later showed that I had added three degrees of dihedral to the wings! No-one had remembered to warn me that the elevators of the Hurricane become heavy at high speed, and tended to freeze when this became excessive. I had no doubt exceeded the maximum speed allowed for this aircraft.

The next few weeks passed quietly, with nothing exciting happening. It cannot be said that we were bored—Simy was too lively and entertaining a companion to let that happen. We gathered much pleasure from sallying forth on our bicycles into the Scottish countryside, enjoying its charm and beauty on sunny summer days, climbing mountains and eating lunch in cosy little country inns. In the evenings we visited the pubs and dance halls of Elgin, and enjoyed the company of the vivacious bonny lasses of Scotland.

Yet, although life was pleasant enough we were dissatisfied—our expectations, and we ourselves, had changed greatly. During the time when I applied for admission to the Air Force I was fully aware of the possibility of having to fight the Germans, and though apprehensive I put on a brave face. I wanted to learn to fly, and although I had patriotic feelings for my mother's country, I hoped that the war would be over by the time that goal had been reached. This now seemed aeons ago—a different century. Now I could hardly wait to get to grips with the enemy. This was of course, to a great extent due to the training I had received, and the confidence it had kindled within me. But there was another underlying reason for this enthusiasm, and that was the spirit that prevailed in the RAF. We considered ourselves better trained and more competent pilots than our adversaries. Furthermore, we were strongly influenced by the prevailing propaganda. The Nazis had shown, without a trace of doubt, that they were villains who did not hesitate to assail unarmed citizens, women and children, whether on the Continent or in Britain, and they had to be wiped out.

In addition to this, there was the ambition lying deep within most fighter pilots; the craving for aerial 'victories'; the desire to prove his worth by shooting down more enemy planes than his buddies.

With all this in mind it is maybe not surprising that Simy and I were restless, and discontented with being detained up there in the north where nothing exciting was happening, and we kept on pestering our superiors for postings to somewhere closer to the 'action'.

Although we constantly had two Hurricanes patrolling over the convoys off the coast, only once did anything happen to break the monotony. At dusk one evening my leader and I had been flying around a convoy for nearly an hour and a half. Fuel was getting low in our tanks, and we were about to set course for home when suddenly the silence was broken and we heard the controller's voice on the R/T:

'GRINGO Blue section (our call sign), SAMSON calling. A bogy (unknown aircraft) approaching from the east at 5000 feet. Steer vector 080 and climb to 6000 feet.' There was an unbroken layer of cloud with a base at 2000 feet, and we had stayed below it to keep an eye on the ships. We now increased power and headed up into the clouds. At 4000 feet we broke out of them and above us the sky was clear with a few bright stars already blinking in the fading light.

'GRINGO Blue, this is SAMSON. Bogy now six miles from you, vector (course to steer) 065.'

A short time later my leader called: 'Tally-ho. Eleven o'clock.' (Observations were always reported in relation to the dial of a clock, 12 being directly ahead, 6 directly astern and so on.)

Yes, there in front of us I saw a small black object against the light background of the clouds, the gap between us closing rapidly. Within seconds it became clear that this was a Ju 88 bomber, and I switched on the reflector sight and removed the gun button safety-catch in preparation for attacking. But just at that moment the enemy must have seen us silhouetted against the lighter background of the western sky, because he turned sharply and dived into the clouds.

'Shit, we've lost him,' my leader exclaimed. 'GRINGO Blue Two, you stay above the clouds and I'll go below.'

I started orbiting, but after a short while the controller told us that the enemy was heading east and we were cleared to return to base. I was getting worried as the fuel gauge was hovering very close to zero. I set the engine at the lowest possible revs and requested a radar vector for the shortest way home, and heard my leader make the same request. Below the clouds it was now pitch dark, and because of the black-out there was not a light to be seen anywhere. I knew I would even have difficulties seeing the airfield due to the subdued lighting, and I was getting really worried about the fuel running out and the engine cutting. If that happened I would have little choice but to bail out, as a dead-stick landing in the dark in this hilly country was virtually the same as committing suicide. However, the radar operator did a good job guiding me home, and shortly I caught sight of the runway lights and put my Hurricane down without delay. GRINGO Blue One landed right behind me, and it could not have been cut any closer, as his engine cut whilst taxying to dispersal.

Admittedly we had managed to do what we were sent out to do. We had protected a convoy from being attacked by an enemy aircraft, and this gave us a certain amount of satisfaction, but it still did not alter the fact that the job was dull and monotonous. Simy and I continued to express our desire for more action and I think our superiors were beginning to get fed up with our incessant grumbling.

Now an event took place that most likely had a bearing on the future realisation of our hopes and dreams.

XII   RINGS UP TO HIS ELBOWS

One sunny Sunday morning our CO suggested that Simy and I should take up a couple of Hurricanes and practice some dog-fighting. After a good deal of hard work throwing our planes around the sky, and 'shooting each other down', we got tired of this game. However, as the weather was so beautiful we decided to do a little sight-seeing.

We flew in formation along the coast and shortly came to a little town called Nairn. It had a nice-looking, sandy beach crowded with people seemingly enjoying themselves splashing in the water and basking in the sun. I gave Simy a sign that I intended to go down for a closer look. I was in high spirits and felt in the mood to give the good people of Nairn a little entertainment. I approached the beach at high speed and flew along the length of it just a few feet above the sea and then pulled up into a vertical roll. I felt quite pleased with the skills that I had demonstrated—we fighter pilots of the RAF most certainly knew how to fly!—and it further pleased me to see that Simy had followed my lead.

We now repeated the fly-past but this time, instead of the vertical rolls, we pulled up into a loop with a roll off the top; again showing what marvellous skills we possessed.

This is where we no doubt should have waggled our wings to our audience and called it a day, but a little devil within me would not let go, and talked me into doing a little bit of provocation. It would be rather good fun to fly very low over the beach and swirl up the dry sand. No sooner had I conceived the idea than I put it into effect.

I was tearing merrily along just over the heads of the sunbathers when I noticed an elderly gentleman standing on the sea front leaning on a walking stick and watching me intently. Furthermore, as I flashed by him, I saw that he was wearing the light blue uniform of the Royal Air Force. And, as if that wasn't enough, he was sporting a broad ring on his tunic sleeve, topped with tiers of narrower ones, seemingly reaching up to his elbow. The peak of his cap was covered with scrambled eggs. All this I noticed during the couple of seconds I was close to him in passing, and I didn't like the look of it at all. I called Simy on the R/T and told him we had better disappear as fast as possible.

We formed up and set course homewards, but we had not gone very far when the call I had been dreading came through on the R/T: 'Gringo Yellow Section, you are to return to base immediately!'

As we taxied into the dispersal we were met by a very serious and worried looking CO. 'I don't know what the hell you boys have been up to, but headquarters at Inverness phoned with a summons for you to go to see the AOC (Air Officer Commanding). It must be very serious for him to wish to see you without delay—and on a Sunday! You'd better take the Tiger Moth. Best of luck.'

Every fighter squadron had a little aeroplane for communications purposes; usually either a Tiger Moth or a Miles Magister. Inverness, where the Fighter Group Headquarters were located, was about a 100 miles to the west of us, or less than an hour's flying away in a Tiger Moth.

Two rather downcast sergeants said farewell to their squadron leader; this was very likely the end of their careers as pilots in the RAF.

However, wailing wasn't going to help; we'd just have to put up a manly front and take what was coming to us. We hurried out to the Tiger Moth and climbed into the cockpits—Simy in front and me in the back—and set course for Inverness. Ahead of us lay a flight of about 45 minutes and, as the weather was sunny and calm, we saw no reason not to enjoy it. Low-flying, skimming just above the ground, is of course one of the most exciting forms of flight, and we succumbed to the temptation to do just that—we had probably nothing to lose anyway.

We flew low over woods and fields and enjoyed the sensation of speed that low-flying imparts. The corn stood tall and was soon ready for harvesting and I challenged Simy, who was flying the machine, to drag the wheels through it. Simy did not need any urging and did this so successfully that the tracks became clearly visible across the field. We were repeating this in the next field when we discovered to our horror that we were heading for a strand of telephone wires that we were unable to avoid. As we lurched into the wires it seemed that the aircraft must surely lose its flying speed and crash, but to our relief this did not happen and we found ourselves still flying. Fortunately none of the wires seemed to have got entangled with the propeller, but we certainly didn't like what we saw. There were deep gashes in the leading edges of the wings and a tangle of wire was wound around the right-hand wings (the Tiger Moth is a biplane) and trailed behind the aircraft.

Well, we definitely had a few problems on our hands now. To start with we would have to get rid of that darned wire before we landed at Inverness—it was far too noticeable. We decided that I would try to climb out onto the wing to remove it, but after I had got both feet out of the cockpit I lost my nerve and came to the conclusion that I would not be able to reach the wire. I hasten to add that I was not in any particular danger as I was wearing a parachute, but gliding down to mother earth in such a way to meet the Air Marshal would take some explaining.

Our only course of action now was to find a suitable field to land in so we could remove the tell-tale wire. After a short while we found a pasture that looked suitable for our purpose. It was not ideal as there were cows dotted around it but we managed to pick a spot to thread our way between them. The surface proved to be more uneven than we had anticipated, but after a few heavy bumps we came to a halt without seemingly having broken anything. We hurriedly removed the offending wire, but the look of the aeroplane caused us some worries; deep cuts in the wings and the fabric torn in places.

However, no good ever came from crying over spilled milk, and we would just have to hope that we were able to park at some remote spot on Inverness aerodrome so that the authorities would not notice the damage before our meeting with the Air Marshal.

But now we were faced with a new problem—the cows proved very inquisitive and collected around the aeroplane. Some had even started to lick it. Shooing them away proved difficult as they kept coming back again, and we could not take the risk of both of us sitting in the cockpit with the engine running as they could easily get in our way, and even walk into the propeller. We solved the problem by having Simy sit in the cockpit and taxying slowly forward while I shooed the cows away. I then chased after him, climbed into the rear cockpit while Simy continued the take-off run.

On landing at Inverness we observed that some airmen were painting a hangar with camouflage paint and, as our Tiger Moth was also decorated in those colours, we saw that this was our lucky break and taxied straight there. One of the airmen promised to cover the gashes with tape, and when we got back to the aircraft later there were hardly any signs of what had happened to it earlier that day.

As there was no point in keeping the Air Marshal waiting we hurried over to the headquarters building to get our ordeal over with. We were naturally rather depressed and felt fairly certain that we could now kiss our wings and stripes good-bye. Most likely we would leave Inverness as a couple of 'erks' of the lowest grade, and we might even have to serve sentences for breach of discipline.

At headquarters we were received by a serious looking sergeant, but I did seem to detect a slight smirk on his face when he said: 'Well, boys. I wouldn't like to be in your shoes at the moment. The Old Man in there is going to have something to say to you lads!' He walked to a door, knocked on it, poked his head through the doorway and said: 'The pilots are here, Sir.'

We heard a deep, gravelly voice say: 'Send them in.'

The sergeant opened the door wide and we marched in, came to attention in front of a desk and saluted.

At the desk sat a grey-haired elderly man with pilot's wings on his left breast above rows of medal ribbons indicating that he had been much decorated during a long career. He stared at us sternly with steely eyes from under bushy eyebrows. There was a severe set to his jaws, and he looked us over for a long time without saying a word. The tension was getting unbearable and I felt sweat running down the back of my neck.

'So, you are the great aviators who were demonstrating to us poor earthlings the art of flying. I've been eagerly awaiting the opportunity to see what such aerobatic geniuses look like.' He then hit the table-top with a clenched fist and continued in a loud voice: 'I can't believe that you are such imbeciles as not to know you have broken a number of important Air Force rules and regulations. This morning you put the lives of numerous peaceful citizens in danger, in addition to disturbing a church service to such an extent that not a word of the sermon could be heard. There is no doubt in my mind that you should be grounded and be demoted to the lowest rank that exists, and even that is too good for you.' And he continued giving us such a thorough dressing down, that I was beginning to hope that the floor would open up and swallow me. Then suddenly he stopped and for a moment a playful smile broke through the stern features of his face, and he said in a lowered voice: 'I'll admit that I enjoyed watching your performance this morning, but don't tell anyone I said so'. And then in a louder voice, 'and don't ever let me catch you at it again! Have you had any lunch?' And when we, gaping in disbelief, shook our heads, he said: 'Tell my driver to take you to the sergeants' mess and wait for you while you have a bite to eat, and then take you to your aircraft'. And with a big grin on his face he added: 'The best of luck lads, and happy landings!'

And so ended that adventure. Instead of being wingless and demoted delinquents we rode up to the sergeants' mess in style flying an Air Marshal's pennant!

Not long after this Simy and I said good-bye to 17 Squadron. Simy was posted to Malta where, I later learned, he lost his life after an heroic performance in the defence of that beleaguered island. I achieved my ambition to be posted 'down south' to 11 Group. I joined 111 Squadron based at North Weald aerodrome, not far north-east of London. This famous squadron was equipped with Spitfires, and a new and exciting chapter of my life was about to begin.

CHAPTER THREE

FIGHTER PILOT

I   TREBLE ONE SQUADRON

I had a bit of luck as I was given the opportunity to fly my Hurricane to North Weald and so avoid a long and tedious journey by rail. Another pilot going on some errand up north would fly it back.

Immediately after landing it became evident to me that this was a far busier place than the one I'd left. Aircraft seemed to be continuously coming and going; things were happening here. The flying controller directed me to the 111 Squadron dispersal.

North Weald was a typical fighter station of the type I have already described. During the Battle of Britain it was severely bombed, but most of the damage had now been repaired. As a matter of fact the ruins of a burned-out hangar were still being torn down by a gang of workers, and various other signs of bombs having fallen were to be seen. Three squadrons were based on the airfield, 111, 222 and 71, the last named being the 'Eagle' Squadron, manned entirely by American volunteers.

I was taken straight in to be introduced to my new CO, Squadron Leader Brotchie, a short, quietly spoken Englishman of indeterminate age. I quickly discovered that he was a highly respected and popular leader. He immediately made me feel at ease, and declared that it was a pleasure to add an Icelander to a squadron that already had such an international flavour. Amongst the pilots, in addition to Britons, there was a Frenchman, an Irishman, a number of Czechs and men from most of the Empire and Dominions. He introduced me to Flight Lieutenant Ronnie Clifford Brown, the commander of 'A' Flight, who would be my immediate superior.

And that was the start of my career with Treble One—a period rich with excitement and adventures, full of joy but also a good deal of sadness.

And indeed, my career with the Squadron started none too happily. I was told to take up a Spitfire to do some circuits and landings for the purpose of getting re-acquainted with the aircraft and to become familiar with the surrounding territory. I wasted no time because I was eager to fly the Spitfire again, and especially this latest model, the Vb.

To keep the control tower's frequency uncluttered and open for essential operational use, aircraft on local practice flying, in reasonable visibility, were instructed not to use the radio except in dire urgency, it being left to the individual pilots to keep an eye out for other traffic. Although North Weald prided itself on two asphalt runways, it was essentially a 'grass-field' with a surface smooth enough to enable pilots to ignore the runways. However, on my first day there I was unaware of this and used a runway for take-off and landing, as indeed I observed another pilot do who was also practising landings. I also noticed that this pilot taxied back beside the runway, rather than along the perimeter track, and as the control tower didn't seem to object to this, I did the same, mainly to prevent the engine overheating from long taxying as it was a fairly hot day.

I was halfway across the airfield after my first landing when I saw a red Verey light being shot up from the tower. At first I did not know what this was supposed to indicate until I saw three Spitfires appear over the brow of a slight rise in the centre of the field heading in my direction, and one of them seemed to be coming directly at me. I decided to make a fast about-turn to get out of the way, but then discovered that the aircraft which had been heading for me had made a slight alteration in course—probably with the intention of going behind me—and was now still coming towards me and getting very close.

At that moment I was sure that the end was coming up, and instinctively hunched, but at the very last second the pilot pulled his aircraft off the ground and shot over the top of me with a terrible roar. However, by the greatest of misfortunes, one of its wheels caught my propeller causing the aircraft to crash into the ground a little way beyond and burst into flames. I jumped out of my aircraft as fast as I could in the hope of doing something to save the pilot, but was unable to get close due to the intensity of the fire. The fire-engine arrived quickly and doused the fire, and I helped the firemen to pull the pilot out of the wreck, feeling my fingers sinking into his burned flesh. He still showed signs of life, but the poor lad died on the way to hospital.

He proved to be a sergeant pilot of my new squadron, who alongside his companions had been 'scrambled' when an unidentified aircraft, which later proved to be friendly, approached the east coast.

I was heartbroken over this incident as I considered myself largely to blame for the death of my comrade-in-arms. If only I'd taxied along the perimeter track in stead of... If only I'd kept going instead of turning around... These thoughts, and others such, burned within me.

My new comrades tried to reassure and comfort me and showed great solicitude and compassion. They tried to impress upon me that this had been an accident, an unforeseeable course of events for which I must not blame myself. Brotchie, our leader, took the same attitude. He called me into his office, put an arm round my shoulders and told me not to take this too personally. He pointed out that I myself had only just missed being killed; what had happened had been unavoidable fate and I should try to drive away any feelings of guilt.

Later that day I was shown to my quarters which were on the first floor of the mess-building. This was a double room and on one of the beds lay a young man reading a book. He stood up, shook hands and introduced himself as Alun Williams. He had been with the Squadron only a short time, so we were both new recruits. We soon became great friends and were destined to remain together practically until the end of the war, first with 111 Squadron and later with 65 Squadron. I think I can safely state that this was unprecedented, and most remarkable when the upheavals of war are taken into consideration.

Alun (who was usually called Bill amongst our comrades) was a Welshman, but now lived with his father and two sisters in Romford, about 15 miles from North Weald. He was slightly under medium height, slim, with wavy black hair and wore a thin moustache which was fashionable in those days. He had a cheerful temperament, although at times he could also be most serious when such a mood was justified, and like me he was as stubborn as a mule. At times our combined stubbornness could cause friction between us, but only for short periods. In most other respects we were very unalike. He was capricious, but resourceful, unselfish and generous, and a more loyal friend was not to be found. We went down to the Bar and there, over a few beers, our friendship started to develop, and I also met a few more of my new comrades.

Next day I was sent on a convoy patrol over the Thames estuary with a Czech pilot by the name of Hruby. As I write these words, Ota Hruby has just recently died (15th May 1993) after suffering a long illness. Ota had led a most remarkable life. He was a pilot in the Czech Air Force before the war, but when the Germans occupied the Sudetenland he went via Poland and the Baltic to France, where he joined the Foreign Legion and was sent as an infantryman to Algeria where, incidentally, his Platoon Sergeant was a German. On the outbreak of war the French took him into their Air Force, but when they were defeated he somehow made his way from Southern France to Gibraltar, and thence to England, where he eventually joined the RAF. He continued fighting the Germans to the end of the war. He gained some victories and was much decorated for valour.

After his country had been liberated he returned to Prague to a hero's welcome and rejoined the Czech Air Force with the rank of Captain.

However, not long after this the Communists grabbed power (1948), Ota, along with many other patriots, was thrown into jail for the crime of having fought alongside the 'wicked imperialists' of the west. While in jail he was 're-educated'. This entailed standing for three hours every morning in line with others up against a brick wall with their noses three inches from the wall. Anyone who wobbled had his nose brutally shoved into the wall. Each morning started with the ritual of scrubbing the wall clean of the blood from the previous day. After rotting in prison for nearly four years he was set 'free' on the condition he only worked at manual labour and kept strictly away from all aviation. And so things remained until finally the Communists lost power (1989), and Hruby and his Czech RAF comrades finally had their honour restored. He ended his career as an Honorary Colonel in the Czech Air Force.

Hruby and I flew around the convoy for close on two uneventful hours until we were relieved by another couple of Spitfires, and I was beginning to wonder whether this was just going to be a continuation of the type of flying I thought I had escaped from when I left Scotland.

Next day the three squadrons that formed the North Weald Wing went on a 'sweep'. When a bunch of fighter planes crossed the Channel and flew around over enemy-held territory for the purpose of enticing the Germans to come up and fight it was called going on a sweep, a show or a circus. Often a few bombers were also sent along to give added reason for the enemy to show himself. The bombers would attack factories or other installations of military significance, such as railway marshalling yards. When I noticed that my name was not entered on the blackboard amongst the names of the pilots taking part in the sweep I asked the Flight Commander when I could expect my turn to come. He smiled and told me not to worry—I'd get my full share of sweeps before long, probably more than I'd bargained for, but in the meantime I should concentrate on practising as much as possible with the squadron, learning its tactics and procedures.

I watched fascinated as the three squadrons took off, one after the other, twelve Spitfires at a time—thirty-six aircraft joining up in an impressive formation that set course in a southerly direction and shortly disappeared into the clouds.

An hour and a half later I observed their return, not in unison as when they left but in small groups and even single aircraft. After they had landed I could see that some of the aircraft were damaged, and holes in the tape over the gun-ports of many of the aircraft indicated that their guns had been fired. There was an atmosphere of excitement and tension as the pilots stood around in groups, smoking cigarettes, drinking cups of tea and excitedly describing aerial combats, often with a great deal of gesticulation, while the 'Spy' wandered around with a writing pad and took down reports. The enemy had put up a strong defensive force of fighters, breaking up the RAF formations and heavy fighting had resulted. Many had fired their guns but only one pilot in our squadron put in a 'claim'. He thought he had probably destroyed a Messerschmitt 109; it had been going steeply downwards with a lot of smoke coming from it when last seen.

Here it is appropriate to say a few words on the system of claiming victory over enemy aircraft. The claims are made on three levels: a) DESTROYED, for which there must be substantiated proof. b) PROBABLE, when it is likely that the enemy was destroyed, and this claim must also be backed up by a witness. c) Enemy aircraft DAMAGED.

The number of aircraft that took part in this battle could be counted in the hundreds and many of them, both friendly and enemy, were witnessed falling out of the sky in flames, and many parachutes seen floating down. Unfortunately one of our comrades was amongst those that did not return.

The pilots of 222 Squadron had destroyed three of the enemy and those of the 'Eagle' Squadron claimed two, so all together the North Weald Wing could claim to have shot down five of the enemy, and probably one more, and to have damaged four. Four of the Wing's planes failed to return.

The next two weeks was a period of intensive training for me. In between going on shows, the squadron had days off from operations which were used for practising formations and tactics, and I eagerly took part in this. I went on another uneventful convoy patrol and also concentrated on getting better acquainted with the aircraft's armaments.

These Spitfires differed considerably from the ones I had flown at the OTU. Not only were they more powerful and therefore faster but they were also differently armed. Instead of the eight Browning .303 machine-guns, there were only four, but in addition they had two 20 mm Oerlikon cannons with barrels sticking out of the wings' leading edges. With these we could fire at longer range with greater destructive power. We could choose to fire either the machine-guns or the cannons separately, or all together. The bullets and shells for these guns were varied such as ball, explosive, armour-piercing or tracer, and were arranged in a certain sequence. I flew to the firing range on a lonely part of the coast and practised shooting at static targets on the ground and moving targets in the air, and was astonished at how much destruction these small cannons could cause if used in the right way.

Then one evening the following words were written on the blackboard at dispersal: 'Sweep tomorrow. The following pilots to appear at Ops at 0900 for briefing.'

On the bottom of the list stood the name Jonsson. A feeling of excitement mixed with apprehension filled me. My manhood and courage were about to be put to test. Would I pass—or would I fail?

II NUMBER TWO

I slept rather badly that night as I continually found myself locked in deadly combat with Me 109s. However, when I climbed out of bed the next morning and looked out the window I didn't like what I saw—low cloud and drizzle with practically no visibility. At the breakfast table my companions were not very optimistic about flying that day and they were proved right. At headquarters we were told that owing to a warm front moving across the Channel the weather was unsuitable and operations were suspended for twenty-four hours.

I felt frustrated, as I had been impatiently awaiting my first sortie against the enemy and had convinced myself that I was ready for it.

The next two days continued to be unsuitable but at last the 'show' was declared 'on'. The ops-room at headquarters was tightly packed with pilots. On the wall behind a dais there was a huge map of Southern England, Northern France, Belgium and Holland. A thin coloured ribbon had been pinned on this map, starting at Dover and continuing across the Channel to Boulogne and thence in an arc inland as far as Lille and back to the Channel again at Dunkirk.

A side-door opened and the Wing Commander strode onto the dais. The pilots stood up but he waved a hand and said: 'Be seated, lads. Well, at last the weather-gods are going to be kind enough to let us nip across the pond to visit our chums. They must be sorely missing us by now. We'll have to give them our greeting and apologies for such a long absence.' There was laughter in the room.

'And now down to business. We'll be flying the route shown on this map, accompanied by the Debden and Hornchurch Wings. The Kenley, Biggin Hill and Tangmere Wings will be synchronized to operate a little further to the west of us. I'll be leading 71 Squadron today at 24,000 feet, 111 will stay slightly behind us at 26 and 222 above at 28. We'll leap into the air in the same order and take-off will be at ten-O-eight. Let's synchronize our watches. The time is now 09.16—55, 56, 57, 58, 59—09.17. I hardly need to tell you that I don't want to hear any unnecessary natter on the R/T, and if someone has something important to say he shall do so clearly and calmly and not scream like a neurotic old hag as too often happens. (Much laughter amongst his audience) And that's about all I have to say, except: Happy hunting, lads!'

The pilots crowded into the trucks that took them to the various dispersal points to prepare for the flight.

In our hut Brotchie discussed our proposed formation: 'We'll fly as usual in three sections. I'll lead NOOKER section, Ronnie leads NOOKER BLUE on the right, and you, Jimmy, NOOKER RED on the left. NOOKER was the squadron's radio callsign. When the squadron flew in the type of battle formation that was common at that time, which consisted of three parallel columns of four aircraft in line astern, the aircraft were numbered One to Four in each column (or section), so for instance NOOKER BLUE Four was the last aircraft in the right-hand column. When in the vicinity of the enemy a distance of about 100 yards was kept between the columns, and 20-30 yards between individual aircraft. If the squadron formation broke up, which practically always happened in combat, it was the duty of the second and fourth pilot in each column to stay with the pilot immediately in front of him, thereby forming a sub-section and he became a 'Number Two' (or a wingman), and his task was to protect his sub-section leader so that the latter could concentrate on attacking the enemy. Although this battle formation was by no means the best, it was a great improvement on its predecessor, when the squadrons flew in four sections of three aircraft in vic formations. In that arrangement the pilots were much too busy trying to hold position on their leader's wing to keep an eye out for the enemy. The Germans were far ahead in battle tactics, and it was most surprising how long it took the RAF to cotton on, and take up the same sort of tactical formation. This was called the 'finger four' formation, and consisted of sections of four aircraft flying as the fingertips of an outspread hand. The sub-sections flew at slightly varying heights, and far enough apart for the pilots not to have to worry about collisions and so able to give each other cross-cover.

'We'll keep fairly close together to start with,' continued the CO, 'and stay on channel B (radio frequency) until you see me start weaving, when we'll open up formation and change over to channel C. *(For the purpose of looking behind, where the greatest danger of attack could be expected, pilots turned their aircraft from side to side, and this was called weaving.)* And as the Wingco said: No unnecessary talking on the R/T. All-right boys, let's get ready. Start your engines when you see me do so. The best of luck!'

Brotchie then walked to where I was standing and said: 'Jonny *(I was called both Jonny and Tony at that time)*, this being your first sweep I firmly advise you to keep well up with the squadron, and not lag behind, because if you do lag we might not be able to come to your aid in time should you be attacked. And remember that whatever happens, you must not lose Dennis, your sub-section leader. He must be able to rely on your alertness to protect him should he get onto the tail of a Hun.'

According to the order on the blackboard I was to fly in the position of BLUE Four—'Tailend Charley'. The rearmost aircraft were always in the greatest danger, as the enemy fighters mostly attacked from behind, and it was incredible that the greenhorns, the least experienced pilots, were traditionally placed in those positions. It could be claimed, I suppose, that this was the best 'school' for those lucky enough to survive until they had earned themselves a 'safer' spot in the formation.

Now the pilots started preparing themselves for going out to their aircraft. It was already October and getting cold in the upper levels so most of us wore our fleece-lined flying boots and Riving jackets. We emptied our pockets of all papers or objects that could give information to the enemy's intelligence service, and wandered out to our Spitfires. This was for me a solemn moment and I was not altogether without fear. I was surprised at the apparent lack of concern amongst my companions. They cracked jokes and behaved as if they were about to go on a joyride.

It was not long, however, before I gained an insight into this side of the RAF nature; a strong tradition that dictated that pilots never showed their true feelings of fear, no matter how deep those feelings might be. As I have already mentioned, the pilots of the RAF came from various parts of the world, but it did not seem to matter what their nationality was, they respected this tradition. Apprehension or worries were not allowed to surface; they had to be covered up with a show of unconcern and gaiety. Everyone had to show an enthusiasm for going on every raid, and express disappointment if they were left out, although without doubt some must have felt relieved at times at being 'forced to stay at home'!

Of course it was inevitable that occasionally men did crop up who had not the moral stamina to endure this deception indefinitely. Such men did not remain on the strength of operational squadrons for very long, but were quietly whisked off to less demanding jobs.

Out by their aircraft the pilots smoked their last cigarettes, chatted with the mechanics and wandered round behind the aircraft to empty their bladders. This was jokingly called 'having a nervous pee' but was the natural thing to do, as once strapped into the cockpit of a Spitfire there was no convenient way of relieving oneself. Next came the time to tie on one's lifejacket, commonly known as the 'Mae West' (named after the well known and buxom Hollywood film star of that period), followed by the parachute with its attached rubber dinghy. Then the climb into the cockpit and the safety straps fastened with the help of the mechanics.

A little while later I saw Brotchie start his engine and the rest of us followed suit. Red warning flares were fired from the tower and we taxied out just as 71 Squadron roared into the air. Thirty seconds later our own 12 Spitfires were bumping at high speed over the grassy surface followed closely by 222 Squadron. All went without a hitch, as was to be expected since it had been frequently rehearsed.

We quickly caught up with 71 Squadron and positioned ourselves to the right of it and slightly above, and in a little while the lads of 222 were in position higher up and out to the left. The weather was beautiful; just a thin layer of wispy clouds, and by the time we reached six thousand feet we were flying in the sunshine under a cloudless sky.

Out to the left I caught sight of numerous small dots that grew larger as they drew closer, and proved to be the Spitfires of the Debden Wing. They took up position out to one side, and shortly we were joined by the Wing from Hornchurch.

I had my right hand on the control column and with my left I operated the throttle to keep my position in the formation, and I let my mind wander. With pride and admiration I cast my eyes on these large and orderly formations speeding purposefully into battle. Oh, how comely and slender the Spitfires looked as they sped effortlessly through the air, but at the same time they were warlike and menacing with the gun-barrels sticking out of the wings lake bared fangs. This must be a terrifying sight to the poor enemy pilots. I was filled with a feeling of confidence and all fear vanished—it was groundless to harbour any anxiety when in company like this. Here was a large group of the world's best fighter planes in the hands of highly trained men who knew how to handle them. No, there was nothing to fear.

Between the intermittent clouds below us we could see the coastline, and in a little while it was behind us with the blue water of the British Channel below and the French coast ahead under a cloudless sky.

Until now the R/T had remained silent, but suddenly we heard our leader's voice: 'OK boys, its time to spread out and get weaving. Change channels.'

Our section moved out a little so that there were about a hundred yards between us and NOOKER section, and we started swinging gently from side to side. I switched on my gunsight which cast its orange-coloured image onto the bullet-proof windscreen in front of me, and I removed the safety catch from the gun-button on the control column.

Suddenly black puffs of smoke appeared in between the aircraft and in the sky around. These were greetings from the coastal-defence anti-aircraft-guns, and although these greetings seemed a little frightening to me, my companions didn't seem to take them too seriously, and in a short while these dirty little black clouds were left behind.

We now heard the Wing Leader call the controller in England to ask for news. The instant reply he got was: 'Radar reports groups of bandits (the word bandit denoted enemy plane) both to the west and south of you, angels (altitude) two five to three zero. Keep your eyes skinned.'

So, the reception committee was on hand. Something was bound to start happening. Involuntarily I started breathing harder and casting my eyes in all directions.

Suddenly the unhurried voice of our Squadron Leader: 'NOOKER aircraft, this is NOOKER leader. Bandits five-o-clock above, heading north. Watch them!'

I felt my stomach muscles contract. Soon all hell would let loose. I swung my aircraft violently to the right but couldn't see any enemy planes.

Now someone shouted: 'A large gaggle of bandits at six-o-clock. DAFFODIL squadron break right immediately!'

Other voices now started reporting bandits in all directions and I swung and swung but was unable to catch sight of a single enemy aircraft. Now I was beginning to get a bit worried. (Much later I realised that in my nervous state I had never rested my eyes long enough on any one spot for them to focus on anything.) I knew I had good eyesight and yet I couldn't see what others all around me were seeing. This made me both frustrated and scared, causing me to swing too violently, so much so that I was beginning to lag behind my comrades in spite of constantly pushing the throttle forward to increase speed. I was flying the rearmost aircraft and 'bandits' were being reported behind us so I didn't dare reduce my weaving—I simply had to be able to see what was coming from that direction.

And now misfortune truly caught up with me. I came out of an unusually steep turn and found myself alone—my squadron had vanished. I swung and strained my eyes in all directions but to no avail—I was alone with not an aircraft of any kind in sight.

Yet the sky was reportedly full of enemy fighters, and now I was alone and really frightened—what should I do? I kept going forward, dazed and near to panic, swinging violently, trying to make up my mind what to do, when suddenly I caught sight of a group of aircraft ahead and slightly below. Thank heavens, I had found my squadron again.

I pushed the throttle fully forward and gradually caught up with them. But . . . oh, something was wrong here—the planes were too numerous and I suddenly noticed that they had struts under their tail planes! I had nearly joined up with a squadron of Me 109s.

Now I really panicked. With my heart thumping in my chest I snap-rolled my Spitfire, pulled the stick back and dived away vertically with full power. All I wanted to do was to increase the distance between those devils and myself as fast as I possibly could and hoped that my speed was sufficient. Perspiration was running off me in spite of the frost. The R/T was alive with shouts, calls, warnings and orders, which indicated that battles were being fought all around me, but I ignored this and concentrated solely on getting out over the Channel as quickly as possible.

By the time I reached the coast I was flying pretty low. Tracer-bullets arose from the ground in graceful curves like red strings of pearls, but I was flying so fast that they disappeared behind me. After a while I had reached far enough out to sea to believe I was out of danger and pulled back the throttle a little—I had been flying at full power for some considerable time. I had escaped.

I wiped the sweat off my face and reflected on what had happened, and felt rather chastened. I had to admit to myself that I had shown very little courage when it came to the test. In truth I had panicked. What had happened to the great warrior who was going to give the Germans hell? Where was that hero now? How would my comrades in the Squadron react to my cowardice? Would I ever be able to vindicate myself?

Such questions were burning in my mind when I happened to look behind and saw two aeroplanes approaching. I figured it would be agreeable to have company whilst crossing the sea, so I further retarded the throttle so they would catch up with me. I was therefore more than a little shaken when I observer tracer-bullets shooting past me, followed almost immediately by a couple of Me 109s, doing a steep climbing turn to the left as they overtook me. So, the enemy had followed me out to sea! I was lucky, however, on two counts. Firstly, their marksmanship had been poor and, secondly, I had slowed down so unexpectedly that they overshot me before they realised what was happening.

I wasted no time in pushing the throttle fully forward, hoping to get away, but that proved to be too optimistic. The Messerschmitts had made a very tight turn and were diving down on me again. The only thing I could do was to turn towards them, and now we started going round and around in hair raising vertical steep-turns with the wingtips just above the waves. Fortunately the Spitfire could hold its own against a Me 109 in such a situation, but against two of them it was a different story. I noticed that one of them pulled away with the obvious intention of coming at me from a different angle whilst his comrade kept me occupied. This struggle could only have ended in one way if it had not been for a bunch of Spitfires suddenly turning up and driving my tormentors away. The last I saw of them, they were heading for France with gun-blazing Spitfires on their tails. I was soaked with perspiration but now I could relax again, and for the second time I set course for England.

My fuel supply was running very low after having flown for long periods on full throttle, so I landed on the first airfield I found after crossing the coast. After refuelling I continued to North Weald where my companions had all landed after an uneventful trip. They had not come across any enemy planes and considered the show to have been rather a 'washout'. No-one had seen me since shortly after crossing the French coast and they had considered me 'lost'. They were greatly amused and cracked benevolent jokes when they heard my story. They sympathetically pointed out that the first sweep was always the worst—I would soon become 'seasoned'.

And I most certainly hoped they were right. Later, when I had gained experience, and more confidence, I often recalled how I had squandered a unique opportunity to shoot down an enemy on my very first sweep.

III   THE ABBEVILLE BOYS

Next afternoon I went on my second sweep. Most likely the reason for the CO sending me over the Channel again so quickly was to help me to regain some of my confidence. Again my position in the squadron's battle formation was BLUE Four, and Brotchie pointed out to me that it was by no means necessary to 'weave' so violently as I had done the day before. My comrades in the other sections were well able to keep a look-out for anyone approaching me from behind and warn me of danger. I should concentrate more on doing the same for them. This was no doubt a well deserved admonition.

This time our assignment was to escort a formation of twelve Douglas Bostons that were to bomb a factory near Mazingarbe in France. They would be cruising at a height of 12,000 feet and we were the close-support squadron. The Wing's other two squadrons would be above and behind us. Other fighter wings would be positioned both sides of us and ahead. The rendezvous was over Dungeness on the south coast.

All this worked as planned. Our protégés were orbiting Dungeness and on our arrival they set course over the Channel and we followed closely behind and above them. At the same time other Spitfire wings took up their positions and the whole 'circus' headed for France.

The sight of this large group of aeroplanes was impressive and gave me a feeling of confidence. It also aroused in me a feeling of pride for being a part of it. Such a show of strength must surely put the wind up the Germans. In the centre there was a tight formation of bombers that formed a sort of kernel around which groups of smaller fighter planes swarmed like flies on a hot summer's day. The weather was ideal; hardly a cloud in the sky and the smooth sea reflected the orange-coloured rays of the late-afternoon sun.

Ahead lay the coast of France with the mouth of the river Somme cutting into it like a fjord. On the banks of this river lay Abbeville aerodrome; home of the 'Abbeville Boys' as we colloquially called the pilots of the famous Jagdgeswade 26 (fighter group). They, along with the pilots of JG

52 at St. Omer near the Belgian border, formed the main German aerial-defence forces of the area. Many of the pilots of these groups had started their careers flying with the famous 'Condor' Legion in the Spanish Civil War, and were greatly experienced. Some of the leaders were already famous, such as Adolf Galland. Probably to distinguish themselves from others—and no doubt to intimidate their opponents—the pilots of these groups had the nose-spinners on their Me 109 fighters painted yellow.

The pilots of the RAF were aware of the fact that they were up against the cream of the enemy fighter pilots, and that they were certainly not to be underestimated, but at the same time they considered themselves to be fully their equals.

The Abbeville Boys are no doubt already airborne and waiting for us, armed to the teeth, I now thought to myself. Not a comforting thought. Some of my new-found confidence was beginning to wane a little.

Over the coast the German ack-ack gunners spent a great deal of gun-powder on us without any visible results, and unflaggingly the formation continued on its way; the bombers in a tight little knot with the fighters swarming around them. On the R/T we would hear that our comrades in other wings had already sighted enemy planes, but so far they had not appeared in our vicinity. Deeper into enemy territory we continued, and the bombers kept up the tight formation that would have been a credit to them at any peacetime air show.

When we reached the target I could not but admire the determination and concentration that their crews showed. The anti-aircraft guns put up a steady stream of fire, and black puffs appeared in the sky all around the bombers, but their pilots didn't budge an inch, and kept on a steady course as if this was just an ordinary practice flight. When the target had been passed the bombers started a gentle left turn, and I waited with anticipation to see where their bombs landed. However, after what would be a normal time for the bombs to reach the ground there were no signs of explosions and I was puzzled. But then, when the bombers kept on turning, it dawned on me that they were about to make another run over the target. This I felt must be the epitome of courage and determination.

We kept on circling around the bombers and we could hear on the R/T that some of the other wings were already fighting the enemy. We could therefore expect German fighters to appear at any moment, and I was beginning to get worried over the seemingly unhurried attitude of our protégés. We had already used up a lot of our fuel and this could become of paramount importance should we become engaged in combat.

The bombs were finally released on the second run over the target and shortly afterwards I watched the factory nearly disappear in a cloud of smoke. The boys had done a good job and now it only remained to get them safely home again. However, it now became evident that one of the bombers had been hit by anti-aircraft fire; smoke poured from one of its engines and it began to fall behind the others.

Suddenly we heard the Wingco's voice on the R/T: 'NOOKER (squadron), you stay close to the lame duck. DAFFODIL, you keep above to the right, and we in HORSESHOE will stay on the left. Keep your eyes skinned. Other wings will take care of the rest of the bombers.'

We certainly had a problem on our hands. The damaged Boston had lost one of its two engines and had consequently slowed down considerably; it would be ages before we reached safety and our fast dwindling fuel supply was a cause of anxiety. My thoughts turned to the crew of the 'lame duck'. I wouldn't like to be in their shoes, but still, it must be a great encouragement for those five or six airmen to see three squadrons of Spitfires staying to give them protection.

After a short while a voice on the R/T called: 'NOOKER leader, NOOKER BLUE One calling. Two "bandits" at three o'clock, about two thousand feet below, flying in same direction.'

The answer came immediately: 'OK. Ronnie, I see them. This may be a trap. We'll keep an eye on them, but leave them alone unless they become aggressive.'

I bet someone has an itchy trigger finger right now, I thought. Two enemy aircraft were sitting there in a perfect position to be jumped, but of course our prime duty was to stay with our ward; we must not leave him unless forced to.

Within a short time it became evident that Brotchie's suspicions had been sound—those two aircraft had been sent to entice us to leave the bomber. Suddenly 10-15 yellow-nosed Messerschmitts appeared out of the sky from a southerly direction. In a steep turn 222 (DAFFODIL) Squadron broke into them and we could see the start of a typical aerial battle.

I did some gentle 'weaving' and tried to keep an eye on what was happening behind us. I was much less scared now than I had been the day before. I was learning to scan the sky rather than dart quick glances here and there, and I was now able to catch sight of other aircraft, both our own and the enemy's. And just then I spied four suspicious looking aircraft at five o'clock, slightly above and about a mile away. They were diving down towards us and as their formation was different from ours I didn't hesitate, and yelled into the microphone 'NOOKER BLUE, break right!'

BLUE leader immediately started a steep turn and the rest of us followed him. We had turned through about ninety degrees when we saw two grey Me 109s with yellow noses streaking towards us in a turn while the other two kept going straight on with the obvious intention of getting at our ward. I now saw BLUE leader, followed by his wingman, roll their aircraft over

Top left: 'GLAXO Baby', May 1922. This photo was used in an advert extolling the virtues of GLAXO milkpowder for rearing 'beautiful babies'.

Top right: With my sister Betty and brother Boyi, 1929.

Above: My parents, 1919.

Top left: 'Steini Boy' c.a.1930. Snapshot taken by the front steps to our home in Reykjavik.

Top right: My English Grandparents, 1890.

Middle left: At ITW, Aberystwyth, August 1940.

Above: Proud airmen wearing their uniforms in public for the first time in Warrington, May 1940. From left: Ian MacLean, unknown, Ronnie Batten and 'Thirsty'.

Top: Hawker Hurricane, the first 'real' fighter in which I did a short flight at SFTS, Montrose, in the spring of 1941, and subsequently posted to 53 OTU (Spitfires) at Heston.

Above: Spitfires, my all time-favourite aircraft. This picture (from a painting by John Young) is of three Spitfires of 111 Squadron, which I joined in September 1941 and served with until March 1943.

Top: Pilots of Treble One. Back row (on wing) L-R: Sgt Plt D J Connolly, Sgt Plt Alun Williams, Sgt Plt 'Scottie' Haine, Sgt Plt 'Blondie' Durnford. Front row L-R: Sgt Davidson (W/Op), Flt Lt L S Pilkington DFM, Sgt Plt E H Schrader, F/O Pannell, P/O Wainwright, Sgt Plt E Cooper, F/Sgt O Hruby, F/Sgt J Naldrett.

Above: Pilots of Treble One, Debden - February 1942. Back row L-R: Sgt T E Jonsson (Iceland), F/O Jiri Hartman (Cz), Sgt P E G Durnford, P/O Wainwright, Flt Lt R Clifford-Brown, Sqn Ldr G F Brotchie, Flt Lt J Clouston (RNZAF), P/O J Prihoda (Cz), P/O D W Mathews (RNZAF), P/O G Stenborg (RNZAF), Sgt Shiells (RAAF) and Sgt L Zadrobilek (Cz). Front row L-R: Sgt Ota Hruby (Cz), Sgt G Warren-Wright, Sgt K Zouhar (Cz), Sgt H V Boyle (RCAF) and Sgt A Williams.

Top left: Ota Hruby.

Top centre: One of our two main adversaries in the air, the Messerschmitt 109. The other was the Focke Wulf 190.

Top right: 'Anyone for transport?' F/Sgt 'Tubby' Roberts (F/Sgt.discip.) at RAF Debden, 1942.

Middle: Sgt Pilot Alun Williams is presented to Brazilian Ambassador, Senhor J J de Lima e'Silva de Aragao with Sqn Ldr P R W Wickham (extreme left) and Group Capt Johnny Peel (Station Cdr), Debden, 12th June 1942.

Bottom right: Treble One CO, S/Ldr 'Butch' Brotchie.

Top: Sharing a joke with my crew (fitter and rigger).

Above left: Descending from a Treble One Spitfire with parachute over shoulder, North Weald, 1941.

Above right: Proud 'Spitfire-owner' with the Icelandic ensign painted on the fuselage.

Right: Tony Bartley, our popular Treble One CO on board the M/V *Hope Crown* enroute to Gibraltar for Operation Torch.

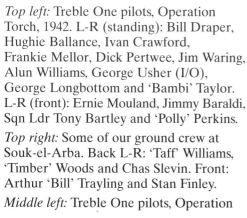

Top left: Treble One pilots, Operation Torch, 1942. L-R (standing): Bill Draper, Hughie Ballance, Ivan Crawford, Frankie Mellor, Dick Pertwee, Jim Waring, Alun Williams, George Usher (I/O), George Longbottom and 'Bambi' Taylor. L-R (front): Ernie Mouland, Jimmy Baraldi, Sqn Ldr Tony Bartley and 'Polly' Perkins.

Top right: Some of our ground crew at Souk-el-Arba. Back L-R: 'Taff' Williams, 'Timber' Woods and Chas Slevin. Front: Arthur 'Bill' Trayling and Stan Finley.

Middle left: Treble One pilots, Operation Torch, 1942. Back L-R: Mel Tushingham, 'Polly' Perkins, Tommy Tinsey, Mac Gilmour (front), J H Johnson, Brian Spranger, 'Bambi' Taylor, 'Tommy' Thomas, 'Tug' Wilson. Front L-R: Dick Pertwee, Barry Gale, George Usher and 'Monty' Falls.

Middle right: Jack Naldrett and Wally Ratcliffe, 'A' & 'B' Flight 'Chiefies'.

Bottom left: 'Quarters' at Souk-el-Kemis.

Bottom right: 'Chow' time for some of our ground crews at Souk-el-Kemis.

Short back and sides.

Shopping.

Saville Row.

Training at 'Sandhurst' - reception committee for German Paras.

into a left turn, in an effort to head off these latter two enemy aircraft. The two 109s that had been heading for us now rolled over and set off after BLUE One and Two, while my sub-section leader, BLUE Three, kept up the steep right turn for the full circle and I followed. At the completion of the circle we found ourselves about 500 yards behind the two Messerschmitts and gave chase with our throttles fully open. In my earphones I now heard BLUE One call NOOKER leader to tell him that two bandits were approaching our ward, and that he himself was too far behind to catch up with them in time.

At this moment we caught sight of four Spitfires diving down from the left, heading for the two 109s that were getting uncomfortably close to the bomber. This was a section from HORSESHOE (71 Squadron), and within seconds one of the Messerschmitts was a burning torch, while the other dived vertically closely followed by four Spitfires.

While this was taking place we had caught up with the two aircraft we were chasing, and BLUE Three started shooting at one of them. I moved slightly over to one side and was about to open fire on the second one when I remembered that my prime function was to protect my leader. I therefore made a gentle turn to have a look behind—and only just in time! Four Me 109s were close behind us and one of them was already shooting. I yelled into the microphone: 'Break right, Mike. Break right!'

We both threw our Spits into a violent right turn, and I could see the tracer bullets curving just behind me. Phew! That had been close. We kept up our tight turn but by now the German pilots must have considered it was time to leave. They went into a vertical dive, and shortly afterwards their camouflaged aircraft were lost to sight against the ground below.

And now suddenly peace and quiet reigned. The sky was empty of enemy planes and we flew unmolested to the coast. There we were greeted by the usual anti-aircraft fire, and there we were also greeted by a swarm of Spitfires sent to relieve us of our role as shepherds. No doubt our 'flock' was greatly relieved to have reached safety and bade us farewell by waggling their wings. Later we heard that they all got safely home.

During debriefing it emerged that 71 Squadron had shot down two Me 109s, and lost one aircraft, but the pilot had escaped by parachute. The pilots of 222 Squadron had destroyed one enemy plane and probably destroyed another. Treble One had less to show this time, but the aircraft that Mike, my section-leader, had fired on was considered damaged as it had been trailing a good deal of black smoke.

After I'd lit a cigarette and answered the Spy's questions I inevitably cast my mind back and started to deliberate about my performance up to now. I had been on two sweeps, and I had had more than one enemy aircraft within firing range, and yet I still had not fired a single shot in combat. My performance in the first sweep was best forgotten, but I felt I could be reasonably pleased this time. I had not been gripped by panic and what was more, I was beginning to 'see'. All that was needed was to stay cool and keep one's eyes skinned. Our Spitfires could out-turn the Messerschmitts and therefore there was no reason to be overly afraid of the Abbeville Boys. And then when Brotchie came to me and patted me on the back and said: 'You're doing nicely, Jonny. Keep it up,' I had a feeling of satisfaction, and I grew taller.

That evening a few of us were having a beer at a local pub when Mike Kellett came over to me and said: 'Tony, I'd like to buy you a pint. No doubt I have your alertness to thank for being here tonight.' I thought to myself that it was a good thing that he didn't know how close I had been to forgetting my role of 'number two', and falling for the temptation of shooting at the enemy. Had I done so neither one of us would most likely be standing here with a pint in his hand.

IV   FIREWORKS DISPLAY

I was now rapidly adjusting to the Squadron and becoming 'one of the boys'. It is difficult to define all the factors that mould an outstanding squadron out of a collection of diverse individuals from far and wide, but of course the leader plays a dominant part in doing so. I regard Treble One to have been just such a squadron; although its pilots were of such divergent nationalities, the dominant characteristic was one of solidarity and brotherhood. This quality remained unchanged for the two years I flew with it. At the end of that time none of the pilots remained of those that were at North Weald when I joined the Squadron, but the spirit still remained unabated.

In most fields there was a healthy competition between the Squadron's two flights, but on the field of battle there was unity and a singleness of purpose. In the air there was strict discipline, but on the ground there was much freedom of action and traditional military discipline was at a minimum. The pilots all used each others' first names irrespective of rank, and the only one to be addressed as Sir was the CO, and even this was often forgotten during parties (usually called 'piss-ups') which were not infrequent.

Dress regulations were not greatly respected, and neck-ties were rarely part of the uniform at dispersal, where rollneck sweaters or scarves were more common. And naturally, even on those rare occasions when full uniform was worn, the top button of the tunic was left undone in the tradition of fighter pilots, to distinguish them from other 'inferior' members of the flying fraternity.

When they were off duty the pilots were free to do as they pleased, but the 'on-duty' could be of two sorts: the '30 minutes readiness', which meant that those on the duty roster must stay within the bounds of the airfield to be readily available if suddenly called, and secondly the 'stand-by readiness' during which the pilots remained at dispersal, prepared for immediate action.

Unless joint action was planned for the Wing it was common practice to 'stand-down' one squadron and give its pilots the day off, unless, of course its CO had other plans. A second squadron was on stand-by readiness, and the third used the time for training and convoy patrols. Every now and again individual pilots were given 48 hours leave, and after longer periods they were given a week or two off. It was a favourite practice to use the two-days leave for a trip to London to see a show, dine at good restaurants and visit popular pubs that were frequented by RAF crews. The Luftwaffe's raids on the capital were abating and caused negligible disruption to the night life.

Two popular pubs were located in the nearest town, Epping, 'The Thatched House' and 'The Cock and Magpie' (usually called 'The Cock'). They were in the traditional style of English country pubs, both regarding adornment and atmosphere, and it did not lessen their popularity that they were usually well attended by the fair sex, and consequently crowded. In one of them there was a piano, and usually someone was found to hammer on it while others gathered around to give loose rein to their voices, the songs becoming bawdier as the evening progressed.

During the next few days I went on a couple of convoy patrols and a sweep without anything of note happening. One evening a few of us were having drinks in the 'Cock' when one of our more experienced pilots, Dennis Wainwright, took me aside and asked: 'How about going with me on a "Rhubarb" tomorrow, Tony?'

Rhubarb was the codename given to a special type of raid carried out by two to four fighters, and was sometimes permitted when weather ruled out normal multi-aircraft 'shows'. These raids were carried out at very low altitudes to avoid detection by radar, and also to make the task of the anti-aircraft gunners more difficult. The targets were ships, railway engines, boats and barges on canals, oil tanks and gasometers and anything else that could be considered of military significance. Rarely did these raids do any worthwhile damage, and frequently resulted in the loss of aircraft and pilots, but the opinion was that they caused the Germans a certain amount of disruption and put heart into the population of the occupied countries.

It surprised and heartened me that Dennis should invite me, the green-horn, to accompany him, especially after the debacle of my first sweep when I had been his number two and lost him as soon as things started warming up. Although I knew that these raids could be dangerous I wasted no time thinking about that and answered immediately: 'Yes, I'd love to.'

'Good man. Lets go to "ops" tomorrow morning and discuss it with Spy and get clearance.'

That day the weather ruled out any sweeps so the permission for our proposed Rhubarb was readily granted. Furthermore, our Spy, George Usher, informed us that a good deal of barge traffic had been observed on the canal between the North Sea and the town of Ghent in Belgium, and Dennis decided that this needed 'looking at closer'. The met officer said he expected unbroken cloud between 1000 and 2000 feet over the area, which was an ideal forecast.

The two of us set off about ten o'clock and in a short while we left Ramsgate behind on a course due east which should lead us to the coast of Belgium just north-east of Ostende.

In close formation we slipped down to the wavetops and in a while there was nothing to be seen but the grey clouds which seemed to blend with the grey-green sea ahead in dwindling visibility. After about 15 minutes we viewed a low sandy coast on our right, and shortly after that the port of Ostende came in sight. We curved slightly away from the town to avoid the ack-ack, and after passing it we turned right in the hopes of cutting across the railway between Ostende and Ghent. We were now heading for the coast and I widened the space between our two Spitfires. The white lather from the waves washed the yellow sand, but there was no sign of life there except a few seagulls. We had to climb slightly to cross over the sand-dunes and we observed anti-aircraft fire coming from the right. The tracer bullets came towards us, and because of our speed they seemed to curve, at first gently, but with the arc of their trajectory seemingly ever-increasing until they passed by us at lightning speed.

We found the railway and followed it towards Ghent, flying very low, and I could see people working in the fields waving to us as we roared past. Ahead of us we saw a train pulling a long line of goods-wagons and we shot at the engine in passing. I looked back and saw that it was nearly hidden in a cloud of steam. A little later we came to the town of Ghent and the great canal was clearly visible. But we also saw a large railway station and many engines. Dennis called me on the R/T and said we should each select an engine and 'finish it off'. We circled the station and started our attack, but now we most certainly received a hot reception—tracer-bullets seemed to come at us from all directions. We were forced continually to slip our aircraft from side to side to make them more difficult targets, but I saw my cannon shells hit the railway engine and a lot of steam emit from it.

Now Dennis called me and said that as we were not very welcome here we'd better look for happier hunting grounds, and I thoroughly agreed with him. I knew that the tracer-shells that were visible were only a small part of what was being thrown at us.

We now headed north alongside the canal and saw quite a few small boats and barges but we ignored them as we were looking for larger prey, and a little later this proved to be the right decision. We saw a tugboat towing three large barges. Dennis, who was about 300 yards ahead of me started shooting at the leading barge and I saw smoke ascending from it. I followed Dennis and as he passed the barge I took over and directed a steady stream of cannon shells at it. Suddenly, when I was just a short distance from the barge, it simply ripped apart in an enormous explosion sending a column of fire and smoke high into the air. My aircraft was jolted by the blast and I had to make a violent turn to try to avoid the debris being thrown into the air. However, I was not able to avoid it all and felt the aircraft jerk as it hit something, and then saw that a dent had been made in the leading edge of the left wing just beyond the cannon muzzle. This did not seem to effect the aircraft's performance and I started looking around for my leader. By now we had spent quite some time over enemy territory and we could expect our German 'colleagues' to show up on the scene at any moment. The two remaining barges were now drifting together and lying crosswise in the canal, and the crew of the tugboat appeared mainly interested in putting as great a distance as possible between themselves and the barges.

I now saw that Dennis was turning around to make another attack, but I also saw that the barges were armed with light ack-ack guns and their crews would obviously try to give as good as they got.

'Dennis,' I called on the R/T. 'The barges are armed with machine-guns'.

'So I notice, lad. Try to keep the gunners occupied while I take a pot-shot at the tubs. I'm just about to start my run in.'

By making a very steep turn I was able to approach the barges at a tangent to my leader's approach and sprayed them with my machine-guns. At the same time I observed flashes on the covers over the holds which obviously were caused by the explosive shells of Dennis's cannons. As I climbed away I looked back and could see that black smoke lay over the barges and was already rising into the sky.

At that moment I became aware of tracer-bullets shooting past me and I threw my Spitfire into a violent turn and saw a group of Messerschmitts not far behind. I kept turning as steeply as I could in a climbing turn towards the clouds, which were by the grace of God not too far away.

'Dennis, look out, the bandits are here!' I yelled into my microphone. There are at least four, and possibly more. I'm in the clouds.'

There was a period of silence and then Dennis's calm, but jubilant voice sounded in my earphones: 'Ho... ho... ho... thanks for the warning Tony. The bastards nearly got me, but now they can piss off home; they can't touch us in these clouds. My, my, did you see those bloody barges? What a fireworks display! I'll stand you a pint of beer this evening. I'm out of ammo. Let's hurry home to momma.'

I now set course in a westerly direction and stayed at 2000 feet in the clouds until I felt sure I was out to sea. I then slipped down out of the clouds and found that I was flying parallel to the coast, which was quite close on my left-hand side. I saw tracers ascend from coastal batteries but that didn't worry me unduly as I presented a ninety-degree deflection shot and no doubt a very difficult target. I had caught sight of a grey ship, about the size of a trawler, just off the coast and decided to use the last of my ammunition on it. I pushed the nose down and when the range was right I pressed the firing button. Two, three bangs... no more. My ammunition was finished.

This is his lucky day, I thought, as I pulled up in a steep turn to avoid the tracer shells curving up towards me from the ship.

Dennis had just landed when I taxied into our dispersal. He strolled over to me as I climbed out of my Spitfire and with a wide grin on his face he punched me on the shoulder and said: 'Good show, old boy. We most certainly gave the Hun something to worry about. We'll celebrate with a couple of beers this evening.'

Next day we were shown the films from our ciné-cameras and they showed how the barge had blown up. All pointed to it having been loaded with high explosives of some sort, and the likelihood was that it would take some time before its remains, and that of its sisters, were removed, and the canal opened to shipping again.

Somehow the press got wind of this raid and now reporters and newspaper photographers turned up. A short paragraph appeared in some of the papers reporting that 'the only Icelander in the RAF had taken part in a successful raid on important military targets on the Continent'.

There was no denying that I was becoming very pleased with myself. Over a short period I had been praised by three experienced pilots. And I had been in the papers—yes, even a photo of me. I was rather proud of all this; I must be getting good. It was not long before I discovered that I still had a good deal more to learn.

*

V   SINGING AND ORBITING

October was drawing to a close and winter setting in; the gloom and murk of shortening days lay over the land. Our Spitfires stood forlorn and deserted at the dispersals with the autumn rain dripping off their wings—operational flying was at a low ebb. On the few occasions when the weather permitted sweeps, I had to reconcile myself to the fact that pilots who had served the squadron longer could claim priority. All pressed for a place on these rare flights. This was a period of boredom and frustration for a young fighter pilot who was in search of adventure and wanted to get to grips with the enemy. And the current state of the war was not exactly conducive to creating joy—the Army had suffered great losses in Greece and Crete, the 'Desert Rats' were playing a game of tag with the Afrika Corps and were in a tight spot in North Africa, German U-boats seemed to be gaining the upper hand on the oceans and the Russians were retreating on all fronts, being pushed back by Hitler's seemingly invincible legions.

Once in a while I went on convoy patrols which, as usual, were uneventful, and on one occasion I set off on a Rhubarb, but that sortie ended in an unexpected, and rather abrupt way.

The four of us that set off for Belgium that morning in November were full of expectation and fighting spirit. I was flying in the position of wingman to NOOKER Three, and as usual on such raids we flew close to the wave-tops to avoid detection by the watchful German radar stations.

When flying in close formation it is the leader who keeps a lookout and conducts the flight whilst the others watch him and concentrate on keeping their position on him. A strong wind was churning up the sea that day and blowing the tops off the white-caps; the unstable air made keeping a tight formation hard work.

Suddenly the tips of my propeller touched a wave-top, the aircraft shuddered and started slowing down. I used what speed I had to gain height and turned back towards land. It quickly became apparent that all available engine power was needed to keep the aircraft flying. The temperature gauge started rising and before long it had reached the red danger mark. Black smoke was pouring from the exhaust-stubs due to over-exertion of the engine, and shortly white steam from the glycol cooling-system started streaming from under the engine cowlings; it wouldn't be long now before the engine seized. I was greatly relieved to see that Zouhar, my section leader, kept close by me like a mother duck. Most likely I would shortly be in the sea, and it was a comfort to know that he would be able to direct the rescue-boat towards me.

Because of the roughness of the sea I decided it would be safer to descend by parachute rather than attempt a dead-stick landing on the waves. Even under the best of conditions it was deemed to be inadvisable to try to 'ditch' the Spitfire. I was at a height of 500 feet, and any lower would lead to doubts whether the parachute would open in time. I therefore slid back the cockpit canopy and undid my safety straps so as to be able to get out in a hurry when the engine stopped.

Slowly the Spitfire inched forward at minimum flying speed, and it shook so much that I could hardly read the airspeed gauge. Visibility was rather poor and ages seemed to go by until I finally caught sight of the coast. Happily, Manston aerodrome, with its enormous runway, was not far beyond. Manston lies closer to the Continent than any other airfield in Britain, and was repeatedly attacked by the Germans during the Battle of Britain, but repairs were always made without delay. It had frequently been a welcome sight to pilots in distress and continued to be so in ever increasing measure up to the end of the war. Now the great runway came into sight, and with immense relief I was able to slide my aircraft onto its firm ground. I turned off the runway as soon as I could and switched off the engine. A cloud of steam arose from it, and from under the cowling could be heard hissing and snapping noises emitted by the tortured metal. There can be no doubt that had we been just a short distance further from the shores of Britain when my prop struck the wave-top, this Spitfire would have ended up on the sea-bed somewhere in the neighbourhood of the Goodwin Sands.

I was dumbfounded when I viewed the propeller. It looked like a three-petal daisy that was starting to wither. About one third of each blade was curled over—forward! It surprised everyone that this deformed piece of junk had kept the Spitfire flying for at least fifteen minutes.

By next morning the propeller had been changed and the aircraft thoroughly inspected. I took it up on a test flight, and as all seemed in order I flew it back to North Weald.

As for the Rhubarb, NOOKER One and Two carried on, and attacked a railway-engine repair shop in the town of Bruges. The target was heavily defended with ack-ack guns and the leader's aircraft was hit, but he managed to return to base despite the damage.

During a two-week period the Wing lost three pilots on Rhubarbs and a fourth lost his life in a crash when returning in bad weather. The gains from these raids seemed very questionable in relation to the losses, so our CO intervened and put a ban on them—at least for the time being.

Around about this time I became the proud owner of a motor-bike. It was a Norton 500, a fast track-bike and was the very first powered vehicle I had ever driven (excluding aeroplanes). It may seem a bit ludicrous these days, but it was not until two years later, when I was already 22 years old, that I drove a car for the first time. My roommate Bill (Alun), and I roared around the countryside on my bike, and even visited London. We frequently stayed at his father's home in Romford as it was only a 20-minute ride from the airfield. In that neighbourhood there were a couple of good-looking damsels we had an eye on at the time. Petrol was of course strictly rationed, but as Bill also owned a motor-bike our combined rations gave us a certain amount of leeway.

At the beginning of November our squadron was posted to Debden aerodrome, about 20 miles north-east of North Weald, for the purpose of practising night flying. We were far from pleased with this scheme con-cocted by the powers-that-be. The original plan called for a two-month sojourn there, but the weather was so atrocious that hardly any flying was possible, and after six weeks we were told that we were going back to North Weald. We celebrated these glad tidings with a grand 'piss-up' in the mess. This did entail some extra expenses for certain repairs to the premises, but none of us wept.

Only three days after returning 'home' to North Weald, events took place which were to cause great changes in the Squadron's activities, and the reason for the mysterious night-flying practice at Debden became evident. The AOC paid us a visit and kindly but firmly informed us that we were going back to Debden to become an operational night-fighter squadron.

Night fighters! Single-engined aircraft without radar. How ridiculous! Many voices were heard to put forward these, and similar arguments, but to no avail—Debden and night fighting it was to be. Voices were also heard objecting to our having to leave North Weald. We were now so well settled-in, and loved our station. It was home to us.

Squadron Leader Brotchie told us that anyone objecting to being a night fighter could request a posting. Every pilot in the squadron turned up at his office with such a request, but of course no-one was really serious; all felt too much respect for the CO, and had too much loyalty towards the Squadron, to really want to leave.

A great many strange suggestions on how to thwart the German night bombers emerged at that time. One of them was this experiment with Spitfires in the role of night fighters. The idea was that the Spitfire should orbit at 10,000 feet around a beam cast up vertically by a searchlight. If an enemy bomber entered the area the controller would, with the aid of radar, direct the Spitfire towards this uninvited guest, which should by then be bathed in the rays from searchlights and form an easy target.

This idea did, of course, have some merit, but it also had a great many drawbacks. Its execution required a nearly cloudless sky, or a very high cloud base, for the searchlights to be of any use, and during the winter months in Britain such conditions were rather rare. Secondly, the search-light crews were none too adept at holding their prey in the light-beams, especially if the pilot made determined efforts to escape, although it must be admitted they improved greatly in this respect as the winter progressed. But, most serious of all from our point of view, was the fact that the German pilots showed no interest in visiting our area, where no major targets were to be found. They directed their attacks against London and other major cities, and in those areas the defences were in the hands of real night fighters, mostly twin-engined Bristol Beaufighters (and later DH Mosquitoes) equipped with radar and a two-man crew.

However, there was no getting away from it—we had to return to Debden, crushed and ill-tempered, but also with a resolution to make the best of it. It was as if the weather gods were shedding tears of sympathy for us—rain continued unabated into the new year, and hardly any flying was done.

The Spitfire was far from being an easy aircraft to fly in the dark. The engine exhaust stubs—so close to the pilot's eyes—emitted a bright jet of fire that tended to reduce his night vision, and this was only partially remedied by fitting so-called glare-baffles (metal plates fitted to the cowling above the exhaust stubs to shield the pilot's eyes from the glare). Further-more, because of the narrow wheelbase, and the limited forward visibility due to the high nose position, night landings could be quite tricky in any kind of crosswind.

Our Spitfires were painted black—probably the world's only black Spitfires. As a matter of interest it can be mentioned that a few years after the war, 111 Squadron distinguished itself by pioneering multi-aircraft formation aerobatics. Its Hawker Hunter aircraft were painted black and the squadron carried out displays at air shows, and became famous as the 'Black Arrows'.

Now we started practising the 'searchlight system' with the co-operation of a Wellington bomber squadron at a nearby station. In the beginning things did not go too well, mainly due to bad weather, but occasionally we did manage to get within range of the 'enemy'. Snow and other adverse weather conditions continued to limit flying, and we spent a great deal of time hanging around dispersal playing cards, reading, chatting and sleeping. We all agreed that this state of affairs was becoming intolerable and many began contemplating the possibility of applying for postings to other squadrons.

Leafing through some RAF newsletters at that time, I came across an article that caught my attention. German long-range Kondor aircraft were attacking convoys in the Atlantic Ocean, beyond the range of land-based fighters, and to counter this menace there was a scheme for fitting some merchant ships with equipment for catapulting a Hurricane into the air to shoot these bombers down. If the convoy was too far out to sea for the Hurricane to reach land the pilot would bale out and be picked up by an escort vessel. Volunteers were being sought to fly these Hurricanes, and to me this seemed to offer a great deal more action than the dreadfully dull job we were now stuck with. I would be able to combine my love of the sea with the excitement of encountering and possibly shooting down enemy planes.

I approached Brotchie and discussed this with him. He said he would not try to prevent me from applying for this post, but firmly advised me against it. Before long, he said, we would be into spring when no doubt I would have plenty of opportunities to encounter the enemy. Indeed, it was by no means certain that things might not start warming up even sooner.

A few days later an incident occurred which, at the time, I hoped would be quickly forgotten.

One of our most popular pilots, Sergeant Peter Durnford, was about to leave the squadron. He was a tall, blond and handsome lad; the sort of dashing Adonis that brings a gleam into the eyes of maidens. Such men are not always approved of by their own sex, no doubt due to envy, but that was not the case with Pete. He was cheerful and amusing, sincere and friendly and very well liked by all. He was also an excellent pilot and had already destroyed a number of enemy planes, but now he was about to leave us for service in North Africa, and we were going to miss him. All the squadron personnel not on duty that evening were going to turn up at a local pub for a farewell drink with him.

To my great annoyance I had drawn the wrong card and was on stand-by readiness that evening. The weather was murky, and there was practically no likelihood of flying, and yet I would have to hang around dispersal all evening, miserable and ill-tempered, while my mates were enjoying themselves. Visibility kept reducing and by about eight o'clock it was down to a few yards in dense fog. I now became convinced there would be no flying—take-off was out of the question, let alone landing. I jumped onto my bike and cycled to the pub as fast as was possible in this fog. The party was in full swing when I got there, and I wasted no time in getting myself a pint of beer to drink a farewell toast to Peter. Someone was playing the piano and the rest of us gathered around it to sing a few songs. Everyone vied to buy a round of drinks, and much beer was swilled. After having verified that the fog still lay thickly on the ground I joined in with gusto. Although the occasion for this party was ostensibly Peter's departure, there is not much doubt that boredom and frustration with our lot was partly the reason for the way we let ourselves go. As the evening progressed the singing became louder and bawdier.

It must have been around ten o'clock when I, once again, had to take a trip to the 'Gents' outside in the yard. This time I received a shock when I passed through the door leading into the yard and found the moon grinning at me from a cloudless sky. The fog had completely disappeared.I got onto my bike in a hurry and pedalled as fast as I could to the dispersal where a worried watch-keeper awaited me. Twenty minutes had passed since Operations had phoned and ordered an aircraft to be sent on patrol.

It now became obvious to Len Hurle, the watch-keeper, that I was far from sober, and with a worried look he said: 'Surely you are not going to fly in this condition, Tony; you're unsteady on your feet.'

'Don't tshu worry oleboy, I'm orrite,' I said and rushed out to the Spitfire where two mechanics awaited me. I jumped up onto the wing to get into the cockpit but lost my footing and found myself sitting on the asphalt. The airmen helped me to my feet and tried to talk me out of proceeding. I took no notice of their pleas, and managed to climb into the cockpit and, while still trying to reason with me, the airmen helped to strap me in. I then started up, taxied out, requested the tower for take-off clearance, and took to the air; all of this without a hitch, although I was told later that my wingtip had missed a parked aircraft by inches when I moved off.

I signed off from the tower, changed over to the control centre and told them that I was airborne and that they could now turn on the searchlight beam. I was surprised when they did not reply, but a short while later the vertical beam appeared in the distance. Obviously they had received my message and were just keeping the radio-traffic down to a minimum, I told myself.

As I climbed towards the beam I took in the scenery. The moon was full and the stars twinkled in a cloudless sky. To the east, as far as the eye could reach an unbroken blanket of white cloud lay over the ground, and to the west the landscape lay bathed in moonlight. Not a light was to be seen anywhere except for the searchlight that I was heading for. I was alone in the sky—yes, even in the whole world! It was a lovely sensation to be flying free as a bird in such a beautiful and clean world of millions of stars and a big white moon. Not a sound to be heard but the hum of the sweet-running Merlin engine. I felt elated and in the mood to sing, so I sang at the top of my voice. It was such fun singing into the microphone in the face-mask—the sound in the earphones was so crystal-clear and I felt like an opera singer. At the time I departed from the merrymaking at the pub we had been singing the bawdiest songs we knew, some of which were certainly not fit to be performed in polite society, and I now carried on in the same spirit. It mattered not that the words were ribald, and that I didn't always stay with the tune—nobody else could hear me.

After about ten minutes I had reached my patrol area, so I called the control centre for instructions.

And I was certainly not kept waiting for them!

'NOOKER One—this is BLACKBIRD. You are to return to base and land immediately. I repeat, immediately. You have kept the radio-channel occupied for a long period, blocking all other traffic. I repeat, you are to land immediately.'

Oh, my god! The transmitting button had stuck in the ON position, and I had held a concert for everyone listening in on the channel. In my mind's eye I saw all the WAAFs working in the control centre, who must have 'benefited' from listening to these refined arias I had presented to them. Oh, well, it had probably done the darlings a world of good—likely taught them something. But, come to think of it, hadn't they heard it all before?

I didn't spend much energy on singing for the rest of the flight, but landed without further incident and hurried to the sergeants' mess where I knew the good-bye party would continue. News of my exploit had preceded me, and I became 'the man of the hour'.

Next day I was interrogated by no less a person than the Station Commander. When we reached the subject of my negligence with regard to the transmitter button I could see that the Group Captain was having difficulties keeping the stern look on his face that such a serious enquiry called for. I was grounded for a week.

For the next few days this incident caused much mirth in places where men gathered, such as the mess bars and the local pubs. To add to its hilarity the story got around that one of the senior WAAF officers had sent the higher-up authorities a complaint about the uncouth, and even vulgar language sometimes used on the R/T by the pilots.

VI   A GAME OF LIFE AND DEATH

We continued to fly round and around the light-beam and occasionally 'shot down' Wellington bombers, but the Germans of course had sense enough to stay away from this 'strongly' defended bastion of ours.

With one exception though. One night we had a most unexpected, and highly audacious visit; an episode that was probably unmatched throughout the war. So that this bizarre scene can be better understood I will try to describe the stage it was played on. The strict wartime black-out regulations applied to an aerodrome like any other place, and the dimmed runway lights were turned on only whilst aircraft were taking off and landing. On dark nights the pilots had to resort to intermittent use of their landing lights for manoeuvring on the ground. At night-time most activity was at a low ebb and consequently not many people were out and about. Indeed the station resembled a sleeping village.

On the night in question the sky was clear but the moon had set and it was therefore quite dark. A couple of Spitfires were practising night flying, so the runway lights were intermittently switched on and off. An airman cycling to the control tower to go on duty observed a twin-engined aircraft, with its landing lights turned on, taxi onto the tarmac in front of the tower. As the airman approached the aircraft, a cockpit window was opened and the pilot leaned well out of it and shouted: 'What aerodrome is this?'

After receiving the requested information the pilot closed the window, turned the aircraft around and taxied out towards the runway. It wasn't until the plane turned, and the airman was no longer blinded by its bright landing lights, that he caught a glimpse of a swastika on its tail and realised that this was a German.

What should he do? There was no vehicle on hand for chasing the aircraft to stop it. The only weapon the airman knew of was the guard's rifle at the main gate. He pedalled as fast as he could to fetch it, but of course it was too late. The aircraft took off and the controller was considerate enough to turn on the runway lights!

I do not doubt that the German pilot smiled gleefully at this evidence of 'British doltishness', and that his comrades heartily slapped his back and drunk his toast in the messes on the other side of the 'ditch'. At least we did in our mess; we could appreciate men with such audacity. What a nerve!

And indeed, the Germans did not lack boldness. Shortly after this incident they were seen to tweak the 'British Lion's' tail with such impertinence that the world stood agape with disbelief. In broad daylight, right in front of the noses of the British they sailed the battle-cruisers *Scharnhorst* and *Gneisenau* and the cruiser *Prinz Eugen* up through the English Channel, all the way from Brest to Germany.

Shamefaced, the British authorities tried to make excuses for suffering this humiliation with weak explanations such as: It had been considered unthinkable that the Germans would try anything so foolhardy... By the use of a new, secret technology the Germans had jumbled the radar and rendered it useless... The greater part of the Royal Navy's torpedo aircraft had been on station in the Mediterranean... Most of the Navy's capital ships were engaged on other tasks around the world... The weather had been atrocious and advantageous to the Germans, and more of the same kind... There was indeed a grain of truth in all of this, and in fact the British damaged the *Scharnhorst* sufficiently for six months to be needed to repair it, and the *Gneisenau* never sailed again. But the unpalatable fact was that

Hitler had made a long nose at Britain and the people felt both hurt and resentful.

Already on the morning of the 12th of February 1942 we perceived that something momentous was happening when all our leaders were summoned to an important meeting. After the meeting we pilots were assembled and told about the voyage of the German ships, which were now approaching the narrowest part of the Channel in the vicinity of Dover, and a large number of Luftwaffe fighters were airborne to provide them with protection. A short while earlier six torpedo carrying planes had made a valiant attempt to sink the ships. These aircraft were the slow Swordfish biplanes affectionately known as 'Stringbags'. In spite of being obsolete they were greatly loved by the men who flew them, and had played a large part in stopping the great battleship *Bismarck* and had sunk the major part of the Italian fleet in the harbour of Taranto. But this time they didn't reap the success that their effort deserved. Because of poor visibility and numerous heavy rain-showers in the area they did not meet up with the Spitfires sent to escort them, and they had all been shot down before they were able to deliver their torpedoes. Of the twelve crew members, only five had been rescued from the sea.

A large number of fighter squadrons had already taken part in this conflict and both sides had lost numerous planes in battles. Because of the low clouds, poor visibility and widespread showers it proved unfeasible for conventional bombers to attack the ships, so it had been decided to try further attacks with torpedo-carrying Swordfish. Our role and that of numerous other fighter squadrons would be to patrol the area in search of enemy fighters to prevent them getting at the torpedo planes.

When we became airborne around about two o'clock the ships were already in the North Sea about 50 miles east of Margate. We kept in formation as far as the coast, but then low cloud and heavy showers made this impracticable so Brotchie ordered us to break up into three independent sections. I flew as number two to Ronnie Brown who led NOOKER Red section. Ronnie was the commander of 'A' Flight, and it became my task for a while to fly as his wingman. There was much clatter on the R/T, shouting, calling and warning, which indicated that aerial battles were being fought, although we had so far not seen any aircraft. We flew in the direction where the ships were supposed to be and kept just below the clouds at 800 feet. Suddenly I caught sight of two Me 109s emerging from a rain shower a short distance ahead of us.

'NOOKER Red! Two bandits at one o'clock, same height, heading south-west,' I called.

'OK Tony, I've got them. Let's go for them!'

Ronnie increased power and shortly we started gaining on our opponents. I stayed to the right and slightly behind Ronnie and saw him open fire on the rear Messerschmitt. I could not see whether his bullets were finding their mark but suddenly the German made a sharp climbing turn and disappeared into the clouds.

Just at that moment I saw another Me 109 at nine o'clock heading straight for us.

'Break sharp left, Ronnie!' I hurriedly yelled and at the same time turned towards the oncoming enemy. Now the German and I were heading directly for each other and the distance between us diminished rapidly. The flashes from his guns indicated that he had opened fire, and now I did the same. There was not much time for thought, but I did, however, reflect on whether he would go under or over when we met. I decided to go under—that way I could keep an eye on him longer—and only hoped that he hadn't made the same decision. No, thank God, he started to turn and climb. I rolled my aircraft so the wings were vertical and pulled back the stick in an attempt to chase this fellow but never saw him again. I was not aware of his shells having hit my aircraft nor had I any idea whether I had hit him.

By now my companions had disappeared and I was all alone. There was much noise on the R/T indicating that combats were taking place far and wide so I had better keep my wits about me. I flew into a black rain shower to catch my breath and settle my nerves. After a short while I came out of it again and a short distance ahead in the murk I caught sight of a grey colossus with a tall tower—one of the warships. Flashes were to be seen here and there and streams of red tracer shells curled upwards, some of them in my direction. I hurried away.

A short while later I saw a group of aircraft, and on closer inspection they turned out to be Spitfires. I considered the wisest course was to join them and was already turning towards them when I became aware of tracer shells passing me on the left. I immediately went into a tight turn to the right and after about half a circle I saw a Me 109 opposite me on the other side of this circle. We were now caught up in a game of 'tag'—the first one to get onto the tail of the other won the game. The ominous thing was that this was a game of life and death.

Actually, in a situation like this I believed that my Spitfire could out-turn the Me 109; it was more agile, and down here near sea level the turbine-boosted engine of the Messerschmitt would not have the advantage it had higher up. But I also knew that a great deal depended on the skill of the pilot; that had become evident during practice dog-fights. This was my first true dog-fight and I sincerely hoped that my opponent was not some kind of a super pilot. My heart beat faster and I could feel the adrenaline flowing, but gradually my confidence grew when it became evident I was gaining the upper hand. Round and round we went and slowly but surely I was creeping up on my adversary; before long I should be able to open fire. We were now right down near the wave tops so there could be no chance of him escaping into the clouds. Surely I had him nailed! I was already beginning to feel the excitement of my first victory.

But now it was about to be demonstrated that the word victory should not be used until the foe lies slain. Suddenly I saw four Me 109s in line-astern diving down and across my line of flight, the first one already shooting. I saw the tracer bullets curving towards me and felt a jolt when something hit my aircraft. I trod heavily on the left rudder pedal to slip the Spitfire out of the path of the bullets and at the same time continued turning so tightly that the aircraft shuddered on the verge of stalling. My former adversary—my first victory!!!—used this opportunity to change course and make good his escape. I could not follow him as then I would become a sitting duck for my new foes. After a few seconds they had sped by behind me, and as they could not turn fast enough I had sufficient time to climb up into the clouds.

I rejoiced over having escaped but at the same time felt resentful about loosing my prey and was determined not to quit just yet. I slipped out of the clouds and started weaving between the showers and flying round in circles, but saw no other aircraft nor the ships. I must have drifted out of the battle area. The radio channel was still cluttered and during a moment's silence I tried to contact my leader but got no reply. I now decided that it was time to set off home and headed in a north-westerly direction in the hopes of hitting the coast somewhere near Manston, where at least I could land if the weather prevented me from continuing to base.

After flying for about 15 minutes in rain and poor visibility, I found myself still over the sea with no land in sight. I must have been much further north than I had assumed so I altered course to due west and shortly I came to a low, flat coast. Although the rain reduced the visibility to less than a mile I had no difficulty in determining that this was Orfordness—I had so often flown over it en route to convoy patrols. I was now able to set course for home and in a short while I found the airfield and landed. After I had parked my aircraft I walked round it and inspected it thoroughly. There was a hole about an inch in diameter in the right aileron, but that was the only damage I could find.

Most of the Squadron's pilots had already landed, but two were still missing, giving us cause for concern until we heard from them. They had had difficulties finding their way home in the poor visibility and had landed at other aerodromes. The Squadron therefore suffered no loss and Pilot Officer Prihoda was credited with having shot down a Me 109, Peter Durnford claimed a probable and Hruby a damaged.

Personally, I was able to reconcile myself with my lot. Admittedly I felt a little peeved over 'the one that got away', but on the other hand I was thankful for having narrowly missed being shot down myself. The important thing was, however, that I was gaining confidence. I was no longer in the grips of terror when I saw aeroplanes with yellow noses and black crosses. I was beginning to feel that I could meet our adversaries on level terms, and I had an unshakeable faith in the Spitfire's superiority over the Me 109 in combat, and that made all the difference.

VII 'INITIATING' REPLACEMENTS

After this welcome diversion, our life slipped back to the previous boring routine; night flying, training flights and convoy patrols. None of this did much to enliven our existence, and even the letter of commendation from the AOC, for our performance in the dramatic events over the Channel, and also for diligent night operations in spite of adverse weather, did nothing to cheer us up. Here was a group of highly trained fighter pilots chafing at the bit. They were becoming very impatient for more action and more thrills.

An incident took place in the middle of March that touched the Squadron deeply—we lost Sqn/Ldr Brotchie, our popular and highly respected CO. During a squadron formation take-off, the aircraft of a Czech pilot accidentally swerved into Brotchie's aircraft, who lost his life in the resulting fire. Three days later we had a new Squadron Commander, Squadron Leader Peter 'Pete' Wickham. He was a highly experienced pilot who had destroyed numerous enemy aircraft in North Africa, Greece and on the Western Front. My association with Pete lasted only a few months on this occasion, as he was shortly to be promoted to the rank of Wing Commander, but two years later I was to fly a great deal under his guidance and leadership.

Finally, in the early days of April, the powers-that-be became aware of a certain fact, which we had known for a long time; i.e., single-engined fighters, such as our Spitfires, which had to rely on searchlights on the ground for finding the enemy, were of very little use at night. Not once had the squadron come anywhere near to finding an enemy aircraft in the night sky. At last, our Spits were allowed to discard their black 'night-gowns' and change back to their ordinary day clothes. With this our spirits rose anew.

Shortly afterwards I personally had a further reason to rejoice. It is the ambition of every fighter pilot to have an aircraft assigned to him as his own personal aircraft, but as the pilots in a squadron are more numerous than the squadron's aircraft, the pilots have to earn the right. The two deciding factors are length of service in the squadron and the position held. By this time I had started flying as a sub-section leader; i.e., in the air I was in charge of a section of two aircraft and I had a No. 2 (or wingman) flying with me. Now I became the proud 'owner' of JU-J. The letters 'JU' were the Squadron's identification code and 'J' the individual aircraft marking.

Pilots naturally became attached to their own aircraft and were jealous of others flying it, although this could not, of course, be avoided. As I have explained earlier, each aircraft was in the care of two mechanics, a fitter and a rigger, who 'owned' it along with the pilot, and normally there was very close co-operation between these three. Most pilots personalised their aircraft with some sort of badge or emblem. I decided to mark mine with a small Icelandic flag, and the 'co-owners' offered to paint this on the side of the fuselage, just in front of the cockpit. They told me that they had a picture of the flag to copy it from. When I saw the result of their work of art I discovered that it was the ensign which is only used by government officials and establishments. Oh well, I decided to let it be, and duly became the Icelandic Air Force!

As we moved into April the fighter sweeps started up again with renewed vigour, and hardly a day passed without some kind of a cross-Channel show. The list of squadron victories grew longer, but at the same time we had to face the sad fact that many of our comrades failed to return. As a matter of fact some of them were seen to bale out, and would most likely become prisoners of war, but others had to be considered dead. In the mess we toasted their memory and passed remarks about so and so having been a nice chap... he's probably playing the harp now... or, he's probably removed the wire from his halo as he did with his cap... or, hopefully St. Peter was able to greet him in Polish... or, let's hope he'll be able to get his favourite tobacco—or other such inane remarks.

In the beginning I found this type of 'sick' humour regarding our dead comrades both heartless and disagreeable, but I quickly learned that it was practically unavoidable—constantly mourning lost friends and comrades was hopeless in war. This type of superficial indifference was a part of the self-defence mechanism. Even though one might privately mourn the loss of a good friend, outwardly one had to show steadfastness, courage and lack of feeling. In our hearts we all knew that it might be our turn next, although we tried to convince ourselves that such things only happened to others. Life must continue, and those of us that remained had to avoid becoming overtly emotional.

New pilots replaced those we lost, and in complete contradiction to what has been described above, we sometimes put on a show of mourning for their benefit. When a new, inexperienced but probably desperately keen pilot appeared in the mess for the first time we might spontaneously decide to tease him a little. Everyone would put on a look of utter depression, each one would drink his beer in his private little world without saying a word to anyone else. A deep silence and an atmosphere of mourning prevailed. The new arrival would cast a look of surprise over this 'stage' and then wander over to the bar in search of a beer. After a little while he would summon up courage and ask the nearest person what the matter was; why was everyone so depressed? The person asked would lift his glass with a shaking hand, sip his beer, sigh and say something in the following manner:

'Are you one of the replacements?'

'Eh . . . yes, I suppose so. I've just come from number 53 OTU.'

Our man would look at him for a long silent moment with mournful eyes and then say:

'Well, I certainly hope you will last longer than the ones we got yesterday. We lost two of them this morning, and the third one this afternoon. It's absolute hell over there, and the Huns are laughing at us. We've lost eighteen pilots during the last three weeks, mostly new recruits although a few of the older ones have also "gone for a Burton" *(slang at the time, meaning killed)*. Thank heavens I'm going on leave in a few days time. That is to say if I am still alive.'

After having delivered this speech he would drink up his beer, pat the new boy's shoulder, wish him the best of luck and walk away. The poor victim would be left alone at the bar, with a worried look on his face as he mulled over these terrible tidings.

After we felt the poor fellow had been tormented sufficiently we would all burst out laughing, gather around him to welcome him to the fold and buy him some beer. Without exception a look of utter relief would appear on his face.

VIII   'DOG-FIGHTING'

Around about this time the new German fighter, the Focke-Wulf 190, started appearing in increasing numbers. It was faster and more nimble than the Me 109 and heavily armed with four 20 mm cannons and two lighter machine guns. It was certainly superior to our Spitfire Vb, and we were very much on guard against it. It wasn't until the Spitfire IX came along in 1943 that the RAF had a fighter to match it.

The Squadron had become more 'international' than ever with the addition of a Norwegian (Yves Henrichsen) and two Rhodesians (Hughie Ballance and Bert Bryson). We now entered into a period of intensive operational flying, both sweeps and rhubarbs, in addition to convoy patrols. Many of my companions started marking up 'victories', and one of our pilots, the New Zealander Gray Stenborg shot down four Fw 190s within a period of four days, two of them in one day. For me, however, this was a period of frustration and disappointment in this respect. I oscillated between flying as No. 2 to Ronnie Brown and leading a sub-section. I frequently took part in aerial combats and dog-fights, and more than once I was given the opportunity of destroying an enemy plane, but somehow never succeeded in making sufficient use of those occasions to enable me to make such a claim.

As an example of this I can mention a sweep to Hazebrouck in France on April 12, when I flew as Ronnie's wingman. Our role was to cover the withdrawal of the twelve Stirling bombers, homeward bound from the target. This stage of a raid was usually considered to be the most dangerous because then the enemy fighters had the advantage of the sun behind them.

The sun over France was shining brightly that day, and to the south, high above us, we could occasionally see the sun's rays twinkling like bright stars when they were reflected off the canopies of enemy fighters hovering there—probably the Abbeville Boys. We knew that before long they would be coming down, and then the 'ball' would start.

But suddenly a gaggle of around fifty enemy fighters appeared from the right and below with the obvious intention of attacking the bombers. We would have to intercept them and try to cut off the attack, but we were also fully aware that the 'hawks' above would then be diving down on us. The three squadrons in our wing were stepped up in an incline, one above the other with a height of 2000 feet separating each squadron. As we were the lowest squadron in this formation we were ordered by the Wing Commander to make the interception whilst the other two squadrons prepared to meet the high flyers who no doubt were about to start their attack.

The Messerschmitts were about 3000 feet below us and were now making a gentle right turn towards the twelve bombers that flew in close formation on a steady northerly course. As we were up-sun it was not certain that our adversaries had seen us yet and we were in a good position for attacking. Of course there was the small matter of the enemy numbering around fifty while we were only twelve.

As he started to slide his Spitfire downwards, our leader said in a calm and unhurried voice: 'Alright boys, let's give them a lesson. I'll go for the leading Huns and you, Jimmy, cover my tail, and, Ronnie, you take care of the rest.' Uh, uh, was that all? Just take care of the rest!

That the skirmish above us had already started was indicated by the shouts and calls on the R/T that form an integral part of aerial battles: 'They're on the way down, break left Yellow Section . . . SHOEBOX Green break hard left . . . Look out Ken, there are four bastards on your tail . . . Yellow, keep on turning left . . . They're 190s! . . . I got him, I got him!' And more of the same.

Ronnie delayed going down for a short while until the others were well on their way, and we could tell from the blue smoke trailing Wickham's aircraft that he was already firing his guns. Now we headed down towards four enemy planes and I could see that they were the new Fw 190s, and it appeared that they had not yet seen us. Ronnie started firing as soon as he was in range, and as his wingman I stayed slightly behind him to keep a look-out. Suddenly I saw two Fw 190s approaching from the right at high speed and I yelled: 'Ronnie, break right!'

And now a real mêlée that defies description commenced. I stayed with Ronnie for all I was worth as we twisted and turned in all directions, upwards and downwards, all over the sky. We were in turn either shooting or dodging enemy bullets. Aircraft seemed to be all over the sky with either black crosses or red and blue roundels on their wings. All happened at such speed that there was never enough leeway to press home an attack before having to break it off and turn towards an oncoming enemy to avoid his bullets.

Before long Ronnie observed that the pilots of a couple of 190s were showing great determination and getting ominously close to the bombers. He immediately went after them and opened fire on one of them, but in a flash another Fw 190 appeared and started to attack him. The R/T was so cluttered that I was unable to warn Ronnie, but I did manage to send his attacker a long burst of fire from fairly short range. I could see from flashes that some of my shells were finding their mark, and I saw something break off the enemy aircraft before the pilot suddenly rolled it over and pulled the nose down into a vertical dive.

I was very much tempted to chase this evidently damaged foe and try to finish him off, but that would have meant leaving my leader whom I was supposed to protect. It testifies to the discipline that had been drummed into us that I didn't do so. A Number Two who left his leader, without being forced to, was in disfavour with his superiors, and was made to feel it. Ronnie had succeeded in driving these two attackers away from their prey and they too had dived vertically, but at the same time he had become aware of the hail of bullets from the enemy I was firing on and had therefore given up further pursuit. All this may seem very confusing to the reader, but that is exactly what these aerial battles were—confusing.

And suddenly, as so frequently happened in these encounters, the sky was empty. The bombers in the distance continued placidly on their homeward flight, and on careful scrutiny small groups of Spitfires could be seen hovering around them. In a few places vertical columns of smoke left by burning aircraft were to be seen, and at one place a pilot was dangling in his parachute. It was evident from the chatter on the R/T that combats were still taking place somewhere, but here there was only peace and tranquility now. As we neared the coast a wing of Spitfires appeared to relieve us and we set course for home.

I was annoyed with myself. From an ideal range, with very little deflection required, I had fired a long stream of bullets from my cannons and machine guns at an enemy plane without achieving tangible results. This indicated that only a small percentage of my shots were finding their mark. I was convinced that a good shot would have needed only a fraction of this ammunition to destroy an enemy under such conditions. Some pilots, of course, were born marksmen, such as the Canadian George 'Screwball' Beurling. His career in the Air Force was extraordinary, although it did not start off particularly well. He was a singular youngster who kept very much to himself and went his own ways, and had difficulties adjusting to squadron life, where discipline and co-operation in the air was called for. He was consequently posted to Malta, where his individuality and outstanding marksmanship came into their own in the tumultuous skies above this Mediterranean island. In a period of four months he shot down no less than 27 enemy aircraft. He was such a painstaking shot that in some of his reports he even specified how many cannon shells had found their mark. In one case, according to an account in the book *Wing Leader* by 'Johnnie' Johnson, he felt he had probably shot down an enemy plane but was not certain enough to claim having destroyed it. He was, however, certain that five shells had hit the cockpit. A little later news reached headquarters that a Me 109 had crash-landed on the island—there were five bullet holes in the cockpit!

I admitted to myself that such accuracy was perhaps not absolutely necessary but on the other hand I had to concentrate on improving my marksmanship. The fact that the ciné-camera confirmed I had damaged a Fw 190 provided scant comfort.

On a sweep shortly after this I felt there was very little doubt that I had managed to destroy a Fw 190, but I was unable to verify this, either to my own satisfaction or anyone else's. This time I was a sub-section leader, and following a hectic encounter with a bunch of enemy fighters at 12,000 feet in the vicinity of St. Omer, my No. 2 and I chased a couple of Fw 190s right down to the ground where they split up and we were then left to chase one each. After much twisting and turning I gradually started creeping up behind my adversary and opened fire on him. Flashes on the nose of the Fw in front of the cockpit indicated that my cannon shells were going home and black smoke started streaming from the cowling round the radial engine. The aircraft slowed down so suddenly that I overtook it, and as I passed by I saw the cockpit canopy come off as if the pilot was about to bale out, but at that moment I became aware of bullets slamming into my own aircraft. I threw it into a steep turn and dived down to below the treetops where I turned and twisted as close to the ground as I dared. After a short while I discovered I had lost my pursuer, so I set course for home and stayed at this low altitude until I was well out to sea. My radio was dead and later I discovered that it had been destroyed by an explosive shell. The radio compartment was just behind the armour-plate against the pilot's back. My wingman had already landed and said he had lost the enemy plane he had been chasing. Most likely it was the German that had nearly clobbered me.

The ciné-film did indeed show that I had hit my adversary—but that was all. Once again I had to settle for a 'damaged'.

But on another occasion I had my Guardian Angels to thank for not becoming a 'confirmed' in some Luftwaffe pilot's log book. Following the usual dog-fight break-up of the squadron, somewhere over France, I found myself alone in the sky. After a short while I saw a lone Fw 190 below. I fish-tailed a couple of times to make sure I wasn't being followed and then dived on him. However, the pilot saw me coming and turned steeply to the left to meet me, and once again the traditional steep turning circle for life or death ensued. As no-one seemed likely to intervene in this duel I became hopeful. My Spitfire should be able to out-turn this Fw 190. We continued turning and turning, the circle becoming ever tighter. The wings stood up vertically, the throttle was fully forward, the aircraft shuddered on the verge of stalling and the blood was being drained from my head so that I started to feel dizzy, and yet the enemy was gaining the upper hand. This was not possible! Within a few more turns I would be in his sights. I couldn't believe it. I, who had been so sure of myself a short while ago. But now the boot was on the other foot, and I was scared. I'd have to do something in a hurry if I was to get out of this mess alive. In despair I decided to try a trick that could possibly save me, but it could also backfire, as a skilful pilot might anticipate it and gain an even better tactical position. This was like a gambit in a game of chess. I pulled the control column sharply towards me and at the same time stamped on the right rudder pedal. The aircraft flicked over into a vicious spin. I quickly recovered from the spin, but kept on going vertically down until I was down to sea level. To my great relief this trick seemed to have succeeded because my opponent had either lost me or decided not to follow me down. I hurried home.

But I was thoroughly shaken. We had great faith in our belief that the

Spitfire could easily out-turn any German fighter, and in the right hands it no doubt could. I had simply come up against a far more skilful pilot than myself. My self-esteem was badly dented.

IX THE JOURNEY THAT NEVER WAS

Hardly a day passed without the Squadron going on sweeps, up to three a day, and if weather conditions prevented these multi-aircraft operations there were always pilots keen on nipping across the 'ditch' on rhubarbs. The foe was not to be given any respite.

And now a new type of attack was instigated, directed mainly against the enemy fighter aerodromes. Hurricanes were modified to carry a couple of bombs, one under each wing, and they became known as Hurribombers. These aircraft were used for making low-level attacks on hangars and installations on the German-held airfields across the Channel. They were preceded by a squadron of Spitfires which attacked the anti-aircraft guns dotted around the perimeters of the airfields, while other Spitfires flew overhead as protection against German fighters. It must be admitted that aerodromes were not our favourite targets as they were usually very heavily defended. Attacks on them often resulted in losses, of which 111 Squadron bore its share.

The first of these Hurribomber raids was carried out on the great aerodrome at St. Omer, one of the citadels of the Luftwaffe's fighter force in the west. This attack caught the foe off guard. The Hurricanes' bombs and the cannons of the Spitfires did much damage both to equipment and aircraft scattered around the airfield. This time no German fighter planes arrived on the scene, but a Hurricane and a Spitfire fell victims to ack-ack guns. On our next visit however, two days later (April 30), we were greeted with a large number of fighters and a hard battle was fought. Gray Stenborg destroyed two Fw 190s but we lost Sergeant Chubb. I myself had potshots at various enemy aircraft without observing any results, and I am in no doubt that I owe my life to my Spitfire's nimbleness. Our Wing lost eight planes in this action, against three of the enemy shot down.

When setting off on sweeps it frequently happened that we had to climb up through layers of cloud, and if these were dense, this entailed an element of risk. In such clouds visibility was often limited to a few yards, and the pilots in each squadron had to fly in very tight formation so as not to lose sight of the next aircraft. Before cloud was entered the leader of each squadron must ensure that ample space was between his formation and the next, to minimise the danger of collision. On occasions this separation was found to have become ominously narrow when emerging from the cloud. Close formation flying in cloud was often very strenuous as both icing and turbulence could be encountered, and it is mainly thanks to excellent training that collisions did not happen more frequently than they did. I only remember one such incident in our squadron.

In thick cloud over the Channel the Spitfires of Sergeants Hollingdale and Hetherington collided. Hollingdale was able to glide his aircraft back to England and force land in a field, but Hetherington had to bale out. It cannot have been a comfortable feeling swinging below a parachute in thick cloud and hearing the engine noises of scores of aircraft passing by. After half an hour in the 'drink' he was picked up unharmed by a fishing vessel, but this was probably an unforgettable day for him.

In June 111 Squadron was honoured by being selected to receive a Spitfire presented by the State of Sao Paulo, Brazil. For the presentation ceremony the Squadron's Spitfires were neatly lined up in front of the dispersal hut where the new plane was unveiled by the Brazilian Ambassador and accepted on behalf of the Squadron by Pete Wickham. The Spitfire bore the name 'O Bandeirante' (The Flag Bearer). The ceremony was followed by a tight Squadron formation flypast.

At the end of the month the Debden Wing, which then consisted of 71, 111 and 350 Squadrons, was for some mysterious reason sent to Gravesend aerodrome where it sat inactive for a week and then returned to Debden. We never did find out the reason.

Towards mid July an announcement came like a bolt from the blue that the Debden Wing had only four days to prepare themselves for going abroad. As was to be expected, this intelligence was received with mixed emotions. The married men, a minority amongst the pilots, were understandably not very enthusiastic about going abroad, while most of the others had little or no objections to this and some, including myself, were even delighted with the prospect. Our destination was a closely kept secret, but generally it was thought to be North Africa.

We were inoculated against various diseases, resulting in most of us having a sore left shoulder for the next few days. The conjecture that North Africa was to be our destination received a boost when we were issued with tropical clothing. But then a new and persistent rumour got around. A few months had passed since Singapore fell to the Japanese who were now in Burma and threatened India. It was now rumoured that we about to be sent there to fight the 'Yellow Devils'. The merits and drawbacks of this move were much discussed and various opinions expressed, but I was enraptured with the prospects of seeing more of the world and meeting alien peoples. Not many Icelanders in those days were given the opportunity to visit such remote places.

We were all given two days embarkation leave, and some of the unattached lads went to London for a final fling before going overseas. To their amazement they were asked by people in various bars when they were to embark for Russia. So much for all the secrecy!

On arrival back on the airfield we received confirmation that indeed our destination had been Russia, but the posting had now been cancelled. In the first place the issue of tropical kit had been a cunning deception, as our destination had not been to southerly environments, but to a more northerly one. Our Spitfires had been shipped ahead of us, but the convoy that carried them had been subjected to ceaseless attacks from German U-boats, aircraft and even warships. Our aircraft now lay on the sea-bed and therefore it was pointless for us to continue our journey. This unexpected disclosure naturally surprised us greatly, and some of us felt that a singular opportunity for adventure had slipped through our fingers. On the Eastern Front we would have been in the ideal situation of flying our delightful Spitfires against German aircraft of lower quality. At that time the Soviet fighters were inferior to their German counterparts, and the Germans were therefore able to make good use of their older types against them, and save their better ones for the British challenge in the West and North Africa. Spitfires in Russia would have caught the Germans by surprise and most likely have played havoc with the Luftwaffe. Furthermore, flying on the Eastern Front would no doubt have been an unforgettable adventure, but it was not to be.

X   A CHARMED LIFE

On our return to Debden we continued where we had left off. It seemed to us that our opponents on the other side, the St. Omer and Abbeville Boys, must have had a kick in the back-side from Hermann Göring, as they now met us with more determination than ever before. Hard battles were fought with heavy losses on both sides. During a short period we lost four of our companions, and much the same applied to the other squadrons in the wing. We were encountering an increasing number of the new Fw 190s and they posed a real danger. In the upper layers of the atmosphere they were, along with the latest model of the Messerschmitt, the Me 109F, far superior to our Spitfire Vb, and it was only thanks to the latter's agility that this superiority was not more decisive.

However, we did not let this discourage us and most pilots sought to be included on every 'show'. We were young, full of confidence and aggressive spirit. It was, of course, unavoidable that the effects of this continuous tension should begin to show in some individuals. As soon as an operation had been decided upon, the pilots started their preparations, each one in his own particular way. Most started off by discussing the state of the aircraft with their mechanics, put on their 'Mae West', studied the weather charts and route-maps and then stood around in groups chatting and making jokes until the time came to climb into the cockpit. But occasionally the odd pilot might be seen to draw aside and furtively inspect his parachute and his escape pack—each pilot was issued a small package containing French money, a small compass, a map printed on silk, a booklet with French phrases and a small phial of Benzedrene tablets. Many pilots had managed to get back to England with the aid of the underground organizations, and these escape packs had frequently come in handy. Pilots were also seen carefully checking their revolvers, writing 'last letters' and other things of that sort, and these pilots were never quite successful in hiding their anxiety. Few pilots were completely free of uneasiness before each raid but most succeeded in pushing it to the back of their minds or covering it up. As soon as pilots began showing this fear their days with the squadron were numbered. They quietly stopped seeking a place on shows and gradually found themselves being continuously omitted. It was then not long until they left the squadron to perform other tasks that suited them better.

The cases of men folding up due to nervous strain or fear were very rare, however, as usually they had been removed from operations before this happened. A completely different case presented itself when pilots, who had flown on operations for a long period, began to show the strain brought on by fatigue. This was readily understood and taken care of by the rule stipulating that pilots having reached 200 hours of operational flying must take a rest from operations for at least six months.

But now we were into mid summer and we enjoyed life to the full. We were light-hearted and carefree; we lived for the passing moment and were happy to let tomorrow take care of itself. Very few of us had any notions of saving money because although it was never discussed we all knew that we might not live long enough to enjoy such savings. We were fans of Omar Khayyam!

On sunny days we played football and tennis and took part in various activities and sporting events on camp. No world records were set at these meetings, but lots of fun was had, and on one occasion I managed to be victorious on behalf of Iceland—I won a pillow fight! No, no, not the kind that's fought in bed, but rather out in the open air. In this type of pillow fight a pole is placed on trestles each side of a small pond, and the opponents sit astride the pole with sacks filled with hay, with which they try to knock each other off the pole into the pond. In the final round my opponent was a New Zealander and the spectators yelled either 'come on Iceland' or 'on with the Kiwis' or other such encouragements. It was obvious that the rivals were favoured in accordance with their squadron membership.

After some skirmishing neither seemed to be getting the better of the other until I managed to deceive my opponent with a cunning trick. I pretended to inadvertently give him an opening, and when he took a mighty swipe at my head I rolled over so that he lost his balance and fell into the pond. I hung upside down on the pole, and was able to propel myself onto dry land. There was, of course, much rejoicing amongst members of Treble One as the opponent belonged to 350 (Belgian) Squadron, there being intense rivalry between the two. The prize awarded was a safety-razor of the newest type and the only prize I have ever won for a 'sporting achievement' with the exception of those I have won playing golf, a game I did not take up until many years later.

The distance to Cambridge, that beautiful and peaceful university city, was less than 20 miles, and on sunny days we occasionally rode there on my bike. The Germans deserve praise for having spared this charming city with its ancient buildings from the vicious bombing that so many other cities were made to suffer.

Memorable are the sunny days when lying in flat-bottomed punts we let the languid current of the River Cam carry us slowly downstream as it wound its way between green lawns, and the old trunks of the weeping willow trees leaned out over the water with their bright yellow clusters: in the background stood the famous old buildings of this noble city of learning. There in the realm of Mother Nature, surrounded by trees and flowers, peace and quiet reigned and we savoured it. It seemed so very, very far from the tumult and ruthlessness of the war that raged so close by. Sometimes our punt was adorned by the presence of pretty maidens and their nearness did nothing to lessen the pleasures. And then, when the evening sun hovered in the west, and occasionally peeped between the ancient spires until the twilight embraced us, it was time to steer the boat into a haven, and pay a visit to one or more of the charming pubs.

Yes, life was wonderful and I was tempted to look upon this ghastly world-wide conflict, which I was taking an active part in, as a 'lovely war'. Those thoughts could, of course, not be expressed aloud, but the fact remained that I was enjoying life and considered myself to be a very lucky fellow. My most optimistic hopes had been fulfilled; hopes that only a little over two years ago had just been remote and unattainable dreams. I enjoyed excellent health, I was flying my dream aircraft and I had passed my ordeal by fire. I was prepared to meet the enemy in aerial combat without losing my nerve and yet I didn't underestimate his ability. I had numerous good friends and plenty of 'sweethearts'. Our wages arrived regularly every fortnight and nearly covered expenses. I had recently received promotion and was now a Flight Sergeant and a full-blown section leader, leading a section of four aircraft. Yes, life was wonderful.

As I have already mentioned I often went up to London on my 48-hour leaves, and on one of these excursions an incident occurred that was an extremely remarkable coincidence. Around midday one day I was strolling in Piccadilly Circus, one of the most crowded thoroughfares in the world. The pavements were swarming with passers-by, and people wearing uniform, both men and women, were predominant. These uniforms were of a great variety both in colour and cut, and the two-tone khaki uniforms of the Americans were becoming conspicuous. Then there were the dark-blue uniforms of the Navy, the Australian airmen and the Free French, the grey uniforms of the Poles and the blue-grey attire of the RAF. On the traditional British uniforms various shoulder badges were to be seen that proclaimed the wearer to be from Czechoslovakia, Canada, New Zealand, Norway, Denmark and various other countries. I myself was proud to display the word Iceland on my shoulders. This attracted a great deal of attention and people even turned round to regard me closer. That little word had already earned me quite a few pints of beer!

Mingling with all these people in uniform were of course numerous civilians. My mind was occupied as I strolled along the pavement, and it was not until I had taken a few paces past an elderly lady going in the opposite direction that it dawned on me that there was something familiar about her. I swung around and caught up with her—and yes, unbelievably, there was my grandmother as large as life. We had a joyous reunion and I steered her into the nearest pub where over a glass of sherry she explained her reason for being there. It transpired that her sister, who lived in a London suburb, had recently died, and my grandmother had attended her funeral. She had not been to London for over 20 years, and as her train did not leave for a couple of hours she had decided to fill in the time with a stroll around town. What a remarkable coincidence. Shortly after this I had a fortnight's leave and spent it visiting the Hawkridge family in Hull and my relatives in Grasby, where I stayed with my grandmother as usual.

The Americans were now busily engaged in building up their military strength in Britain, and units of their air forces had already given the Axis powers a taste of what was to come. Their B-17 bombers, generally known as Flying Fortresses, had by now carried out raids on targets on the Continent, escorted by RAF fighters. The three American Eagle Squadrons in the RAF now joined their fellow countrymen and formed the nucleus of the 4th Fighter Group of the US Army Air Force, which along with the 56th Fighter Group, were to make a name for themselves with numerous victories over the Luftwaffe. When the American forces first arrived in Britain their own fighter planes were no match for the Germans, so to start with their squadrons were equipped with Spitfires. It therefore became a common sight to see Spitfires with white stars on their fuselages instead of red, white and blue roundels. In the spring of 1943, however, American fighter squadrons began re-equipping with their own aircraft; first P-38s (Lightning) and P-47s (Thunderbolt) and later the outstanding P-51s (Mustang).

But now Debden was about to be turned into one of the main bases for the American fighters and we had to make way for them. Treble One Squadron was moved to Kenley airfield, just south of London, and our place at Debden was taken by our old friends of 71 (Eagle) Squadron, which now became the 334th Squadron of the US Army Air Force.

They threw us a good-bye party and as was to be expected from the Americans there was no sign of austerity. One of their leaders proclaimed in a speech that the experience they had gained in the RAF would create the foundation for building up the US fighter squadrons. The new units being formed would be led by veteran pilots of the Eagle Squadrons, and it certainly did no harm that they were to retain their beloved Spitfires. Some wag evoked laughter by interceding with the remark that it also was causing no harm that their pay was about to be doubled. Amongst these friends that we were bidding farewell to, were men such as James Clark, Duane Beeson, Howard Hively and others, who had already claimed many victories over the Germans and were to make names for themselves later with outstanding performances.

Although we had by now become adjusted to Debden and its surroundings we were, in our hearts, not greatly grieved over having to leave. The airfield was deep in the countryside, fairly far from any of the larger towns, and communications with the outside world were sparse. On the other hand Kenley was ideally situated and we were delighted with the transfer. It was a short distance from built-up areas with many pubs, dancehalls and cinemas, and it only took half an hour by train to reach the centre of London.

In the latter part of August combined military forces carried out a one-day raid on the French port of Dieppe. Over 6000 soldiers, predominantly Canadians, challenged the Germans and fought their way ashore against strong defences. Officially the object of the operation was to destroy defences, airfields, radar installations, harbour structures, power stations and railway facilities. Furthermore, the intention was to take prisoners, capture secret documents and samples of German invasion craft. Probably the more likely explanation was that German defences were being tested with an eye to the invasion of the Continent and the establishment of the 'Second Front' that the Soviets were constantly demanding. A tremendous battle was fought, and at the end of the day only a fraction of the attacking force managed to return to England. It was a saga of countless heroic deeds and enormous sacrifices that only succeeded in gaining a limited number of the objectives sought. The planners had intended aircraft to give the ground forces powerful support, but in fact this proved almost impossible when the latter were locked in such close combat as in this case. Indeed many lessons were learned that were to be of advantage in later operations, but this was of little comfort to the Canadians now fighting for their lives.

The fighting in the skies above the battle area was more furious than most of the squadron pilots had so far encountered. I felt frustrated over not being able to participate due to being in hospital with an attack of yellow jaundice.The Wing's task, along with other Spitfire wings, was to fly protective patrols over the ships carrying the raiders. The Kenley Wing entered the fray four times that day, and in the first sortie managed to repel a very determined attack on the ships by Ju 88 bombers, three of which were shot down. Treble One and 402 (RCAF) Squadrons were pitted against the fighters that escorted these bombers and a hard battle ensued. Two of our pilots, Franz Vancl and Brian Spranger managed to get at the bombers, and between them they shot down a Do 217. Sgt Hindley failed to return.

The second flight that day was even more hectic than the first. From a long way off the pilots could see the cloud of smoke lying over the battle-field, and as they came closer they observed that aerial battles were being fought over the town and the ships in the Channel. Messerschmitts, Focke Wulfs and Spitfires were seen twisting, turning, climbing and diving trailing blue smoke as they fired their guns, and columns of black smoke hung in the air caused by burning aircraft. As one of my pals related to me: 'We approached at 20,000 feet and immediately joined in the affray. A little way ahead and below I could see four Fw 190s and reported this to my leader'.

'OK, NOOKER Red, get them!' was the answer I received. 'My section followed me as I dived down on the Focke Wulfs but they saw us coming and turned to meet the attack. Now followed the usual steep turning that is typical of combat between fighters, but a group of Me 109s appeared from above, and by holding my Spitfire in as steep a turn as possible I managed to rid myself of an attacker on my tail and suddenly I was alone.' Of course, that was typical for aerial combat—one moment the sky is full of aircraft milling around, and the next moment the sky is empty.

Frank Tyrrell had a rather comical, but at the same time frightening experience. His aircraft was hit by Flak and after having escaped from his burning Spitfire, he floated down in his parachute and landed in the sea a short distance from the Dieppe harbour mouth. He inflated and climbed into his rubber dinghy and, to his horror, the rising tide carried him slowly but surely into the centre of the harbour where the racket of the battle engulfed him and bullets whizzed over his head. After the tide changed sometime later the ebb flow carried him out through the harbour entrance again, and in the falling dusk he was picked up by an Air-Sea Rescue Launch. His ordeal was, however, still not over, as the launch was strafed by German fighters and some of the crew were wounded, although Frank was landed safely at Dover.

I may add further that during the day's fighting Jimmy Baraldi and Yves Henrichsen each shot down a Dornier 217 and Barry Gale a Fw 190, making the Squadron's score for the day four enemy aircraft destroyed and quite a few damaged.

XI   RUM AT SEA

The sweeps across the Channel continued but now certain changes were taking place within 111 Squadron. We were sorely disappointed when our highly regarded leader, Pete Wickham, left us at the end of August and the Squadron was taken over by Anthony Bartley. The word had quickly got around that Anthony had done well in the Battle of Britain and shot down a number of enemy planes. Furthermore, he had spent some time as a test pilot with Supermarines, the designers and builders of the Spitfire, so we felt the Squadron was getting a promising leader to replace Pete. He had been promoted and had taken temporary command of his preceding squadron, but this was for all intents and purposes his first full post as Squadron Leader, and we awaited his arrival with some expectancy. But to our surprise, and disgust, he started his leadership in an unexpected, and from our point of view, entirely negative way.

His first act was to line up the whole squadron, ground staff and pilots, on the station parade ground. We were not used to this kind of 'military bullshit', and we didn't like it a bit. Then Bartley stepped onto a rostrum and made a tub-thumping speech about obedience and discipline, and ranted about 'playing ball'! We pilots certainly didn't like the way this was going and agreed that we had been landed with some sort of a dandy—a bloody conceited cock who hadn't flown on operations for ages and was now lecturing a group of pilots, who daily faced the enemy, on discipline. Consequently, we lost respect for him immediately. But then the unexpected happened—within a short period he had won back our hearts and respect so emphatically that we would not hesitate to follow him wherever he led.

A few days after this parade we were given the opportunity to observe his remarkable mastery of the Spitfire. Because of the complex conflict at the eastern end of the Mediterranean, Britain had persistently attempted to get the Turks to enter into the war on the side of the Allies, but the Turks vacillated because of the superiority the Axis powers were displaying on all fronts. Just then a group of Turkish generals were visiting London for discussions and they were dispatched to Kenley aerodrome to be introduced to the Spitfire, and watch a demonstration of its flying qualities. And a demonstration they certainly got—Tony Bartley saw to that. He performed such a daring aerobatics display just above ground level that we stood gaping, and we were no novices. We had never before seen such skill and daring and our reluctant respect for Tony rose by some degrees. There was no doubt about his flying ability. During the next few weeks we were to discover that he also had extraordinary qualities of leadership combined with an admirable concern for the safety of his pilots.

Throughout September and most of October the Squadron did an unusual amount of flying training, with much emphasis placed on air firing, both through the use of the ciné-camera guns and actually firing our guns at target drogues towed by aircraft. For this training we spent a few days at Martlesham Heath aerodrome near the east coast of Essex. No doubt my marksmanship improved somewhat due to this, but even so it still left much to be desired. From Martlesham the Squadron moved to Fowlmere, near Cambridge, and we were all given a week's leave. This gave voice to a great deal of speculation—obviously something special was being planned for the Squadron, and most of us guessed that an overseas posting was about to be sprung on us. And indeed, so it was. On 19th October 1942 Tony Bartley told the Squadron personnel to start preparing for a trip overseas at short notice. New members were inoculated and once again we were issued with tropical kit. This time however, we were not going to be deceived as easily as last time, although a variety of guesses were afoot about our destination. Russia had now been added to the list of possibilities, and the issue of tropical clothing rather added to the likelihood of a northerly destination.

It was not long however, before we learned that we were going to North

Africa. To us this meant Egypt and the desert. The Allied invasion of Algeria and French Morocco, under the codename 'Torch' was now in the planning stages, but was kept very secret and was completely unknown to us.

Bill and I had a rather unlucky break—the 'short notice' turned out to be *very* short notice. We had been given permission to nip in our Spitfires to Hornchurch airfield, not far from Bill's home, to say good-bye to his father and sisters. While we were there the weather closed in, ruling out all flying. Confidently we telephoned base expecting to be told to fly back the next day, but to our horror we were told to grab our parachutes and travel back by train as quickly as possible. By a roundabout route via London we eventually got back to base just in time to be bundled into transport for a night journey to Liverpool. Everyone else had been given a special meal to sustain them on the long ride in the back of a lorry, but Bill and I had to put up with both cold and hunger.

Our officers travelled to Manchester where they embarked on a large passenger steamer that had been converted into a troop ship. We, the NCO pilots were sent to Londonderry in Northern Ireland, where we were placed in small groups on the warships that escorted the convoy. Mel 'Tush' Tushingham, a Canadian pilot, and I sailed on a mine sweeper by the name of HMS *Bideford*, and we were given a comfortable berth in the Chief Petty Officers' mess. We were, however, not just inactive passengers on the voyage as we had to stand look-out watches up on the open bridge. We were issued with powerful binoculars and assigned a section of the ocean to scan.

As I'm blessed with the quality of not being seasick I enjoyed the voyage right from the start. Tush was sick the first three days but after that he felt better—that is to say until the storm hit us. This storm was one of the worst that the oldest sea dogs on board could remember and even many of them became seasick. Due to its role as an escort vessel the tub had to be darting about all over the place and consequently was hit by the weather and waves from all quarters, and until then I would never have believed that a ship could roll so much without rolling right over. In one of these vicious lurches the ship's skipper had the misfortune of receiving the contents of my coffee mug in his face, but he managed to smile. I was thankful for not being sick no matter how much the ship was thrown about. This condition bore the consequences, however, that I had to stand watches for those who were too overcome with seasickness to do so themselves, but as I was enjoying myself I did not mind at all. And this also had other positive benefits.

In those days it was still a tradition in the Royal Navy to issue each person a daily tot of dark-red rum which generally was called 'Nelson's Blood', and as so many of my messmates did not feel well enough to go after it I did so for them. In that way I managed to hoard two bottles of this potent tipple to celebrate arrival at our destination. Strictly speaking this hoarding was not allowed, but the bo's'n in charge followed Nelson's example and 'turned a blind eye'.

This convoy that we escorted was the largest ever to set sail until then, and indeed it not only carried a manifold invasion force, but also all the equipment and stores required for such a complex undertaking. It had, of course, been impossible to hide the preparations for such a large convoy, so every effort was made to give the impression that its purpose was to reinforce Montgomery in Egypt and also break the siege of Malta. Various deceptions were effected for this purpose and later it was confirmed that the Germans had fallen for them. They prepared to attack this great convoy in the channel south of Sicily where the Mediterranean is narrowest, and for that purpose they had built up a strong fleet of aircraft in Sardinia, Sicily and Southern Italy. With scouting planes they carefully kept a watch on the convoy's progress along the Mediterranean, and on the evening of 7 November it had reached a position north-east of Algiers. But early next morning the convoy had disappeared—it had been turned around towards the invasion ports in Algeria. This was most frustrating to the Germans, for now only a few of their long-range bombers could reach it, and these would have to do so without the protection of fighter planes.

However, so far we had no knowledge of the cargo nor its destination. As was customary for convoys we continually kept altering course, but I saw on the charts that we went much further out into the Atlantic than I had expected, bearing in mind that we were supposed to be heading for the Mediterranean.

Twice we became aware of U-boats and in one of these instances I saw the streaks made by a couple of torpedoes as they passed close behind us heading into the centre of the crowd of ships in the convoy. We were not aware of any explosions so the missiles must have missed their mark. In both these instances our ship took part in the action against these submarines, darting hither and thither, dropping numerous depth-charges, but I was unaware of whether we did any damage to these deep-sea snipers. Anyway, the defences proved adequate as not a single ship of this large convoy was lost.

On one of my watches I saw in the distance a small dark object that now and again appeared on top of a wave. We steamed towards it at full speed and as we got closer we could see that it was a lifeboat crowded with castaways, men and women, and we immediately set to rescuing them on board. They totalled 26 and were part of the crew and passengers of a South African ship en route from New York to Cape Town. It had been sunk three days earlier, and four crowded lifeboats had been known to get away. It was around nine o'clock in the morning that we picked up these survivors, and for the rest of the day we, and another escort vessel, searched for the lifeboats—without success. When darkness fell we had to set off at full speed to catch up with our charges and by daybreak we were back on station.

Our great armada sailed through the Straits of Gibraltar in darkness two weeks after leaving Londonderry, and to our surprise Tush and I were put ashore in Gibraltar. He was delighted to have his feet on dry land again as he was not greatly enchanted with the sea, but I bid HMS *Bideford* and its crew farewell with a feeling of regret. I was attracted to the sea and had enjoyed the voyage and felt at home on board. I had made many new friends that I would probably never see again. They would continue their unwavering fight against the harsh forces of nature and the enemy in the deep whilst I would be turning to new adventures up in the skies above them.

XII   OUT OF THE CRATES

A new epoch in my life was about to begin. Outside the British Isles, Gibraltar was the first foreign soil I stepped on, and here were many interesting and exciting sights to be seen. This large and majestic rock was in fact an impregnable fort. Within its interior there were miles of tunnels connecting fortifications, headquarters, billets, hospital, power plant, communication centre, fuel storage and stores. And also, deep within its interior there was a large reservoir kept topped up with distilled sea water. Most of the debris from the tunnelling had been used for building an airport. A long and wide runway had been laid over the neck of land that connected the rock with the mainland, and this runway reached some distance out into the bay.

On the airport tarmac, work was in progress taking dis-assembled Spitfires and Hurricanes out of crates and assembling them, and during the next few days long lines of these aircraft grew steadily. This, naturally, caused us some speculation because as far as we knew we were going to either Malta or Cairo, and these aircraft certainly did not have the range to fly that far. Our best guess was that in one way or another the aircraft would be loaded onto an aircraft carrier and flown off it when within range of their destination. Malta, that 'Island Fortress', had for a long time been a thorn in the flesh of the Axis Powers and was subjected by them to nearly incessant air raids. With their large fleet of aircraft in Sicily and Southern Italy they had caused Britain a considerable loss of ships when attempts were made to reinforce the island. Nevertheless, Malta's force of fighter aircraft had been successfully replenished using the above-mentioned method, and we thought it likely that this was now to be repeated. As the assembly of these aircraft took place right under the noses of German spies across the border in Spain, less than a quarter of a mile away, it seemed likely that they must reach the same conclusion.

Incidentally, the tempting target these rows of aircraft standing on the open tarmac presented no doubt worried the military authorities in Gibraltar, but to their great relief they were left untouched.

On our second evening ashore a crowd of us from Treble One went to a cinema and saw a film named *The First of the Few*, an epic about the Battle of Britain. It caused much hilarity amongst us when Tony Bartley appeared on the screen. He was in a scene showing a group of pilots sitting on deck chairs and lying in the grass in the sunshine outside a dispersal hut awaiting the peal of the bell that would send them sprinting out to their Spitfires. Tony was made to utter a few words in the film but what they were I no longer remember. He never became an actor after the war, but did maintain an association with the film world by marrying the famous film star Deborah Kerr.

On the morning of 8 November the news of the Allied landings at Algiers, Oran and Casablanca broke, and at last we discovered where we were going. Under the codename 'Torch' and led by the American General Eisenhower, the Allies intended to gain control of North-West Africa and then move with all haste eastwards. The 8th Army under General Montgomery had broken out of Egypt after a decisive victory over Rommel's Afrika Corps at El Alamein and was now chasing the enemy westwards. The forces of the Axis powers would be caught between these two advancing armies and pushed into the sea. The whole coast of North Africa would then be in Allied hands, securing shipping lanes through the Mediterranean. As Morocco, Algeria and Tunisia were French colonies, the Allies had hopes of being received with open arms, or at the worst passively, but unfortunately these hopes were dashed.

The French colonies in Africa were governed by the Vichy regime in the unoccupied part of France, and Admiral Darlan was the Minister of Defence in that government. By pure coincidence he happened to be in Algeria when the Allies arrived—he was visiting a sick son—and he immediately took control as Supreme Commander and ordered all French forces to oppose the Allied landings. This opposition was greatest in Oran and caused much bloodshed. On the other hand the defence of Algiers was not nearly as determined, thanks mainly to the attitude of General A P

Juin, who disregarded Admiral Darlan's orders. By the evening of 10 November the Allies had established bridgeheads at all these places and Darlan, deciding that further opposition was useless, ordered his troops to lay down their weapons. Vichy's reaction was to declare him a traitor and dismiss him from power. Darlan now considered that he had done his duty to Vichy and could now join the British and Americans without loss of honour. A few days later he was assassinated by a fanatical young Frenchman.

The Allies had not expected this French opposition, which delayed the advance of their armies and gave the Germans the opportunity to make preparations to meet the threat. They therefore wasted no time in sending powerful forces to Tunisia where they built strong defensive positions. Two major airfields fell into their hands there, which were to play an important part in the struggle during the coming months.

As soon as the landing forces had secured the Maison Blanche aerodrome at Algiers it was intended that we should fly there to help protect the ships and ground forces against attacks by German and Italian bombers. Auxiliary fuel tanks were now fitted to our Spitfires. Without them Algiers would have been near the limit of our range. It now transpired that we were to escort some Hudson bombers which were much slower than our Spitfires, so even with this additional fuel we were liable to have problems reaching our destination, and in fact this proved to be the case for some of our pilots.

From the time we heard of the landings we were on readiness for immediate departure, but due to the resistance put up by French Army units, it was not until after kicking our heels for the next three days that we were able to set off.

CHAPTER FOUR

UNDER A
PROTECTIVE WING

I ALGIERS AND ELENA

On the morning of 11 November, 1942, 111 Squadron took off from Gibraltar and headed for Algiers. Alongside us flew the Hurricanes of 43 Squadron. We were assigned to escort two Hudson bombers which I believe carried Air Marshal Welsh, the Chief of Air Staff, and his assistants, in addition to a group of war correspondents, which would account for such a strong escort. The Hudsons were a good deal slower than the fighters and naturally we were not particularly happy about having to 'loiter' on the way and spend four hours over the ocean in single-engine aircraft. Moreover, they had been assembled straight out of the boxes and pushed aside without being test flown.

We had, of course, to accept this and in fact we were only too happy to be airborne again after such a long period away from flying. The weather was beautiful and the sun shimmered on the glassy-blue Mediterranean far below. We were setting off on new adventures, and optimism flew with us. Indeed, we were at the head of a tremendous military operation that was to change the course of the war.

In spite of the extra fuel tanks not all of us reached our destination. Two or three had to crash-land on the beaches of Algeria and among them was our popular flight commander, Mac Gilmour. He damaged his back, which caused him pain for many weeks, but in spite of that he was to be one of the most outstanding pilots of our squadron in the months that followed.

These Spitfires looked quite different from the ones we had left behind. Gone were the green and grey camouflage colours, to be replaced with the brown colours of the desert. Nor were they as slim-looking for there was a bulge below the nose housing an air filter. And indeed it became evident that this filter effected performance and reduced speed.

Finally, after what seemed an endless flight, we sighted the snow-covered Atlas mountains rising in a blue haze above the distant Algerian coast, and as we drew closer we could see the whitewashed city of Algiers. The setting was beautiful, the town forming a semi-circle around the cobalt blue waters of a wide bay. Climbing up the slopes of the surrounding dark green hills were rows upon rows of snow-white houses with red roofs. A large number of ships were scattered about the bay and black smoke rose high into the sky from the harbour area, no doubt caused by German bombs. Until now the only opposition the bombers had met with was Flak from the anti-aircraft guns of the escort vessels. Now they had better look out—the fighters had arrived.

Those of us who made it all the way, landed on the last few drops of petrol, and we immediately began removing the auxiliary tanks and preparing our planes for the impending action. The squadron's ground staff was still somewhere out on the ocean, so we pilots had to do most of this ourselves, ably assisted by newly-formed RAF Commando units. Provisions, ammunition and petrol, (in five gallon cans), were transported from the harbour by soldiers using a variety of vehicles, including horse-carts, hand-carts and even wheelbarrows. They also helped us to pour the petrol into the tanks through funnels and chamois leather which we had brought along precisely for this purpose.

While we were busily engaged in these activities, bombers arrived over the harbour and started dropping their loads. We had not been aware of any warning signal being given, and the first indications of an impending air raid were the black smoke-puffs in the sky made by the anti-aircraft guns of the escort ships. The first aircraft was half way through being filled with petrol, but without any hesitation Tony Bartley climbed into the cockpit and started the engine. Without bothering to don his parachute or fasten the safety straps he taxied in leaps and bounds to the boundary, spun around and without further ado took off.

The last of the bombers had just finished dropping its bombs and was turning out to sea again when we saw Tony approach it, and we eagerly awaited the inevitable conclusion. We watched the Spitfire creep close up to the bomber and then, to our amazement, it turned sharply away without achieving any apparent results, and the enemy continued unperturbed out to sea. A short while later Tony slid down onto the airfield.

'What a bloody balls-up. I had the bastard in my sights at short range, and when I pressed the tit nothing happened. Not a single bloody shot.'

For some reason the guns had let him down. The bomber's gunners must have been amazed, and highly delighted with this deliverance. They'd had no gun problems of their own to contend with—at least two of their bullets had hit the Spitfire. A thorough search was now made for the cause of the failure, which was not easy to find as we had no armourers, but eventually it was traced to an unconnected wire.

For the rest of the day we had two Spitfires on standing patrol over the harbour, but it was not until dusk that a group of Junkers 88 bombers appeared. As before, the first indication of their arrival was given by the ships' guns, but unfortunately at that moment the two patrolling aircraft were just touching down. As there were no runway lights available they were making use of the last vestige of daylight for landing. The control radio equipment had as yet not been installed, so there were no means of contacting them. As a matter of fact the radio set of one of the aircraft on the ground could have been used for this purpose, but it entailed starting up the aircraft to obtain the alternating current for the VHF radio, and then warming up the set, and all this would have taken too long.

Tony Bartley, who was standing near me, ran towards his aircraft and called to me: 'Follow me, Jonny.' I jumped into my Spitfire, started the engine and followed my leader's aircraft, which I could only barely see in the failing light.

Suddenly the airfield's anti-aircraft guns started shooting and bombs fell close to one of the Air France hangars not far away from us. Tony ignored this and continued taxiing to the eastern boundary of the field, and when he saw that I had caught up, and was lined up by his side, he opened his throttle and I followed him into the air. There was still some light in the western sky from the sun which was now well below the horizon.

I heard my leader's calm voice in my earphones: 'OK, Jonny, lets go and clobber a few of those bastards. Follow me.'

Ahead the myriad of lights of Algiers glimmered like an ocean of diamonds, and I was enchanted with this sight after all the blackout darkness of Britain. In the harbour area fires were burning, testifying to the madness and destructive nature that repeatedly overtakes mankind.

The sky was lighter than the ground below so I flew slightly below and behind Tony and had no difficulties staying with him. The coastline was easily discernible and we flew out over the bay hoping to find the enemy bombers, but we had to depart in a hurry as the ships started shooting at us. The fact that the guns were not shooting at any other target indicated that we were too late—the bombers had dropped their bombs and left. We flew a good distance out to sea but found no enemy and feeling disappointed, headed back home.

Tony suggested we switch on our navigation lights so that trigger-happy gunners were less likely to open fire on us. A waxing moon, still low in the starlit sky, cast a faint light so we could discern the landscape below. Most houses were whitewashed and stood out clearly against the dark background. In the countryside beyond the town scattered lights were to be seen, and we easily found the aerodrome—a black hole with no visible lights.

'Right, Jonny, come in close and follow my lead.'

I knew I was in good hands and had nothing to worry about, Tony would get us safely onto the ground. I formed up on his right side and we flew a circuit around the 'black hole' with our landing lights on. After a moment a floodlight was switched on and it lit up a section of the airfield and we slid in a gentle arc towards the ground. When Tony lowered his wheels I followed suit, and also when he lowered his flaps, and before I knew it we were rolling gently along the smooth surface and taxied to our dispersal. Expectant colleagues surrounded us as we climbed out of our cockpits but unfortunately we had to disappoint them. Our efforts had not produced the hoped-for results.

No provisions had been made for billeting us that night, so a couple of airliners that the Italians had abandoned were requisitioned for night quarters. Bill and I found a little shack where we tried to sleep on the floor with newspapers for bedclothes. Most of us had little sleep that night as enemy bombers were active overhead and sent us occasional greetings. However, they did little other damage than robbing us of sleep.

The next three days we flew continuous patrols over the harbour and the ports of Bougie and Philippeville a little further along the coast to the east. Most of the time there was nearly unbroken cloud over these places facilitating the German and Italian bombers' escape. However, our presence disturbed the crews of these bombers sufficiently to make their bombing erratic and less effective. Occasionally we managed to get within range of these raiders for short periods, and sometimes we even damaged them, although we were not able to claim their destruction. An entry in my log book on 12 November is typical for those days:

> "Chased a Ju 88 in and out of cloud for nearly 20 minutes, and before it
> eventually got away I had a good squirt at him and saw black and white
> smoke pouring out of his S-board engine. One Ju 88 damaged."

For the next couple of nights we were billeted in a small hostel close to the airport, and having access to ablutions was a great improvement. Our baggage consisted only of toilet articles and what little underwear could be stuffed into a small hold-all. Our personal possessions were due to arrive by ship later on, but in fact never did, as the vessel was sunk. Our blue uniforms had been left behind and we wore khaki battledress like the army. We also wore a webbing belt with a revolver attached to it, and most of us wore flying boots.

On our second evening in Algeria we nipped into town and wandered around in the city centre, drinking a glass of beer or two and observing the population. It was interesting, and even a little comical to observe the reaction of the French to this unexpected invasion. They had been governed by the Vichy regime of Marshal Pétain, whom many worshipped as a national hero, and they had been remarkably submissive to the Germans. Furthermore, many Frenchmen felt antipathy towards Britain, whom they accused of abandoning them during the Battle for France, and also for attacking and sinking French warships in Oran, Dakar and Madagascar. Because of this the Allies placed much emphasis on Torch being made to look like an all-American operation, but trying to disguise the large number of British ships, aircraft and soldiers was of course hopeless.

In the beginning the French showed little signs of welcome. It was obvious that they feared the Germans and were not convinced the Allies had come to stay. But once it became manifest that 'les Bosch' would not be returning they became a good deal more sociable towards us.

On this first visit of mine to Algiers I had an amusing experience. A few of us entered a tavern in the town centre and sat down at a table and ordered some beer. The place was half empty and a good-looking young woman sat alone at the bar and appeared to be deep in thought. I mentioned jokingly to the boys that there was a comely lass that I wouldn't mind getting to know closer. Some wag in the party offered a bet that I wouldn't get very far with her, and the rest of the gang wasted no time following his lead. I attempted to back out but was overpowered, and anyway I had to admit to myself that I wouldn't mind trying. It was now a long time since I'd had a woman in my arms.

I sat down beside the girl and ordered a drink. I then turned to her and asked if I might be allowed to buy her one. She looked straight ahead, frowning and didn't bother to answer.

Oh well, the damsel probably doesn't speak English, I told myself, and that certainly complicated matters a bit. The trouble was that my knowledge of French was practically nil. In fact I had started studying the language just before I left school, but what little I had learned would not be of much use to me now. However, it wouldn't do to give up after only one attempt. Somehow I would have to get her to understand that I only wished to cheer her up as she looked so unhappy. My French vocabulary was, to say the least, quite inadequate to express this. The word 'jolie' came to my mind as I had come across it recently and I associated it with the English word 'jolly'.

I pulled myself together, fished out my packet of cigarettes and offered one to the girl as I smiled and said in my best French accent:

'Vous nest pa tray sholie, mamsell.'

For those readers that lack the command of French that I have I will explain that this was supposed to mean: 'You are not very gay, miss.'

The young lady gave me such a look of contempt that I felt uncomfortable. But when she saw the look of bewilderment on my face she burst out laughing. She took a cigarette out of the packet and said in nearly faultless English: 'Have you no manners, young man? You won't get very far by telling girls that they're not pretty.' And she laughed some more.

I'd certainly made a mess of things. By telling this girl that she was not pretty I had most likely ruined any chances of making headway with her. But now she stopped laughing, winked at me and said with a smile: 'You can tell your comrades that they have lost their bets—I heard what was going on between you.'

It now became evident that she had good command of English. She accepted a glass of apéritif and we introduced ourselves. Her name was Elena and she was Hungarian of Jewish descent. She had lived for two years in Algiers and was a school teacher, but occasionally eked out her earnings with a little prostitution. She told me that she had meant to take this evening off, but seeing that we got on so well together I was welcome to see her home if I cared. We had another drink and then bade my companions farewell. I could see that they envied me and it gave me a certain amount of malicious satisfaction. I wasn't going to tell them that this delightful girl was a prostitute and that I was going to have to pay for her charms. Furthermore, I had a suspicion that she might be rather expensive.

She lived in a pleasant flat in the neighbourhood and it was obvious that it took more than a teacher's salary to furnish it so comfortably. I spent an enjoyable night with her, and next morning the darling refused to take my money. She said that since I was fighting the hated Nazis this was the least she could do for me in return.

In our conversations I mentioned that I had a fondness for Hungarian goulash and she said I simply must come back again the next evening so she could show me how it really should taste. The day after that the Squadron left Algiers, but a firm friendship had been forged between Elena and me, and a few weeks later when I spent some leave in the city, I stayed with her in her flat in great comfort.

II   BITTEN TO LIFE

After the Allies had captured Algiers the army groups moved fairly rapidly forward. The British forces raced along the coast and occupied the ports of Bougie, Djidjelli and Philippeville, and British paratroops captured the

important port and airfield at Bone. This ancient city, which h
reclaimed the name Annaba by which it was known before French
only 50 miles from the Tunisian border, and its port was a vital link in the
Allied supply system. The American army units captured towns and
villages on the border of the Sahara desert, such as Biskra, Youks, Tebessa
and Gafsa.

The French resistance, during the first days of the landings, had given the
Axis powers valuable time to occupy Tunisia and build up counter-
measures. It was only a relatively short distance from Italy, and because of
local mastery in the air they were able to keep the sea-lanes open. With
their well-known flair for organization and enterprise, the Germans had
brought over well-equipped forces and organised strong defensive
positions. Here the Allied forces under Eisenhower came to a halt while
reinforcements were built up for the later engagements, when the
combined armies of von Arnim and Rommel were finally annihilated.
Montgomery's 'Desert Rats' had already broken through at El Alamein
and Rommel's Afrika Korps was being pushed out of Egypt, to be driven
finally into Tunisia. During this period the Red Army at Stalingrad won its
first great victory against Hitler's war machine, and these events proved to
be the beginning of his end.

At this time however, the Luftwaffe in Tunisia didn't sit back empty-
handed, but built up a strong force both of bombers and fighters. During
the next weeks they had the upper hand in the air, and ceaselessly carried
out attacks on the Allied armies, their communications and airfields. They
also prepared for a strong counter-attack in Tunisia which was to cause
Eisenhower and his forces great problems, as we shall see later.

Three days after our arrival in Algeria, Treble One was advanced to the
forward airfield at Bone, about 250 miles along the coast east of Algiers,
and now things really started warming up. At Bone we became most
unpleasantly aware of our closeness to the important aerodromes at Bizerta
(Banzart) and Tunis—as the German fighters and bombers based there
seldom gave us much peace.

Although it was cloudy along the coast the day we moved, we had no
difficulty finding Bone, as thick black smoke caused by German air raids
arose from the harbour. Bone was a pretty little town that snuggled up
against the hills enclosing a small plain along the coast. The airfield,
situated about three miles outside the town, had two runways. One was
long and narrow and the other shorter and wider and had obviously not
been completed, as one end was just a coarse foundation awaiting a top-
layer dressing.

The paratroops that had landed there the day before, welcomed us with
open arms—they had been constantly subjected to virtually unopposed

German air attacks. In spite of this, they had already moved considerable amounts of fuel and provisions from the harbour to the airfield, and now they quickly helped us refuel our aircraft to be ready for the next attack.

While this was going on, balls of black smoke appeared in the sky over the harbour and, as in Algiers, this indicated that an air raid was in progress. We were quickly able to discern a formation of bombers at a height of about 6000 feet over the harbour.

Now we had to get airborne in a hurry. Refuelling was stopped, tanks closed and engines started. In this manner five or six Spitfires managed to get into the air within a short time. But it was already too late. The bombers were Junkers 88s, an aircraft which can, without doubt, be regarded as one of the finest and most versatile aircraft of WW II, and which because of its speed and manoeuvrability was used in a variety of roles such as bomber, night fighter, torpedo-bomber and reconnaissance-plane to mention a few.

By the time we were airborne the enemy had completed his task and the aircraft were already on their way out to sea again, and because of their speed it would be nearly impossible for our desert-equipped Spitfires to catch up with them. With the throttle fully open I headed for one of the Ju 88s and only very slowly did the distance between us show any signs of decreasing. A large bank of clouds loomed ahead, and to my great annoyance I had to watch the bomber disappearing into this just before I got within range for opening fire. The same happened to my colleagues with the exception of Mac Gilmour. In spite of his injuries he had been the first to get airborne, and was able to take a shot at one of the Ju 88s from extreme range before it disappeared into the cloud.

The lack of warning of impending attack was our greatest problem, and caused us untold difficulties. The only answer we had was to keep Spitfires constantly patrolling the harbour and airfield and this demanded a great deal of hard work. The Squadron's ground staff had not yet arrived and we ourselves, with help from a few soldiers and RAF Commando units, had to do the refuelling and rearming of our Spitfires, and any other jobs that fell within our capacity.

In addition to the aircraft on patrol, we placed two on standby near the end of the runway. The pilots sat strapped in their cockpits ready to press the starter button, and leap into the air at the first sign of enemy action. This was not a very popular assignment, because on the day after our arrival at Bone the Germans started sending fighters to attack the aerodrome, and they were able to come in low from off the sea with very little warning. Admittedly, the army boys had placed a few anti-aircraft guns around the perimeter, which did have the effect of distracting the Germans, and they even managed to shoot down one or two, but those stand-by Spits by the runway were very exposed, and had very little time to get into position to meet the enemy.

Close to the airfield there was a farmhouse that had belonged to an Italian family which left in a hurry when the paratroopers arrived. The spacious house was turned into a headquarters and billet. We found various mattresses and blankets and that first evening we bedded down in preparation for a good night's rest. I had hardly closed my eyes when I started itching all over. At first I tried to put up with it, but after a while it became unbearable. I also became aware that most of my colleagues were having similar problems.

Now flashlights were being turned on and we discovered that fleas were jumping about all over the place! Sleeping in these circumstances was obviously out of the question. Most of us took our blankets outside and shook them hard. Fortunately the rainy season, which was shortly to make life miserable, was not upon us yet and the ground was dry. We found a hollow in the terrain not far from the farmhouse and bedded down there for the second time that evening. During the night a bomber came over and, with great precision, dropped a bomb on our erstwhile residence. A few persons were still in the house, and most of them lost their lives. Undoubtedly I can thank the fleas for still retaining mine.

At dawn patrolling began again. It was also the start of one of the most eventful and memorable days of my life. On this day, November 15 1942, I scored my first 'victory', came very close to being blown sky-high and suffered my first, and only wound from enemy action. As during the previous days, the sky was partly covered with ragged clouds, and a heavy cloud-bank hung over the horizon out at sea. All this cloud made the standing-patrol's task more difficult, and enabled the enemy aircraft to sneak, mostly unseen, to the vicinity of the harbour and aerodrome. It also facilitated their escape, and this we found most annoying.

At first light I led a section of four aircraft on a patrol line between the harbour and the aerodrome. As on previous occasions black puffs over the harbour from the ack-ack guns were the first indications of the approach of enemy aircraft. Shortly after this warning I caught sight of a formation of six bombers nearing the harbour flying at about 3000 feet, just below the clouds. We immediately turned towards them, and as we got closer we could see that they were Heinkel 111 bombers. This was very encouraging because the Heinkels were much slower than the Ju 88s, and we should be able to catch them easily enough providing they did not reach cloud cover in time. I switched on my reflector sight, thumbed off the safety catch for the guns, pressed the R/T button and announced as calmly as I could: 'OK lads, now's our chance. I'll go for the leader and each one picks his own target. Lets clobber the lot!'

When the bomber crews saw us approaching they seemed to panic and the formation broke up. We could see columns of spray erupting on the surface of the sea below, indicating that the bombs were being dropped at random far from any targets. The adversary that I had chosen was already in a tight climbing turn heading for the clouds and just before he disappeared I sent him a long burst from my cannons at maximum range. I saw no signs of having hit him, and once again I had reason to curse my poor marksmanship. But this time I was determined not to let him escape; the clouds were ragged and not too large, and I was bound to find him again and ... Oh yes, there he was, slightly out to the right. But before I got within firing range he again disappeared into cloud. I ground my teeth and cursed some more. Hell, this one simply must not get away!

The pilot of the Heinkel was cunning and continually changed course in the clouds so that each time he emerged again he was out of range. I tried to anticipate his moves, but without much success at first. At last, after about ten minutes of this grotesque game of hide-and-seek, I guessed right. We came out of a cloud flying line-abreast about a hundred yards apart, and by making a sharp right turn I was able to get in a burst of machine-gun and cannon fire. Even I could not miss at this short range, and just before we entered cloud again I observed bright flashes near the right wing-root. At first I thought these flashes came from the enemy's guns but then realised that no guns were positioned there so obviously the flashes were caused by the explosive shells from my cannons.

Now I was bound to get him. My heart was beating a tattoo and I had a feeling of euphoria. A few seconds later we both came out of the cloud. The German had turned to starboard and I now found myself slightly above and behind him—he was a sitting duck. I saw tracer-bullets curving towards me from the Heinkel's gun turret but this I ignored, and from very close range I sent him a long burst of fire and saw the right-hand engine explode. I had to take fast evasive action to avoid flying into debris from it, and once again we were both engulfed in cloud. About thirty seconds later I emerged from the cloud but could see no other aeroplane. A short time later however, I caught sight of a column of smoke and then a great splash on the surface of the sea a short distance off the coast.

I felt a great elation over this victory, and my pleasure was no less when I observed four parachutes hanging in the air below, and a small warship on the sea heading towards us. These airmen had put up a good fight and, although they were the enemy, I was glad to see that they had survived. I flew slowly past the top parachute and saw the airman wave to me. Two years later another German pilot waved to me—but that's another tale.

On landing I discovered that Dennis Hogan had shot down a Heinkel just outside the harbour and Nobby Clarke had probably destroyed another, but the rest of the bombers had escaped in cloud. Later that day our CO, Tony Bartley, shot down a Ju 88 and another one was probably clobbered by Ernie Mouland.

A sort of headquarters had been set up near the southern perimeter of the airfield. There the army had raised a couple of tents for us, and in one of them we kept what meagre baggage we had in addition to our parachutes and flying kit. The other served as a dispersal hut where the CO and flight commanders had their 'office', and it also contained a few chairs and tables where we could relax during the rare occasions that we weren't either flying or taking shelter in ditches or slit-trenches. This was also our mess and the kitchen was located just outside the tents. The stoves consisted of petrol cans that had been cut in half and filled with sand; petrol was then poured into them for fuel. They were mainly used for boiling water for tea, as our main diet at that time consisted of Field Rations. These came in strong cardboard boxes which each held a day's ration for 14 men. The contents were mainly various types of canned food, which could be eaten cold, although heating it did no harm if facilities were on hand. In addition to the cans there were all sorts of goodies such as chocolate, raisins, biscuits, cheese and butter in tins, coffee, tea, milk-powder, salt and pepper, cigarettes, matches and toilet-paper. Some of us quite liked these rations, whilst others detested them.

Amongst the desert equipment we had been issued with were eating utensils and a billy-can. This was an elongated aluminium container with a lid, and could be used as a casserole or a dish. The handle was designed in such a way that it served as a bar to keep the lid closed. Inside this we kept our utensils and a collapsible mug.

A memorable incident happened just after I had eaten my midday meal. Not far from the mess tent, behind a large stone, there was a fairly deep hole in the ground that served as our toilet. During lunch I could not find my spoon so I borrowed Bill's. After eating I placed my utensils with my other belongings in the tent, lit a cigarette and wandered in the direction of the toilet. I was about half-way there when I heard Bill call:

'Tony, you bastard, give me back my spoon. I need it now.'

I cursed under my breath, returned to the tent for the spoon which I handed to Bill with thanks. I then set off again for the toilet and had only gone a short way when the ground ahead of me lifted up in an explosion and I was thrown onto my back-side. On investigation it emerged that our toilet-hole had been made by a delayed-action bomb dropped from an aircraft some time earlier! My guardian angels had most certainly been alert and doing their job, but I trembled at the thought of how close I had been to meeting my creator with my pants down.

After an uneventful patrol in the afternoon, my wingman and I were walking from our aircraft to the tents when suddenly four Me 109s swooped in low from the sea spraying a hail of fire. One of them seemed to head straight for us and the bullets from its guns kicked up the earth around us. We didn't waste any time, dropped our parachutes and sprinted for the nearest ditch less than 100 yards away. No doubt we set a new world record for that distance, and the hail of bullets seemed to follow us as we dived head-first into the ditch. That is where I received the wound I mentioned earlier. The sun had been shining spasmodically and the weather had been sufficiently warm for me to wear shorts, and I now cut a knee on a rusty tin lying there in the ditch. However, I soon stopped feeling sorry for myself when I saw the plight of my poor colleague. Someone, probably an Arab, had answered the call of nature there in the ditch and my friend had landed with his face in the 'goodies'! When I saw him again a few hours later his face was still red and shiny from much-repeated scrubbing.

Excrement was to play another roll before this day was over, but we will come to that a little later. As for my wounded knee, it posed no immediate problem. The Squadron's ground forces, including our MO, had not yet arrived, but I got an army medical orderly to clean and dress the wound. Nevertheless it became infected and a few days later I had to go for further treatment in a local field-hospital.

It was decided that the Squadron's pilots would be quartered in the town's best hotel. This was of course a great improvement on the previous billet, but it did have one great draw-back: it was very close to the harbour where the Luftwaffe was a regular visitor. Furthermore, a large anti-aircraft gun was located in the hotel's back garden, and the noise it made was enough to awaken the dead. An uninterrupted night's sleep was out of the question.

Three of us were to share a room on the top floor, George 'Titch' Heighington, Bill and myself. Before going up to our room I invited my pals to join me at the hotel bar to celebrate my first confirmed victory. I drank beer, but the other two preferred red wine. After a couple of glasses I started to feel queer in the stomach and we decided to call it a day and get up to our room. At this time an air raid on the harbour was in progress, and just as we were about to enter the lift a bomb fell close to the hotel and the electricity went off. We had therefore to grope our way in the dark up five flights of stairs to the top floor. On the way up my intestines started playing merry hell, and it was becoming obvious that I must reach a WC without delay. We had problems fitting the key into the latch, and by the time we eventually managed to open the door to our room I had no time to lose. By the little moonlight that came in through the window I was able to discern a sink against a wall and, thankfully, by the side of it a water closet. My trousers were down before I reached it and with great relief I plonked myself on the seat and let go! It was then that it occurred to me that the shape of the seat was unusual, but I put it down to French eccentricity—they seemed inclined to be different from other civilized people in so many ways.

I now felt a great deal better and looked around for a chain to flush the toilet as I didn't wish to expose my roommates to the rather pungent smell any longer than necessary. It was then that I discovered two oddities. Firstly, I could find no chain, or handle, for the purpose of flushing, but instead there were two taps on the rear rim of the basin. This was of course rather odd, but obviously very French. The other thing that I found peculiar was that those two idiots, who were supposed to be my roommates, had gone off their rockers and were hooting with laughter. Personally I could not see anything very funny about being attacked by a bout of diarrhoea. After a while one of them managed, in between spasms of laughter, to groan: 'That's not a bog, you clot. It's a bidet!' Then he resumed his hooting.

I was totally at a loss. I had never either heard of nor seen one of those 'bottom bathing' appliances that the French are so fond of. However, the last laugh was now mine. The drain was half clogged, and we only partly managed to rinse out the basin. Consequently, my mates were forced to lie in bed and try to drift off to sleep with the aroma of my diarrhoea in their nostrils.

Yes, it had certainly been an eventful day.

III   YOU CAN KEEP THIS GUN

The next few months spent in Africa were so eventful that a whole book could be written about just this one segment of the great adventure that my life in the RAF was becoming. I will, however treat this period as a series of stepping stones and limit my narrative to a few of the more memorable incidents.

The first took place the very next morning. As we were preparing to go on the first patrol at daybreak, I discovered, by sheer chance, something that could have had the most serious consequences had it gone unobserved. When I collected my parachute from the storage tent I noticed that one of the two snap-fasteners, that hold a little flap in place over the retaining pin, was undone. I can give no plausible reason for my actions when I saw this.

Instead of pressing the snap into place, as I would have done nine times out of ten, I undid the other one and lifted up the flap. What I saw in the beam of my flashlight gave me a jolt and produced an outburst of profanity.

To explain this reaction I must try to describe how these parachutes were designed.

The large silk canopy was folded in a specific way and then placed into a canvas cover designed rather like a bulging letter envelope. Four triangular flaps, like the back side of the envelope, were stretched over the folded canopy and on the tips of these flaps, where they came together, there were loops through which a pin was passed to hold them together. This pin was connected by a wire to the pilot's release handle, which when pulled drew the pin out of the loops, allowing the elastic in the flaps to pull them apart and thus releasing the canopy. To form a little resistance to prevent the pin from inadvertently being pulled out of these loops, a thin strand of red cotton was attached to it. The flap with the snap-fasteners was folded over the pin to give it protection.

What now stared me in the face was the fact that the end of the retaining pin had been bent over in such a way that there was no way of pulling it out of the loops. The seriousness of this needs no explanation.

My companions looked into the tent to see what had caused my outburst and were naturally astonished when they saw the reason. On inspection they found that their own parachutes had been treated in the same way, and further examination revealed that all the parachutes in the tent had been tampered with in the same fashion.

Our first thought was that this was an act of sabotage by an enemy agent. It was known that the Germans had secretly trained many Arabs in North Africa to commit acts of sabotage, appealing to their nationalism and promising them independence after a German victory. These agents had already caused some damage to lines of communication and storage depots, and a sorry state of affairs had been reached when nervous soldiers on guard-duties shot at any Arabs they thought behaved suspiciously. The military authorities thus found reason to impose a fine of fourteen pounds sterling for killing an Arab without adequate proof of his guilt.

We went in search of the soldier who was supposed to have guarded the tents during the night—he was certainly going to be in trouble for having slept on watch. When we found him he was astonished at our reactions: 'Wasn't it obvious to everyone that the thin strand of cotton was pretty useless?' With a touch of pride he declared that he had got hold of a pair of pliers and made improvements. We were flabbergasted. The man in his naiveté had thought he was doing us a favour.

It was most fortunate that he had failed to fasten that stud on my parachute flap, and also that it should have been the very first parachute to be picked up that morning. Before the day was over two pilots had taken to their parachutes to save their lives.

This was a strenuous day—the enemy kept up constant attacks on us and seemed determined to force us to abandon the airfield. Aircraft burned on the aerodrome and so did petrol dumps, but by the end of the day at least seven raiders had fallen to the anti-aircraft guns and those of our Spitfires. Tinsey and Stevenson each got a Ju 88 and Christian shared one with a pilot from another squadron. I myself had attacked at least three Ju 88s but was only able to claim to have damaged one of them after seeing black smoke pouring from its port engine as it disappeared into cloud. This was not the first time that my marksmanship was found wanting. One of our pilots was killed and many of our aircraft were destroyed or damaged. We tried to keep our Spitfires flying as much as possible, as that way they were less vulnerable, but of course we had to land to replenish fuel and ammunition, and in that way we lost a few of them on the ground.

Now our squadron's fleet of aircraft was becoming seriously depleted, but fortunately the situation improved next morning when a bunch of ferry pilots brought us some new ones. The Squadron's score of enemy planes destroyed kept growing. Tony Bartley, Dennis Hogan, Hughie Ballance and Tush each shot down a Macchi 202 fighter of the Italian air force as they were doing low-level attacks on our aerodrome. For some inexplicable reason the one that Tony Bartley shot was flying upside down at the time.

Next evening, as the dusk was gathering, we witnessed a very valiant act by Mac Gilmour. Such acts were of course only to be expected of him, but this one was exceptionally gallant. As on numerous former occasions four Me 109s appeared suddenly off the sea to strafe the aerodrome. At that moment two of our Spitfires, which had been on patrol, were landing and the leading one, flown by Sgt Stevenson, was caught by their bullets and crashed in flames. Ivan Crawford, flying the second Spitfire, saw what was happening in time to abandon the landing and turn to face the attackers. We, his companions, were forced to watch passively from the safety of our trenches while he fought off his four attackers—that is to say all of us except Mac who certainly didn't remain inactive. He ran to the nearest Spitfire and without bothering to put on a parachute or fasten his safety straps he started the engine and sped off. With full throttle he raced across the airfield in leaps and bounds. Such a take-off had never been attempted before, and he was even forced to swerve around bomb craters. At the very moment he lifted off the ground, even before he could retract his undercarriage, a Messerschmitt passing in front of him burst into flames from his bullets. The other three turned tail and Ivan shot down one of them just outside the airfield boundary. We had witnessed an act of great valour, but the pleasure it gave us was dampened by also having watched one of our comrades lose his life in a ball of fire.

Earlier that day Mac Gilmour and Titch Heighington had each destroyed a Ju 88 and I also managed to shoot one down and badly damage another. I had been on patrol with two of my companions when a large gaggle of Ju 88s attacked the harbour. We chased them out to sea and on my third attack on one of them it blew up. While I was firing this burst I became aware of an almost unbelievable occurrence—one of the doomed crew's comrades tried to come to their aid by attacking me from behind, and in so doing showed extraordinary courage. I had not expected such audacity, and only first became aware of the attack when my aircraft jolted and I saw a large hole in the right wing. Also, damage was done to my aircraft's pitot system, depriving me of airspeed indication. I immediately turned towards my assailant and after a few tight turns I was in a good position to send him a long burst from my guns. I saw pieces break off the aircraft and it went into a dive emitting black smoke.

Just at that moment I caught sight of another Ju 88 within good range and turned towards it. The pilot of that bomber made very determined attempts to evade me, displaying great skill, but it was an uneven match and soon I had him in my sights and pressed the firing button. There were a couple of bangs and that was all—the guns were empty! There, by the grace of God, went one lucky German.

On my return to the airfield I found it was about to be attacked by another bunch of Ju 88s. I silently cursed being out of ammunition, and had to make do with imitation attacks on the bombers. This sufficed however, to intimidate some of them, causing them to drop their bombs rather haphazardly, doing very little damage.

The air raids on the harbour and aerodrome continued, but it became obvious that the Germans stood in awe of the small force of Spitfires defending these targets. They started synchronizing bomber raids from Sicily with attacks by fighters from the airfields around Tunis. The bombers ignored the aerodrome to a large extent and concentrated on the harbour, while the task of the fighters was to provide the bombers with protection and carry out strafing attacks on the aerodrome. In fact we were rather surprised at how limited the destruction was that the fighters achieved. The army had built up strong anti-aircraft defences that succeeded in not only disrupting these attacks but also in shooting down a number of the attackers. Our soldiers were also becoming adept in camouflaging our Spitfires and at the same time displaying, in prominent places, those aircraft that were considered too damaged to be repaired and therefore fit to be sacrificed.

So the battle went on and the Squadron's tally of enemy planes shot down mounted, with victories by the CO, Dick Pertwee, Tush Tushingham, Tommy Tinsey, Bill Draper and others.

New aeroplanes and pilots started arriving. In a period of a few days the Squadron was strengthened by the addition of Robertson, Roy Pool, Dennis Moss, Freddie Mellors, 'Tommy' Thomas, George Longbottom and Peter Nickless. These last two were inseparable friends, and for some reason they were called the 'Quiz Kids' by the rest of the Squadron, and their names inevitably became altered to Nicklebottom and Longass. We also began to feel how much we missed our regular ground staff, especially the mechanics and armourers. We kept on flying our Spitfires without any inspections or repairs being carried out, and all sorts of niggling defects, both large and small, started affecting them. For instance, my plane had a hole the size of a fist in its right wing which did not appear to affect its flying characteristics but flying without any airspeed indication was rather a nuisance, although it could be done. Furthermore, the engine-temperature gauge was unserviceable. Most of our aircraft suffered from similar minor defects, which could easily have been remedied by our mechanics.

One of the most serious problems we faced was reloading the magazines for our guns. This was a task requiring much precision, and the smallest mistake or oversight could render the guns useless. Although some of the RAF Commandos were specially trained for this task, there were too few of them, and they often had to do the job in too much of a hurry, either because of an impending attack or an impatient pilot. Most of us had tales to tell about guns that failed when the firing button was pressed with the enemy in the sights. For instance I remember the frustration I felt after chasing a Heinkel 111 in and out of cloud for a long time and nothing happening when I finally pressed the gun button. And I was no less sore when after strenuous twisting and turning in combat with a Me 109, I had him in my sights and the same thing happened. The day of reckoning had been postponed for those Germans!

Then there was also another German pilot who was lucky, even though I did shoot him down. He was about to strafe Bone airfield in a Me 109 when my bullets hit his engine, so he crash-landed on the field. When I landed shortly afterwards, the pilot stood by his wrecked plane and was chatting with a bunch of soldiers that had surrounded him. The circle of soldiers opened up as I approached and someone said: 'Leutnant, here's the pilot that shot you down.'

The German approached me smiling, offered me his hand and said in faultless English: 'Sergeant, I am thankful that your bullets hit the engine and not the cockpit. Now the war is over for me and I shall survive. I hope you have the same luck.' He then handed me his Luger, saying: 'You can keep this gun, it's no use to me any more.'

This took place in the morning, and the rest of the day he spent with us at dispersal, completely unfettered. He showed us a snapshot of his wife and two children and claimed to be pleased with being a prisoner of war as that meant that he would live to see his family again. He denounced the Nazis (as in fact most Germans seemed to do before the end of the war) and said it was obvious that the Germans could not win. We tried to discuss flying and tactics with him, but he refused to be drawn into that subject, and we respected his discretion. We were beginning to form a liking for this ex-adversary and felt a little sad when a group of soldiers came to take him away.

Presently the American bombers, based on the edge of the desert south of the Atlas Mountains, stepped up their raids on the Axis Powers' airfields and centres of communications in Tunisia. This had the effect of forcing the German fighters into a more defensive role with a corresponding reduction in their attacks on our forward airfields. We were now in a position to become more offensive ourselves, and started paying visits into enemy territory. One day I led a section of four aircraft on a low-flying tactical reconnaissance along the valleys between the hills a short distance south-west of Tunis. It was obvious that the Germans considered this their own territory and were not expecting uninvited guests like us. We found a long convoy of covered lorries, and by the time we had spent our ammunition a large number of them were burning brightly.

My ever-watchful guardian angels were once again kept busy. Bill and I had met a charming French married couple who invited us to dinner one evening. At the end of the day's flying we persuaded a soldier to drive us into town for our date. On the way we had a flat tyre which took a while to fix, for the jeep was not carrying a tool kit. While we were thus delayed, the harbour at Bone had one of its numerous visits from enemy bombers. This would hardly be worth mentioning except for the fact that when we finally arrived at our destination all we found was a smoking pile of rubble. We never saw the couple again.

At the end of the month the long-awaited ship carrying our ground crew arrived in Bone harbour. It goes without saying that this particular convoy had an especially numerous escort of Spitfires on the last stage of its voyage, and we had a most joyous reunion with our comrades. It was great to see such good old friends as 'Chiefy' Jack Naldrett and his loyal mechanics, together with 'Basher' Gumbrell's and Chas Cooper's well-trained armourers. Also others such as 'Tubby' Roberts and other ground crew, in addition to George Usher our 'Spy' and Doc Angus our 'Pillpusher' and Ken Mason our 'Chief Plumber'. We had now reclaimed our much-needed and longed-for specialists to attend to our aeroplanes, load our guns, fill our tanks, dress our wounds and cook our meals, just a few of the chores they would perform.

A few days later we left Bone and moved to an airfield near a village called Souk-el-Arba, inside Tunisia about 90 miles from the capital. This field, formerly used by small aircraft, had been occupied by paratroopers and the Army Engineers had bulldozed a strip long enough for our Spitfires.

Before leaving Bone we were relieved by an American fighter squadron flying Spitfires.[1] Until now we hadn't had any direct relations with these allies of ours, and we were curious to see their reaction to taking over this dump of wrecked and burned-out aircraft that the airfield inevitably had become. The wrecks were allowed to stand where they were in the hope that they would confuse attacking enemy aircraft and draw their fire.

We locals knew our aerodrome well and avoided using the short runway unless there was a fairly strong wind blowing down it. When the Americans arrived there was only a slight breeze, but to our surprise they chose to land on this runway. They arrived overhead in a tidy formation, broke up and spread out in a most professional way, and started their approach in a long line astern.

We stood in a group and watched fascinated as they approached the short runway. Someone offered a bet that the first one would overshoot, and I didn't hear anyone take him on. And, of course, overshoot it did, and finished up on its nose on the rocky, unfinished, extension to the runway. The second followed close behind, as did the third and, before we knew, three Spitfires stood there with their tails high in the air, with the fourth tearing along the runway towards them at high speed. However, in some inexplicable way the pilot of this aircraft managed to do a ground-loop with the wingtip scraping the surface. But, he even went one better—he also forced the rest of us to fall flat onto our bellies as during this spin, he pressed the firing button and sprayed the bullets from his guns round the airfield!

The next pilot in the file abandoned his landing when he became aware that his companions were having some problems. It now dawned upon the rest of them that it might be better to use the other runway even though there was a slight cross wind to contend with.

We harboured no feelings of nostalgia when we said farewell to Bone.

---

[1] 2nd Fighter Squadron, 52nd Fighter Group.

IV   IT WAS EXPERIENCE THAT COUNTED

Our stay at Souk-el-Arba was short. As in Bone, the area had been captured by paratroops who had driven the Germans out. The landing strip laid down by the Army Engineers was covered with wire netting that made it usable after the rainy season had started. The rain, which in the coming weeks was to cause us so much trouble, had not started in earnest, and when the ground was dry our aircraft stirred up a great cloud of dust each time they moved. We lived in tents for the next few days, until the landing strip that was being constructed for us at Souk-el-Kemis, about 12 miles further north, was ready.

On our first sortie from Souk-el-Arba my pal Bill Williams had a very narrow escape. We were escorting a small Taylorcraft Auster on a reconnaissance flight over enemy-held territory when a group of Me 109s jumped us. Bill, who was leading 'B' Flight, spotted the impending attack and shouted for the Squadron to break right to face the attackers. He waded into the enemy formation thinking that the Squadron was behind him, but suddenly discovered that he was all alone, surrounded by Messerschmitts. The Squadron was already engaged with other enemy planes, and Spitfires and Me 109s were milling around the sky. In between all the shouts and warnings on the R/T, I suddenly heard a distress call from Bill. He was in a fight with two 109s and getting the worse of it. I believed him to be a short distance behind us and turned back with my wingman to search for him. We reached him only just in time—his aircraft was already damaged, and he had been wounded in one arm. The enemy planes fled when they saw us coming, and Bill was able to make a successful forced landing back at base.

Another of our mates, Jim Waring, was shot down on this flight, but after roaming around the countryside for twelve hours he came across some forward elements of the British Army who transported him, elated, back to the mess. This was the second time that Jimmy had returned to the squadron after being shot down. The first time he brought in a bunch of Italian soldiers. They had seen him walking and hurried towards him with their hands in the air, asking to be taken prisoners. They had had enough of German domineering arrogance and wished to be out of the war.

As on previous occasions, I had only myself to blame for not bringing down an enemy plane on this sortie. More than once I'd had the opportunity, but each time my poor marksmanship had let the enemy escape. It did little to bolster my ego when I witnessed our CO send a Me 109 down in flames with a two-second burst from his guns.

During the next few days we carried out some sweeps and got into a few scraps. In one of them Tony Bartley shot down two Ju 87 dive-bombers and Mac Gilmour probably shot down a 109. Tush Tushingham was shot down, but to our delight turned up unhurt the same evening. We were also visited by bomb-carrying Me 109s and Fw 190s, which managed to damage three of our aircraft on the ground. Tommy Thomas and Jim Waring, who were on standing patrol, chased them, Tommy shooting one down and Jim damaging another. The Fw 190 fighters were now starting to turn up in greater numbers which was not exactly good news.

As at Bone, our dispersal consisted of a couple of sizable tents, a few chairs, a table and an assortment of crates and boxes. When not flying we passed the time with various activities such as card games, chess, horse-shoe throwing and ant-baiting. With the aid of a shovel we would transport a colony of red ants onto a black-ant heap (or vice versa) and watch the ensuing battle. It was remarkable how well organized the ants were in warfare. They even carried their dead off the battlefield and laid them in rows during the height of the combat. Also during this period a new pastime became popular. It so happened that an abandoned German ammunition dump was discovered near the airfield, and amongst other things we found a large quantity of bullets that fitted into our service revolvers. With this abundance of ammunition being available to us we did a lot of target shooting. In addition to the traditional ways of shooting at targets, we indulged in the Hollywood Wild West 'quick on the draw' mode, and some of us became quite skilful 'gun-slingers'. The incredible fact was that the speed I attained in this clowning was to come in handy a few weeks later. But, that's another story.

Tommy Tinsey and the Canadian Bill Draper became the squadron's self-appointed scroungers. Whenever something was needed—which was a frequent occurrence—they were dispatched to acquire it, in one way or another, and they became incredibly adept, and at times unscrupulous, in this activity. If Bill got hold of a car, Tommy would even the score with a case of Scotch whiskey. When Bill turned up with a much-needed cooking range, Tommy turned up with some turkeys. Their greatest worry was that they might accidentally acquire something legally.

Once, however, they got thoroughly beaten at their own game. They had gone to the Souk (market place) in one of the villages to acquire some fruit. It goes without saying that every trick available would be used to acquire the goods as cheaply as possible. As we hadn't received any pay for a lengthy period we had no other recourse but to turn to our escape pack for some cash. On this occasion Tommy opened his and found a goodly amount of Sterling, US dollars and French franc notes, and also four small 20 franc coins. He showed one of these coins to an Arab stall keeper and pointed to the fruit on his cart. The Arab studied the coin carefully and then pointed at a half full sack of oranges. Tommy shook his head as he intended to buy assorted fruit. The Arab then pointed at a full sack of oranges and indicated that Tommy should take it. Tommy and Bill winked at each other, convinced that the Arab was out of his mind to sell a full sack of oranges for a lousy 20 franc coin. Each one quickly grabbed an end of the sack and scurried away with it. Back at camp they triumphantly described how they had tricked 'the stupid Ay-rab'. The smile quickly disappeared off their faces when George Usher, our spy, pointed out to them that these were gold coins dating from the Louis dynasty, usually called Louis-d'ors, and were worth at least 3000 francs each. Of course they never found the Arab again.

A few days later a squadron of Hurribombers took over the airfield and we moved to the new strip at Souk-el-Kemis, which was constructed in a similar way to that at Souk-el-Arba. We settled into a large farm nearby and raised our tents in a grove of Eucalyptus trees. The officers acquired a small cottage as a mess, and we sergeants were given the use of a barn. We cleaned it thoroughly, built an attractive bar and acquired some chairs and tables. As I had dabbled a bit at painting, it befell me to decorate the main wall with a mural depicting a reclining naked beauty. Unfortunately no maiden was available to pose as a model, so I had to rely on memory. My memory must have been good enough—at least I heard no complaints. When our decorations were completed we had quite a cosy little mess, which even the officers envied. Admittedly the place was infested with rats during the night, due to it being next door to a chicken coop, and anything edible had to be carefully removed.

These rats proved to be extraordinary wily, however. One of our members, Hughie Ballance, who came from Rhodesia and was experienced in all sorts of hunting and trapping, set up a variety of traps to catch them, but eventually had to admit to defeat. Usually one rat got caught in every new type of trap, but after that no more. One of the traps consisted of a small plank that stuck out over the edge of the bar counter, and below it was a barrel half full of water. A piece of cheese was placed on the end of the plank in such a way that the plank would tip up when the rat tried to reach the cheese. And true enough it worked. Next morning a drowned rat was found in the barrel, but never again. The plank was always in its place, but the cheese gone! Yes, the rats of Souk-el-Kemis were remarkably bright. At a general mess-meeting in the bar it was agreed that these neighbours of ours were sufficiently intelligent to be considered sergeants and admitted to the mess as full-blown members.

Our two-man supply committee discovered a monastery in the neigh-bouring hills that produced barely passable red wine, and a barrel of the stuff stood on a trestle in the bar. Although we did receive a small ration of beer and spirits, the wine formed the main foundation of our boozing, and was aptly called 'screech'. Occasionally our scroungers were able to augment our booze rations by dubious means, about which we did not ask too many questions. Once Bill managed to divert a large consignment of beer that was on its way to another destination. It must be admitted that we did not suffer any great pangs of remorse whilst we were swilling it. The consignment might so easily have been destroyed by a wandering German fighter plane, or worse still, it could have fallen into enemy hands.

During this period, our flying became more and more offensive rather than defensive. However, we nearly always had two aircraft on a standing patrol in the neighbourhood of the airfield, as the Germans were far from admitting defeat, and lost no chance to repay the uninvited visits we paid them. Most of the time we escorted Hurribombers over raids on enemy airfields, supply dumps and other military installations. The list of enemy planes shot down by the squadron continued to grow longer, but we also suffered the loss of some of our comrades, such as Monty Falls, George Longbottom and Chris Christian.

We were infuriated when Chris was shot down by American anti-aircraft guns on the way home from a successful raid. Unfortunately such mistakes did occasionally happen, and no doubt it was due to inexperience that the Americans so frequently mistook friend for foe.

Another example of such a mistake made by them was the one that took place on a nice clear day a few weeks later. We had just returned to base from a sortie, and Spy was debriefing us outside the dispersal tent when, high up in the blue sky we saw a large formation of Flying Fortresses coming from the south and heading towards Tunis. We had hardly finished shouting into the air: 'Give it to them, boys!' and other such encouragements, when we heard the awful screaming sound that precedes falling bombs. We threw ourselves flat on the ground as bombs exploded all around us with a terrifying din and showers of earth and mud descended upon us. When the infernal racket had subsided, and we dared lift our heads, we saw aircraft and fuel dumps burning in many places on the airfield, and on closer investigation it was confirmed that two airmen had been killed and many injured. Eight of the squadron's Spitfires were written off, and others damaged. Later we were given the explanation that the navigator of the lead bomber had somehow or other got the grid references on his map confused.

By now Bill and I were among the most experienced pilots in the squadron, and we frequently led 'B' Flight in the air when Jimmy Baraldi, our flight commander, did not fly. In mid-December I led the whole squadron for the first time, even though I still only held the rank of Flight

Sergeant. I mention this to confirm my earlier statement to the effect, that when it came to serious operational flying, experience counted far more than rank. In the air a NCO pilot could be in a position to give orders even to high-ranking officers, although this of course could not happen on the ground.

V   SCABIES

The rainy season now set in earnestly causing us a great deal of difficulty and annoyance. Not only because we were frequently wet and cold, but also because the earth turned into clinging, ankle-deep mud that bogged our aircraft down, and made moving them on the ground difficult. Because of the wire-mesh on the runway the take-offs and landings posed no problems, but off the runway we risked standing our aircraft on end whenever we tried to taxi. After two Spitfires had tipped up on their noses it was decided that a couple of airmen should sit on the tailplane of each aircraft while it was taxied out onto the runway. Once there the pilot would give a sign by waving a hand above the cockpit and the airmen would jump clear.

However, once this did not work out right, and I witnessed a singular incident. The Squadron was going on a sweep and I was right behind Tommy Tinsey as we taxied out. When he reached the runway I saw that one of the airmen sitting on the tail of his aircraft jumped off, but the other didn't move. Because of the driving rain and spattering mud he had failed to observe Tommy's signal.

In an effort to keep the enemy in the dark about our movements a strict radio-silence was ordered until reaching enemy territory. Because of this I had not even switched on my radio set and was therefore unable to warn Tommy, and forced to watch helplessly as a dramatic incident unfolded. As Tommy advanced the throttle to fully open, the airman got thrown sideways so that he was pressed against the stabilizer. The strong slipstream held him in place there with his legs hooked under the tailplane as the aircraft rushed forward. When it became obvious that the airman would not fall off onto the runway I hurriedly followed Tommy into the air and flew alongside him. I could see that he was fully aware of what was happening so there was nothing more for me to do. I flew the circuit with him, and I could see the look of distress on the poor airman's face—and no wonder. The landing was rather heavy, and the airman was in such a great hurry to end

Training for the 'Camel Corps'!

Elementary School.

Target practice.

Exercising the grey cells.

Sampling the 'Screech'.

Entering log book.

'Ballance'-trapping.

TREBLE ONE CHARACTERS

Top left: George D Usher, 'Spy'.
Top right: 'Doc' Angus. (Served with 111 Sqdn, 1939-1945 - surely a record!).
Bottom left: Roy Poole.
Bottom right: Ernie Mouland (RCAF).

Top left: Mel 'Tush' Tushingham (RCAF).
Top right: Freddie Mellors.
Bottom left: Fred 'Bambi' Taylor and
Brian Spranger.
Bottom right: Barry Gale (RAAF) and
Ivan Crawford, loading his pipe.

Top left: Dick Pertwee.
Top right: Tony Fowler (RNZAF).
Bottom left: Johnny Church (RNZAF).
Bottom right: Barry E Gale (RAAF).

TREBLE ONE CHARACTERS

Top left: 'Nobby' Clark.
Middle left: Chris Le Roux (RSAAF).
Bottom left: Jimmy Waring.
Top right: Bill Draper (RCAF).
Bottom right: George Hill, with his Spitfire 'Thelma' named after his wife.

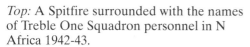

Top: A Spitfire surrounded with the names of Treble One Squadron personnel in N Africa 1942-43.

Bottom left: 65 Squadron pilots and Mustang at Ford in June 1944. L-R: S/Ldr Westenra (RNZAF), CO 65 Squadron, Basil Clapin, Chris Nyrrod (Royal Norwegian Air Force) and 'Ned' Kelly (RAAF). Note 500lbs bomb with small arming propellor suspended under wing.

Bottom right: 65 Squadron flying Mustang IIIs Sitting on engine from L-R: F/O Taylor, RAF; P/O Williams, RAF; F/O Hillman, RCAF; F/Sgt Sumner, RAF; Capt. Nyrrod, Royal Norwegian Air Force; F/O Wally, RAF.

Sitting on wing L-R: F/Sgt Webb, RAF; F/Sgt Smith, RAF; F/O Jonsson, DFM RAF (Iceland); F/Lt Stillwell, RAF; F/Sgt Williams, RAF; Squadron Leader Westenra, DFC RNZAF; F/O Ashworth, RNZAF; Sgt Morton, RAF.

Front row standing L-R: F/Lt Sutherland, RCAF; F/Sgt Kelly, DFM RAAF; F/Lt Will, RAF; F/Sgt Dinsdale, RAF; F/O Lloyd, RAF; F/O Hughes, RAF; F/Lt Cooper, RAF; W/O Boon, RAF; F/O Mizener, RCAF; F/O Muir, RCAF; F/Lt Clapin, RAF; F/O Rafford, RAF.

Photograph supplied by F/Sgt Kelly, taken 16 June 1944 at Ford Aerodrome, Sussex.

Top left: Mustang III, introduced to service with the Desert Air Force in March 1944.

Top centre: 'Suds' Sutherland (RCAF). Funtington 1944. Killed in action 26th June 1944.

Top right: Cooper. Ex-Treble One comrade (North Weald and Debden 1941- 42). Failed to return from a dive-bombing mission to Dreux, May 1944.

Above centre: At the Reykjavik aerodrome on VE-Day 1945.

Above left: In Cairo (on the India trooping-run) 1946 with 'Ginger' Swann and Frank Leary.

Right: 1945.

this unexpected flight that threw himself off before the aircraft came to a halt, and in doing so broke an ankle. But he was triumphant at being down on Mother Earth again in one piece, and said: 'To hell with the ankle!'

For understandable reasons we soon found a new name for our aerodrome and called it Waterloo, but in spite of the rain and mud we were not uncomfortable in our camp. The tents were scattered about the small woods and hard to spot from the air, but in spite of that it did not take the enemy long to ferret us out, probably with information from spies. Bombs fell in the area but did minimal damage. The tents were fairly spacious, each one housing four persons issued with field-cots and three blankets apiece. Further furnishing consisted of a table and chairs, washbasins and even a folding bath-tub. All this furniture could be folded for ease of transportation. Most of us dug trenches to place our cots in for protection against bomb-blast, and going to bed was usually referred to as creeping into one's hole.

At the end of the day's work we were driven in a lorry back to camp where a hot meal awaited us. The basis of our diet was still the contents of the cardboard boxes mentioned earlier, but our cooks were geniuses at concealing this. They were able to concoct a variety of dishes from this canned food with the aid of vegetables and eggs bought from local pedlars, who were frequent visitors with their wares loaded onto the backs of donkeys. One, whom we named Mohammed, appeared nearly daily and became our favourite. We taught him a few well chosen words and phrases in English, but these will not be recited here. After the evening meal we would get together in our respective messes for drinks. Much robust singing was done, often to the accompaniment of a harmonica, and I'm afraid that here again many of the texts would be unsuitable for rendering in public. Some played cards or chess, but by midnight most had crept into their holes for the day started early. We were awoken before dawn, had a mug of hot tea and a sandwich and were then driven to the airfield where the first patrol got airborne in the early twilight.

At this stage I went through a very difficult period. Unaccountably, I had become infected with Scabies, a small insect *(Sarcoptes scabiei)* that lays its eggs under the infected person's skin, causing irritation. In the beginning I experienced only slight discomfort, but then the infection started to spread over most of my body and the irritation grew until it was becoming nearly unbearable. I suffered most when having to remain in the same posture for any length of time, such as when sitting in my Spitfire for long periods on standby-readiness, or lying in my warm bed not being able to sleep due to the itching. A stage was reached when I deliberately got drunk before going to bed in the hope of getting some sleep. In the end I stopped going to bed.

When my companions left the mess I tried to make myself comfortable in an armchair with glasses of screech beside me. When peace and quiet settled in, the rats came out to play, first up on the beams but no doubt they made themselves at home in the rest of 'their' mess. I had my revolver by my side and every now and then, while I still retained consciousness, I took a pot-shot at the rats on the beams. I may no doubt be reproached for showing these messmates of ours such hostility, but I don't think I ever hit one of these 'sergeant' rats, nor was I ever aware of being molested by them. When the gun reports finally ceased I am told that my comrades told each other that Jonny had passed out at last, and now they could get some sleep.

It goes without saying that I was not exactly sparkling in the early hours of the mornings when we went to the airfield, but I tried to bear up, for I was determined not to let the consequences of my indisposition be borne by my comrades. Angus, our Doctor, (or 'Quack' as we affectionately called him) naturally had most of the medicines required for dressing wounds and curing common ailments, but no remedies for fighting this loathsome parasite that was afflicting me. Finally he proclaimed me unfit for duty and sent me to hospital in Algiers for a cure, to be followed by a few days of rest.

The cure consisted of lying submerged in hot water until the skin became soaked and soft. The affected parts of my body were then scrubbed with a stiff brush leaving me covered in small sores which were brushed over with some clear fluid. All this was most painful, to say the least, and I certainly do not include *Sarcoptes scabiei* amongst my favourites of God's creations. Next day I was released from hospital, and my enchanting girl-friend, 'Elena the Ugly', as I jokingly called her, kindly invited me to stay at her flat. I spent a few days with her and thoroughly enjoyed life.

One evening she had to attend a Zionist meeting, or something of that sort, so I used the opportunity to take a look at the 'Sphinx'. This was the name given to one of the world's most splendid brothels of that era. Among the Allied personnel it was out of bounds to 'other ranks'; only officers were allowed to visit it. This posed no problem to me, for as a Flight Sergeant I wore a brass crown above my chevrons. I simply removed the stripes and placed the crowns on my shoulders and became a Major!

The brothel, an imposing multi-story building, was situated in a rather isolated spot near the harbour, and not far from the city's main hotel. Wide marble steps led up to a large oak door with a small inspection shutter that was opened when I pressed the bellbutton. After the doorkeeper had carefully made sure that I wasn't just some wretched lowly soldier wanting entry, but a high ranking officer, he opened the door, and bowing deeply, bade me enter. I stepped into a spacious foyer with a marble floor. Deep armchairs were scattered around under potted palms, and opposite the entrance a large and imposing negress sat on a chair beside the entrance to the lift.

To the left were swing-doors leading into a large, and beautifully decorated dining hall where uniformed waiters served guests sitting at tables covered with snow-white linen tablecloths, adorned with silver candlesticks and gleaming utensils. In the background an orchestra played subdued dinner music.

To the right was the entrance to a large and comfortable looking bar room. The bar itself was at least 30 yards long and appeared to be stocked with just about every kind of drink one could wish for. In front of the bar were zebra-skin covered stools and along the wall a row of cosy stalls. These stalls contained sofas on either side of candle-lit tables, and heavy curtains could be drawn to give them privacy. Scantily clad women sat on settees scattered around the room and were available for anyone who wished to approach them, yet they did not in any conspicuous way try to solicit customers.

I invited a good-looking girl to sit with me at the bar but she spoke no English so she fetched a friend that did. We drank a bottle of champagne between us and she filled me in on the workings of the establishment, which was run by the state and subject to strictly enforced rules. The girls, who were of various nationalities and races, lived on the premises and each one had her own studio flat. They were examined by a doctor every week and their certificate of health was displayed on a wall in their flat. One hour spent with them in their flat cost 200 francs, and the whole night 500. The aforementioned negress, who was addressed as Madame, collected the fee before the lift was entered. The girls were satisfied with their circumstances and there were more applicants for positions than situations available.

When the bottle of champagne was empty I said good-bye to this lady, as I had no need for her charms while I enjoyed Elena's hospitality. After leaving, I had to walk along a practically deserted and badly lit road. When I stopped for a moment to light a cigarette two Arabs emerged from an alley and came towards me. One of them had a cigarette in his hand which he held out to me and asked for a light. As I passed him my matchbox he grabbed my wrist with one hand and at the same time I saw a glint from a knife held aloft in his other hand. My reactions were instinctive and fast—I kicked him in the groin so that he staggered away. I became aware of the other Arab behind me, looked over my shoulder and saw him approaching. I jumped aside, and now our 'cowboy' practices came in good stead. In a flash I drew my revolver from its holster and fired at this attacker. He fell screaming to the ground, and the knife he dropped from his hand rattled among the cobblestones. I turned towards the other one but he was already sprinting away, and disappeared between the houses.

After a short while two policemen arrived. They ascertained that my assailant had a bullet wound in his thigh, and it wasn't long before I began to feel sorry for the fellow, so roughly did they treat him. They asked me to accompany them to the police station to make a report, and gave the impression that they were very sorry I had been caused so much bother. Robbery and violence was becoming much too common, and this criminal had got what he deserved—it was really a pity that I hadn't killed the blighter. Then they roared with laughter over the whole incident and offered me coffee and cognac.

I spent a few more luxurious days with Elena and then flew back to my mates—'deloused', well rested and raring to go.

VI   IS THERE A REAL MAN HERE?

Relentless rain did little to enhance our 1942 Christmas celebrations for water and moisture were everywhere and it was impossible to avoid having to wade through oceans of mud, both at the airfield and in the camp. In fact on Christmas Day all flying was cancelled because of the weather, so all but the cooks had a day off and were free to take part in the festivities. In accordance with tradition the officers served the Christmas dinner to the 'other ranks' in the big mess marquee. Bill Draper and Tommy Tinsey, our caterers had done a good job acquiring turkeys and other choice items of food, and all this fine fare was washed down with a plentiful supply of screech. After dinner an amusing show was put on by the Squadron's 'entertainers', followed by a general sing-song session accompanied by an airman playing a piano, which our supply officers had in some mysterious way managed to procure. Not all the songs could be classified as Christmas Carols, however.

The ground staff's lot as they tended our aeroplanes was not enviable. They carried out their tasks in the open air, often in appalling weather conditions. Furthermore, the airfield was frequently attacked by enemy aircraft with little or no warning, making them take to their feet for survival, and not always successfully. Yet, they were ever-ready to carry out all our wishes—even those of the most whimsical of pilots—and they performed their tasks conscientiously and with courage.

Weather continued to restrict flying during the early part of January 1943, but then it improved and we got down to business once again. Three Spitfire squadrons were now based at Souk-el-Kemis operating as a wing, carrying out sweeps or escorting Hurribombers on raids. With the improvements in the weather it appeared that the enemy had received a shot in the arm—they now met us with increased ferocity and hard-fought air battles were common. Treble One continued to be successful, although this was not achieved without sacrifices.

Fairly typical of the activities of that period was a raid carried out by six Hurribombers on an important bridge a short distance south of Tunis on January 18. Treble One and 72 Squadron were given the task of escorting them, and near the target we were met by a gaggle of enemy fighters determined to intercept the Hurricanes. We were just as determined to protect them and this resulted in a violent battle. As was usual in such situations the squadron split up into small groups and individual combats developed. German fighters seemed to be all over the sky and each time I was about to open fire on one of them my wingman would warn me to break left or right to dodge other enemy planes.

We were being forced to throw our Spitfires violently around, and my wingman, a fairly new lad by the name of Dennis Moss, did an excellent job keeping up with me. Unfortunately this was to be his last battle. In one of our tight orbits I saw cannon shells from a Me 109 hit the forward part of his plane causing the engine to seize. At the same moment I became aware of tracer bullets shooting past me and I had to take very sharp avoiding action. I managed to escape my attacker and shortly caught sight of Dennis below me, gliding down with smoke coming from his aircraft. As the landscape below was very uneven and rocky, and most unsuitable for belly-landing, I called Dennis on the R/T and suggested he'd better bale out, but got no reply. At that moment I again had to take evasive action, and by the time I had got the enemy off my tail I saw that Dennis was down to about 1000 feet above the ground and still had not abandoned his aircraft. I called him once again with the same results as before, and just at that moment I caught sight of a Me 109 far below me heading for Dennis. I wasted no time in diving down towards this enemy who apparently was not aware of me, and I quickly caught up with him. By the time he was getting within range of Dennis, the 109's wings more than spanned my reflector sight and I pressed the firing button. The Messerschmitt exploded and fell burning to the ground.

From force of habit I looked behind and saw an aircraft approaching and immediately went into a defensive turn but quickly became aware of it being a Spitfire, and on closer scrutiny the pilot turned out to be Chris Le Roux, our new flight commander. His voice came on the R/T: 'Well done, Jonny! Let's follow Dennis.'

Chris made repeated attempts to call him without results and we watched as he tried a forced-landing on a ridge in the hills. The ground was strewn with boulders and the aircraft burst into flames as soon as it touched down.

Chris and I flew circles around the burning wreck but saw no signs of life. All indications were that Dennis had been too badly wounded to save himself, as he had made no attempt to bale out nor had he answered our calls.

On this raid Wing Commander Gilroy shot down a Me 109, Chris Le Roux also shot one down and probably another, and Barry Gale damaged one.

A few days later I had an experience which in a way was amusing but could easily have been deadly serious. My No. 2 and I had sat for about thirty minutes in our Spitfires on stand-by readiness at the end of the runway when a red flare warned of an imminent attack. We hurried into the air and within a short while we were chasing two Me 109s. They climbed as steeply as they could and we followed them at full throttle. Higher and higher we went but we were gradually being left behind as the 109s out-climbed us. We were above 21,000 feet when suddenly I felt nauseated and giddy, and lost concentration. No doubt my flying had become somewhat unsteady because I vaguely heard my wingman calling: 'Is something wrong, Jonny?'

I am unable to describe from memory what now followed, but my No. 2 told me later that it appeared as if my aircraft was out of control and commenced to fall like a leaf down to 10,000 feet, where it came under control again. All that time he was unsuccessfully calling me on the R/T. After I regained consciousness I discovered that my oxygen tube was unconnected, and the lack of oxygen had caused me to pass out. The situation could so easily have become worse.

Towards the latter part of the month Tony Bartley ran out of operational hours, and sadly we said good-bye to our highly esteemed and respected leader. A little earlier Jimmy Baraldi, the popular commander of 'B' Flight had left due to eye trouble, and he had been replaced by a new lad, the South African Chris Le Roux who now took over the leadership of the squadron.

Shortly before Tony left us there was a strong rumour afoot about the Axis powers planning a counter-attack on the ground and the possibility of our airstrip being surrounded or even attacked by paratroops. Under the direction of F/O Cohen, the RAF Regiment officer attached to the Squadron, defensive trenches were dug at various points along the perimeter, and we were all issued with rifles and assigned to these trenches to defend the airstrip against these airborne raiders should they be dropped during the night. Of course, in the event of any danger of the strip being surrounded we pilots could fly our aircraft out and thus escape; to save our mechanics from falling into enemy hands, however, our CO concocted an ingenious scheme. The idea was to make strong canvas sacks with a loop that could be slipped over the barrels of the cannons protruding from the wings of our Spitfires. The mechanics would lie in these sacks, one on each wing, and thus be flown to safety. Fortunately the occasion for putting this amazing project into effect never arose, but the fact that the mechanics never voiced any objections bears testimony to the faith they had in Tony and his knowledge of the Spitfire's capabilities.

A month later the Germans did indeed stage a heavy counter-attack through the Kasserine Gap in the mountains to the south of us, but were stopped before posing any direct threat to our airfield. The weather during the early stages of this German thrust was atrocious for flying—much rain and low cloud—yet we flew whenever possible. In mist and poor visibility, with the hilltops shrouded in cloud we flew along narrow valleys attacking German transport and military vehicles wherever we found them. There is no doubt that our fighters and bombers played an important role in halting the German threat.

These were hectic days with little sleep or rest, but the urgency and the weather cost us sacrifices. Our squadron lost a pilot who flew into a hillside in the poor visibility, and another one was shot down by Flak, but he managed to get back to the airfield a few days later, after many adventures. At one time he had to spend a few hours perched up in a tree surrounded by aggressive wild boars, until a group of soldiers rescued him. The wing's other squadrons also lost pilots during this strenuous period.

The weather now improved and we continued to harass Rommel's forces wherever we found them. German fighters made valiant efforts to defend these forces, but were becoming overpowered, for they also had to defend harbours and other important military targets in Tunisia against increasing attacks by Allied heavy bombers.

Bill Draper downed a Fw 190 in an unusual way. He and the enemy attacked each other head on, at a combined speed of about 700 mph, and both obstinately refused to give way. At the last moment the German went over the top and his propeller shattered against the tail of Bill's Spitfire. This happened at a low altitude and the Focke Wulf crashed into the ground, while Bill managed to nurse his damaged plane back to base.

The Squadron's pilots were now given a few days rest. Some chose to spend the time in a hotel we had discovered up in the Atlas mountains not too far away. There were wild boars in the wood surrounding the hotel and I had on one occasion participated in an exciting hunt in the area. The rest of us under the guidance of Chris Le Roux got a lift on a Dakota to Algiers.

The first evening in town we got thrown out of the Sphinx. We were far from sober when we arrived and headed straight for the bar. It was not long before someone suggested that we should order an 'exhibition' to be put on for us, the name given to an event when two prostitutes, privately, put on a special show. This was immediately deemed an excellent idea and someone was sent to make the arrangements with Madame.

After stocking up on booze—most of us bought bottles of champagne—we were shown into a room down in the basement. A couch had been placed in the middle of the floor and armchairs and tables along the walls. We sat down and sipped our drinks while we waited for the arrival of the girls. We were in a hilarious mood, giggling, cracking jokes and roaring with laughter. It was obvious that we needed to let off steam after the strain and tension of the last few weeks. Our merriment was not lessened when two women entered through a side door, stark naked and smiling broadly, and bade us welcome. With an artificial aid one of them acted the role of a male and with great skill and experience these two maidens demonstrated the act of copulation. We exhorted them with unabashed gaiety, and drank toasts to them—everyone seemed to be having an uproarious time. Considering the tender age of some of the onlookers, and the morals of those years, I do not doubt that there would have been some red and embarrassed faces amongst the lads if Bacchus had not been present for encouragement.

However, looks of evasion and embarrassment did appear on most faces when the lady who had played the role of the male smiled provocatively and said: 'Well, is there a real man here, who can show us how this should be done?'

We giggled, cast enquiring glances at each other or looked evasively into far corners; no-one seemed likely to take up the challenge. It was not long, however, before one of our senior pilots stood up unsteadily and said: 'Whatta bunch of girl-guides y'all are. Hass nobody got'n'y guts? Is nobody gonna schow s'm manhood? I'll schow you that'n'all Trebbleone are chicken!'

Having said that he wobbled over to the girls and plonked himself down on the couch. And now the laughter really got going again, growing in intensity until tears were streaming down our cheeks and we were holding our bellies, literally screaming. Without doubt these two Aphrodites were experienced and knew their jobs, but no matter what they tried, they were unable to arouse our hero's manhood. We thought this was screamingly funny. After protracted attempts they patted the poor fellow on the cheek and with wiggling back-sides disappeared through the door, leaving our hero lying dejected on the couch and the rest of us writhing.

We wandered up to the bar, and as by now we were becoming highly intoxicated and still very hilarious, the laughter and uproar continued. Other more sedate customers were beginning to give us askance looks, and after a little while two large Negroes dressed in doormen's uniforms approached and asked us kindly to leave the premises. One or two of our companions started to argue, but we quickly steered them out onto the street with us. The bouncers were very large, and beginning to look threatening.

I may add that our hero had his leg mercilessly pulled and became known as Romeo. But the poor fellow did not suffer his notoriety for very long, for a few days after our return to Souk-el-Kemis he became another victim in our continued attacks on Rommel's forces.

My guardian angels were back on the job again the night we arrived back from Algiers. As I have already mentioned, we placed our field-cots in slit-trenches in our tents for protection against possible bomb or shell blast. On leaving the mess to go to bed we usually did not bother to light our oil lanterns or candles, but undressed in the dark and slipped in between the blankets. For some inexplicable reason I broke the routine this evening. I lifted up a corner of the blanket and shone under it with my flashlight and discovered a coiled-up snake. I grabbed my revolver and sent this would-be bedfellow to join his ancestors. It turned out to be about three feet long and there were various opinions about how poisonous it was. However, I believed in safety first; I had no desire to go to bed with a snake.

But now changes were impending and my adventures in Africa were drawing to a close for the time being. In years to come however, I was destined to experience many more adventures on this fascinating Continent.

VII   INTERLUDE

At the end of February my pal Bill and I were declared time-expired and sent to Britain for a 'rest'. The RAF ruled that fighter pilots were only allowed to fly 200 operational hours before having to take a rest, and the period it took to amass those hours were called a 'Tour of Operations'. Now, to the reader, 200 hours may seem rather a short period, but it must be kept in mind that the average operational flight in the fighter planes of that era lasted about one hour, and during that time the pilot was often subjected to considerable tension. On the completion of a tour the pilot was removed from the line of fire for a period of at least six months to 'rest' and recouperate. I put the word rest within quotation marks because it usually involved instructing novice fighter pilots at OTUs. (Operational Training Units), and rarely gave the individual concerned much rest. Not only was it a rather boring job, for the comradeship and excitement of an operational squadron were missing, but also this instruction was not without its dangers. More about which later.

Bill and I stubbornly fought against relegation, but as I had by now flown close to 200 hours on operations, and Bill even more, it was not to be evaded. Although we would never have admitted it, there is little doubt that we were in need of a break—the accumulated strain of constant exposure to danger takes its toll. We were now the senior pilots of the squadron; most of our old comrades had either been sent away on rest, or gone for the 'final rest'. Yet we were greatly disappointed over having to leave at this momentous time. Things were now really going downhill for the Axis in this theatre of war and the final chapter of the African Campaign was about to be written. The Allies were inexorably gaining the upper hand in the air and many tempting targets were likely to be offered to our fighter pilots in the near future. The Germans would probably resort in desperation to using transport planes to save whatever was possible, and presumably numerous opportunities for shooting down enemy planes would present themselves. This attitude that I express may suggest a certain thirst for blood, but it must be borne in mind that we were highly trained fighter pilots whose ambitions were to shoot down enemy planes, just as a football player's greatest ambition is to score goals.

However, no more than Tony Bartley and other comrades before us, were we able to stay the bureaucratic hand of the rule-makers, and we were firmly informed that our time was up. Our new CO was indeed tactful enough to express frustration over losing his most experienced pilots, but declared that there was simply nothing he could do about it.

The following entry in my log book on 27 February 1943, records my last flight with 111 Squadron:

> "Sweep north of Medjez-el-Bab. Close escort to 9 Hurribombers which bombed a road chock-full of German transport. Lots of Flak."

On this last flight Chris did me the honour of putting me in charge of the Squadron. Together with the rest of the wing we escorted the Hurribombers and saw them do an excellent job, attacking a long convoy of German road transports and leaving many 'flamers' in spite of heavy Flak. There were no signs of enemy fighters, and once we had escorted our charges most of the way back home I returned with my companions to the convoy. After we had finished attacking it with our machine-guns and cannons there were not many transports left that were not burning. My Spitfire—my trusty EP500— that had carried me on many a sortie against the enemy, was hit by a piece of shrapnel, but once more brought me safely back.

And with that I said goodbye to the war in Africa, and to Treble One. In the evening I had a few drinks with my close friends amongst the ground staff, and a few days later I caught a transport plane to Algiers, along with Bill, Hughie Ballance and Tommy Tinsey, who were also time-expired. The evening before our departure we had a boozy goodbye party with the Squadron's officers and pilots. I dearly loved this superb squadron that had such character, and such a spirit of unity and comradeship in spite of (or possibly because of) being made up of such a mixture of nationalities, and I felt sad to be leaving it.

Within the Squadron we never felt aware of any real difference between officer and NCO pilots, but now on reaching Algiers and the outside world the distinction became manifest. My three companions were officers—Bill had just recently been commissioned—and I was a Flight Sergeant, so our paths diverged. Two days later I flew to Gibraltar where, with five other NCO pilots, I boarded a ship bound for Cardiff in Wales.

The voyage was uneventful, but two things about it stand out in my memory. With the exception of the ship's officers all the crew were Chinese, and for the first time I became acquainted with Oriental cuisine, which has ever since been a favourite of mine.

The other memory was an incident that took place after we had reached Cardiff. Our baggage was carefully inspected by a young customs officer before we were allowed ashore, and he mercilessly made us pay for any cigarettes we had over the duty-free allowance. At the completion of this inspection we were unexpectedly ordered up to the captain's cabin where we were made to undress so a Medical Officer could examine our physical condition. In addition to the MO, the captain and the chief customs officer were present in the cabin. One of my companions was a short, timid young lad who showed a reluctance to undress, but he was given no exemption and had to remove every stitch of clothing like the rest of us. And now the reason for his unwillingness to disrobe became clear—his underwear differed very greatly from that normally worn by pilots. While others present roared and rolled with laughter the poor fellow, blushing profusely, removed his uniform which was then followed by a few brassieres, silk-panties, girdles and other items of silk underwear meant to be worn by the fair sex. In wartime Britain such articles in silk were luxuries that few women could indulge in, and obviously this young fellow had intended to smuggle these treasures into the country to delight a wife or sweetheart. He had evidently not expected to have to play the role of a striptease artist. The customs officer was so entertained by this show that he let the stripper go scot-free, and when the captain had finished drying the tears off his cheeks, he produced a bottle of whisky and glasses from a cupboard and poured us all a drink. He said that a toast simply must be drunk for the star of this show.

On arrival in Cardiff I was handed orders to proceed to the Air Ministry in London to receive a commission. I was now Pilot Officer Thorsteinn Elton Jonsson, No 143687, in the service of His Majesty King George VI. Pilot Officer (abbr. P/O) is the lowest commissioned rank in the RAF, and although my salary would rise slightly with this promotion from Flight Sergeant, I would in fact be worse off financially, at least until I got promotion to the rank of Flying Officer (F/O). This was because officers were subject to various expenses that did not apply to the non-commissioned ranks. For example officers were obliged to buy 1st class tickets when travelling by rail; in their messes they had to bear part of the catering and service expenses, and although they received a subsidy for their first uniform they had from then on to clothe themselves at their own expense. In contrast to this all the 'other ranks' received their service clothing directly from the Air Force.

I now had to stay in London for a few days to have my uniform tailored and open a bank account. Non-commissioned ranks get paid in cash every fortnight but officers' salaries are paid into their bank accounts monthly. Those days spent in London were most enjoyable. In addition to going to theatres, restaurants and pubs where I met old friends, I made a point of visiting various famous historical places and museums. I was urged to do this by one of my 'patrons', the well-known publisher, Sir Stanley Unwin. This gentleman was greatly attracted to Iceland, where he had been a frequent visitor before the war, usually staying in my parents' home. He was one of the group of my father's friends who had persuaded the authorities to accept my application for joining the RAF. I now paid him a visit for the first time and a more cordial welcome I could not have wished for. Throughout the war he proved to be a true friend and advisor.

The fortunes of war were beginning to favour the Allies and the frequent defeats of bygone days were mostly a part of history. The Germans' retreat on the Eastern Front was under way; their fate in North Africa was sealed, and the invasion of Sicily was being prepared. Furthermore, the United States had gained the upper hand in the Pacific Ocean. Their military strength in the British Isles continued to grow and there were strong rumours about the 'invasion' being just around the corner. Optimism and expectancy were everywhere.

From London I went to visit my friends in Hull and then continued onwards to my grandmother in the peaceful little village in Lincolnshire. Spring was in the air and the sweet scent from blossoming fruit trees blended with the earthy smell of the green cornfields and the fragrance of grass as the sun evaporated the overnight dew, and the plain below the village shimmered in the distance. Exquisite butterflies fluttered their wings and let the light breeze carry them between the colourful blooms that adorned both flower gardens and hedgerows. In the fields and meadows the cattle ruminated while the sun warmed their hides, and the birds sang unceasingly. The din of war felt so infinitely far off from this peaceful haven where nature's fragrance and the music of the birds filled one's senses. I was enchanted by the beauty and fertility of the earth here in this place where the people lived in harmony with the universe. How well I understood the poet when he said with yearning: 'Oh, to be in England now that April's there!'

Life was wonderful just now. I was home, safe and sound, from adventures involving life and death, and had achieved success beyond my wildest hopes. Intellectually I had come a long way since I went on my first sweeps. Then I had been terrified, but gradually that fear had been pushed aside by a growing confidence. To say that I no longer felt fear would be nonsense; naturally I sensed fear like any other human being. Those who say they do no know fear are immature fools that are not likely to live for very long in war. On my early sweeps I had been greatly handicapped by my inability to see the enemy planes that other pilots kept reporting, but it soon emerged that this was due to nervousness. In fact my eyesight was excellent and before long I was beginning to see our adversaries even sooner than most of my companions. After a while I was nicknamed 'The eyes of the Squadron' and I'm in no doubt that not only myself, but many of my comrades owed our lives to my good vision.

Gradually my responsibilities within the squadron had grown and I had been placed in positions of leadership, and as far as I knew I had let neither myself nor others down. I had even received a letter summoning me to Buckingham Palace in a few weeks time to receive a decoration from the King.

Yes, life was sweet.

VIII   WITH GRANDMA TO MEET THE KING

After spending about two weeks in this rural idyll I was becoming restless, but then I received orders from the Air Force to proceed to Dundee in Scotland to take up a post as an instructor at 56 OTU, flying Hurricanes.

Earlier in this narrative I placed flying instructors in categories according to the enthusiasm they had for the task, and being true to that classification I no doubt came low down on the scale. I yearned for the excitement and special atmosphere of comradeship that was part of life in a fighter squadron. Oh, I was fully aware of the responsibility attached to preparing young, inexperienced pilots for facing a ruthless and well-trained opponent, and I think I may say that I tried conscientiously to do this to the best of my ability.

In the beginning there was a certain gratification to be felt due to the respect—yes, even veneration—with which these young men treated us veterans. They hankered for information about the enemy's battle tactics and the performance of his aircraft, and eagerly absorbed all we could tell them. They asked endless questions, and to start with we undeniably had a tendency to feel smug, but after a while the repetition and monotony became boring, and higher authority began to be pestered with our requests for postings back to a squadron.

I started this period of instructing as an assistant flight commander, but after a while I was put in charge of the flight. The job involved teaching these prospective fighter pilots both defensive and offensive tactics. We tried to create an atmosphere similar to that found in fighter squadrons. For instance we practised 'scrambles' as realistically as possible, getting bombers from other OTUs to act the role of the enemy. We also enacted rhubarbs and sweeps, with instructors playing the role of the Abbeville Boys.

Training inexperienced pilots was not without its dangers. Instructors had lost their lives in collisions with eager pupils a little too full of enthusiasm. I myself was lucky to escape unscathed from such an incident.

One of the elements of training on which we placed much emphasis was formation flying which fighter pilots were required to perform with a certain amount of skill. It is obvious that in the nature of things a certain risk is involved in teaching beginners the art of flying in close proximity to oneself, and of this I became manifestly aware. Frequently pupils' aircraft came very close to colliding with my own, and eventually this did happen. A pupil cut off half the tail of my Hurricane with his propeller, but in spite of control difficulties I managed a forced landing in a field. The pupil baled out and floated safely down in his parachute.

In spite of the monotony of the job, and a yearning for the squadron spirit, I was thoroughly enjoying life. Dundee was a charming town that nestled on the banks of the Firth of Forth, with colourful high ground to the north. I enjoyed visiting the town for I found the citizens extremely hospitable and easy to befriend. It was also an added pleasure that my pal Bill Williams was instructing at Tealing, a nearby OTU, and I got posted there so that we were together again.

Suddenly the Sunday in late summer when I was due to visit the King in his palace, drew close. I was permitted to take two guests along, and of course my grandmother was automatically my first choice. Apart from my love and respect for her, I felt she had earned a visit to Buckingham Palace. She had lost three of her sons on the battlefields of the First World War. That was a sacrifice for which she herself deserved a decoration.

I had a few days leave so I collected my Grandma in Grasby and we spent the Saturday night in London. At the appointed time we drove in a taxi through the main gates in front of the Palace. A soldier stood on guard on each side, but it was just an ordinary Bobby that glanced through the car window and waved us onwards. Now, in the ninth decade of this century I can but wonder at the homely security arrangements of fifty years ago, but then modern terrorism was not a problem.

With my grandmother on my arm we went up the wide steps leading to a foyer and from there we were directed to a large ceremonial hall. After my grandmother had settled down in one of the rows of seats laid out for the guests, I joined a group of men that were obviously present for the same reason as I. Amongst them I met an old friend from 222 Squadron which had been at North Weald at the same time as Treble One.

A Master-of-Ceremonies arrived on the scene and lined us up along one of the walls, and I estimate that we were around fifty servicemen, soldiers, sailors and airmen of various ranks. Centrally in front of the wall opposite us, a dais had been placed with red runners and steps leading to and from it. An orchestra played Viennese waltzes and other light music, and people conversed softly while awaiting the arrival of the monarch. After a while His Majesty King George VI arrived, dressed in the uniform of an Admiral of the Fleet, and all arose from their seats. The King gave the Master-of-Ceremonies a sign, and the latter then invited everyone to be seated again. Two aides stood beside the King on the dais; one of them held a tray on which the decorations were laid out.

In a loud and clear voice the MC read from a list which he held in his hand the names and the decoration each individual was to receive. The person addressed would then march along the red carpet, climb the steps onto the dais, make a smart right turn towards the King, take a step forward and salute. The King would then say a few words to him which we others could not hear, pin the decoration on his chest and offer him a handshake. The honoured person would shake the King's hand, bow and take a step backwards, salute, turn smartly to the left and march off the dais. All this took less than a minute.

I was somewhere near the middle of the group and when my turn came the MC called: 'Flying Officer Thorsteinn Elton Jonsson, Royal Air Force, Distinguished Flying Medal.'

Distinguished Flying Medal and Distinguished Flying Cross are basically the same decorations; the Cross awarded to officers and the Medal to other ranks, and this is a typical example of the division between the classes that existed in Britain. I had been a NCO in North Africa when I had been nominated for this trinket.

I marched onto the dais and went through the ritual. I noticed that the King paid special attention to my shoulders that bore a tab with my country's name on it. He looked at me inquiringly and said: 'Well, young man, I see you come from Iceland. Are there many of your countrymen among us?'

'As far as I know, Sir, I am the only Icelander in the Air Force, but there may possibly be one or two in the Army,' I replied. He then asked what had inspired me to leave Iceland and join the RAF. I answered this to the best of my ability and he then asked me various questions about my country. He asked if it was right that all houses in our capital were about to be heated with hot spring water. This he thought was a notable undertaking. The King had now conversed with me much longer than was customary at these functions. There were still many awaiting their turn and the MC was beginning to become uneasy—probably there was a tight schedule to be kept. The King smiled at me knowingly, pinned the bauble on my tunic and said as he offered me his hand: 'It was a pleasure meeting you, young man, and I wish you the best of luck.'

As I left the dais I was met by an Air Force officer acting in the role of a courtier. He introduced me to the two young Princesses standing nearby and I bowed to them as was the custom. It never entered my mind that nearly half a century later I would be introduced to the elder one again, when on that occasion she paid Iceland a state visit as Queen Elizabeth II.

At the completion of the ceremony I led my grandmother out into the sunshine and outside the palace gates we unexpectedly ran into Mr Björn Björnsson, a wholesale merchant from Iceland, and his wife, who were out for a stroll in the good weather. It was a delightful coincidence that they should be there just then, for there were not many Icelanders in London at that time.

The press were there too, and the next day a small article appeared in the papers about the only Icelander in the RAF being decorated. Outwardly I tried to appear modest and hint that this was just a meaningless trifle, but inside me there was a feeling of pride. I felt that in a small way I had repaid the faith my father, Commander Hawkridge, Mr Mitchell, Sir Stanley Unwin and others had placed in me when they supported me.

That evening my Grandma and I celebrated with a bottle of champagne.

*

IX AMERICAN JUNK

My new sweetheart was undeniably a beauty. She had graceful feminine curves, but she was also robust and provocative. With fascination I admired her from a little distance and then walked over to her with outstretched arms and joy in my heart. I had longed for this moment ever since I had said goodbye to her elder sister in North Africa nine months ago. I was divinely blissful and looked forward to a long and happy relationship with this goddess of my dreams.

It proved, however, to be a short-lived relationship. No sooner had I cast eyes on her than higher powers intervened and took her away from me. These same higher powers admittedly tried to compensate and comfort me by offering me her cousin from America. She was not as beautiful, being more masculine with angular limbs and even a bit of a paunch, but she was also both dynamic and submissive, and it was not long before I developed a great affection for her.

That was the situation in January 1944 when at last I had obtained a posting back onto operations, this time with a squadron that was equipped with Spitfire IXs, the marvellous fighter aircraft I had so long dreamed of flying. But I didn't even get as far as sitting in the cockpit before it was whipped away and replaced with a Mustang.

My new squadron, 65, was stationed at Gravesend, a short distance east of London. Drizzle and low cloud ruled out flying on January 12, the day I presented myself to my new leader at the dispersal hut. Standing outside was the Spitfire IX, one of the best fighters built during WWII. I walked around admiring its beautiful lines and looked forward to the next day when I was going to put it through its paces.

In the mess that evening I met a few of my new squadron mates, and as we chatted over pints of beer I discovered that Tony Bartley had flown with the squadron in the Battle of Britain and made a name for himself. They also informed me that in early 1939 the squadron had been one of the first to be equipped with Spitfires, and had flown various marks of that famous fighter ever since. The pilots were very enthusiastic about the Mark IX which they considered superior to all other fighters, including the best the Germans could offer. Granted, some new and doubtlessly excellent fighters had recently been developed, such as the Typhoon and Tempest from the Hawker factories, but that made no difference; the Spitfire was still the best and the only one they were interested in flying.

Next morning the 'bomb' exploded. The Gravesend Wing, composed of 19, 65 and 122 Squadrons, and led by my old CO Pete Wickham, was informed that the Spitfires were to be replaced with Mustangs.

Men stood open mouthed with disbelief. This simply couldn't be true. Mustangs! P-51s! American junk! To exchange our beloved Spitfires for such rubbish! Had the bloody Air Ministry brass gone off their rockers? This was intolerable! Mustangs! How low could they sink? That evening the pilots gave vent to their anger in a drunken brawl, resulting in fairly expensive repairs having to be carried out to the mess.

I had better explain the reason for this violently negative reaction. In early 1940 Britain had looked to the United States for a supply of fighter planes to supplement her own production, which at that time could hardly sustain her requirements. However, there was not much to be had from American sources, as their best fighter then was the Curtiss P-40 Tomahawk. This aircraft was not held in very high esteem by the RAF, as it was inferior to current British and German fighters, but in spite of that, it was considered better than nothing at all. However, at that time all production from the Curtiss factories went to the American Army Air Corps, so the British negotiators turned to another aircraft manufacturer, North American Aviation, which was already building Harvard trainers for Britain, and offered them a contract to mass-produce the P-40. However, Kindelberger, the chief executive of that company was not at all enthusiastic about producing an aircraft designed by others, but instead offered to design and produce a new fighter plane based on performance requirements put forward by Britain. The negotiators agreed to this, which resulted in the Mustang being launched, followed by deliveries to the RAF in October 1941. The first version, powered by an Allison engine, was fast and had good handling qualities, but above 15,000 feet it proved useless as the engine had only a single-stage compressor. By now Britain was self-sufficient in building fighter aircraft, so it was decided to use the Mustang in the role of an Army co-operation aircraft.

In the light of this it was easy to understand the reaction of my comrades at Gravesend. They were unaware of the fact that on the quiet so many modifications had already been made to the Mustang that it was by now a very different aircraft. A Rolls-Royce test pilot suggested fitting it with a Merlin engine (of the same type as in the Spitfire IX), and in April 1942 this Mustang model flew for the first time. The success of this match exceeded all expectations and resulted in one of the best fighters of WWII appearing on the scene. Further minor modifications were made to this aircraft, such as a 'bubble' canopy replacing the original 'straight' one, and now the Mustang III (P-51C) came into service.

In the early stages the US Army Air Force had shown little interest in the Mustang, but now there was a dramatic change in their attitude. The Packard factories in America began to build the Merlin engine and this led to Mustang IIIs rolling off the production lines in large numbers.

Already next morning ferry pilots started bringing in our new planes and departing with our Spitfires. I could swear that some of my comrades had watery eyes when they looked longingly after their trusted 'Spits' disappearing into the grey distance. Of course it is possible that this dewiness was due to the activities of the evening before, but I suspect there were other more sentimental causes.

The first one to try out our new mount was Squadron Leader Johnston, our CO. After the flight he taxied into the dispersal area, climbed out of the cockpit and stood on the wing smiling broadly.

'Well, boys, quite a good kite,' he said, beaming. 'Handles beautifully and it's just as fast as the Nine. The visibility from the cockpit is excellent, especially rearward. You'd better try it out for yourselves, but I'm sure you are going to like it.'

A look of doubt on the faces of some of the pilots present indicated that it would be hard to convince them that any aircraft would be acceptable after the Spitfire IX. It was now up to the aircraft itself to convince them, and convince them it did.

During the next couple of weeks we did much training flying in these new aircraft of ours, not only in single planes but in sections, squadrons, and as a wing. The general opinion was that it was an excellent aircraft and a worthy companion for the Spitfire. It was, however, admitted that in a dogfight between a Mustang and a Spitfire, flown by pilots of equal ability, the Spitfire would have the upper hand as it was just that little bit more agile. The speed in level flight and the climb performance of both aircraft were similiar, but when it came to speed in a dive the Mustang was faster—a quality that was to stand us in good stead in the following months. Another advantage the Mustang had, which made an enormous difference, was its long-range capabilities. The built-in wing and fuselage tanks carried sufficient fuel to keep it flying for over four hours, and in addition two disposable drop-tanks could be carried, which added another three hours. The Mustang could therefore remain aloft for more than seven hours— longer than any other single-engine fighter. In place of the drop-tanks, bombs could be carried—more about which later.

The early versions of the Mustang III did have a slight drawback, which we just had to put up with; it was armed with only four machine guns of .50 calibre. In comparison, the other main American fighter, the P-47 Thunderbolt, was armed with eight such guns, and the Spitfires, as already mentioned, carried four machine guns and two 20mm cannons. The Mustang's rather limited firepower demanded greater accuracy on behalf of the pilots, and as we were not all first class marksmen, this no doubt allowed many an enemy to escape. The reason for my voluble comparison between the Spitfire and the Mustang is because I have so frequently been asked about it; my answer is that no fighter compared with the Spitfire in the defensive role, whereas the Mustang was an outstanding offensive fighter because of its range and load-carrying capacity.

One of my first tasks after joining the squadron was to suggest to my new CO that he put in a request for an experienced fighter pilot who I knew was eagerly awaiting a posting back onto ops; I was of course alluding to my pal Alun Williams, or Bill as he was usually called in the RAF. We had kept in close touch after arriving back in the UK, and had even spent leaves together. We had agreed that the first one to be posted to a squadron would do all he could to get the other accepted on the same team. Squadron Leader Johnston was amenable and within a few days we had a joyous reunion—we were team-mates and room-mates once more.

Gravesend, with its important docks, had many good pubs well-attended by both airmen and seamen, but the most favoured pub amongst the pilots was the 'White Hart', on the outskirts of the town. Albert, the landlord, was very favourably disposed towards us, doubtlessly because his beautiful daughter, already a widow, had been married to a fighter pilot. It may be added that the poor girl experienced further bereavement. A few months later she announced her engagement to a Canadian pilot in our squadron, Bob Sutherland, but a few days after that he lost his life over France.

The White Hart was a large, popular, modern pub and, as I have already mentioned, much frequented by the pilots of our wing. This was not only due to its being well attended by the fair sex—it was there that I met the girl that later became my first wife—but also because Albert pampered us in a special way. He ran a secret cafeteria in the basement where only pilots were admitted. There we were treated to all sorts of gastronomic delights which, due to rationing, were rarely to be had in normal restaurants. No doubt he obtained the goods through an acquaintance with farmers and suppliers on the 'grey' market. The guardians of the law had wind of this but did not interfere as they knew it was only for the benefit of the lads in the fighter squadrons. It was often good to be one of the boys.

It was on one of our visits to the White Hart shortly after I joined the squadron that I drove a car for the first time. 10-12 of us had as usual piled into (and onto) flight commander Ron Barrett's jeep for a pub crawl. The jeep had been designed to carry four persons, but was considered suitable for twelve, and was frequently called upon to prove so. On arrival at the White Hart I could not find the girl I was dating at the time, so I called her on the phone and she asked me to come and fetch her. I had already drunk enough pints of beer to make me reckless so I asked Ron for the loan of the jeep, which was readily granted. I had often watched others drive and considered it to be a fairly simple task, which indeed it proved to be—that is to say until I had to turn the jeep around. I simply could not find the reverse gear. Oh well, there was only one thing to do—carry on until I found a roundabout, of which there are plenty in England. Shortly after this I learned to use the reverse gear and from then on drove cars like a veteran.

In early March I received an unexpected telegram from my brother Boyi who was a seaman on a ship docked in Hull. He was five years younger than I, seventeen at the time, and I had not seen him in four years. In spite of his youth he had already led a highly adventurous life. Shortly after I left Iceland he mustered on a Danish tramp steamer and sailed out into the wide world. In less than four years he had been shipwrecked three times. One ship was sunk by German bombs, the second hit a mine and the third was sunk by a U-boat. The last time he had spent many days adrift on a raft in the North Atlantic. Of the sixteen men on the raft only two survived.

I may add that he sailed as an able seaman for the rest of the war, after which he attended a navigation school at Greenwich in England and obtained his Master's Ticket. He then continued sailing the 'Seven Seas', first as a mate and then as captain on large Shell tankers until he switched to cargo vessels, serving mainly the west coast of Africa.

Boyi had discovered my whereabouts with the help of Commander Hawkridge, and in his telegram he informed me that he would be in port for a few days. It so happened that Pete Wickham had kept a Spitfire IX for his personal use, and so he lent me this plane to visit my brother in Hull. This was the first time I flew the IX, and I was thrilled with how sweetly it handled, and how strongly one felt in unison with the aircraft, a feeling rarely experienced when flying the Mustang, probably due to its considerably roomier cockpit.

We had a joyful reunion on board the ship, but as it was undergoing repairs, and was consequently rather untidy and cheerless, we decided that Boyi should come back to Gravesend with me. The Spitfire is only designed to carry one person, but I had heard that two people had successfully flown in it, so we decided to give it a try. The cockpit is very confined, but by lowering the seat as much as possible, and having Boyi sit on a cushion instead of the parachute, which I tucked into the rear, I was able to sit on his lap without my head rising above the windscreen. This was naturally a rather uncomfortable posture for poor Boyi, but as the flight to Gravesend was only about half an hour he put up with it. He enjoyed a few days stay with me and then travelled back to Hull by rail.

After a while we were considered to be well enough acquainted with our new mounts to return to operational flying, and we went on a few fighter sweeps. The Abbeville Boys stayed away and these sweeps were mostly without incident. We did, however, learn to keep a weary eye out for our American allies, as they seemed to have great difficulties in telling the difference between friend and foe. Their training in aircraft identification left a lot to be desired. Because of its angular wings, the Mustang was not dissimilar in appearance to the Me 109 when seen from certain angles. It was therefore possible to mistake the one for the other, and this our American friends did incessantly. Frequently we had to turn sharply to escape threats by P-47s and P-38s, but fortunately the pilots of these aircraft all discovered that we were friends before opening fire. Not all of us, however, were so fortunate, for a few months later we watched a trigger-happy P-47 pilot shoot down and kill one of our comrades test-flying his Mustang in the circuit of our landing strip in Normandy.

American bombers were now stepping up their daylight raids on Continental targets, and because of our long-range capabilities we were temporarily given the task of escorting them deep into enemy territory. This role mainly befell the American fighter squadrons, which by now were mostly equipped with long-range fighter aircraft, but as we were still the only RAF wing flying Mustangs we were sent along to reinforce them. On 20 February, 1944 I flew over the German border for the first time. We spent a short period over the Ruhr, and even at the height of 25,000 feet the Flak was frightening. However, most of the time we were assigned to escorting the bombers on the latter stages of their homeward leg, and by then most of the air battles were over and done with. We therefore seldom saw enemy fighters, although occasionally it did happen.

Once, when we arrived over Holland in our role of shepherds, we saw a B-17 (Flying Fortress) far below and behind the main stream of bombers. The plane was obviously damaged for it was trailing smoke, and suddenly I saw a new threat to its safety when a group of black dots emerged from the cloud cover below, and a little to the south. This could only mean one thing: a gaggle of German fighters was climbing up to the attack. On this particular show I was flying wingman to Pete Wickham who was leading 65 Squadron, and when I announced sighting the enemy, I had great hopes that he would lead us down onto them—it would be rather fun to try out our new planes against them, especially as we had the advantage of height. I was therefore quite disappointed when he ordered 19 Squadron to attend to the visitors, 122 was to send a section to escort the lame duck, and the rest of us would continue with the main bomber formation. We watched the 19 Squadron lads jettison their drop-tanks and shove their noses down towards the enemy. On the R/T we were able to listen to the progress of the engagement below, and later we were to learn that they shot down two 190s and damaged others, losing one aircraft from which the pilot was seen to be floating down in his parachute.

As for the damaged bomber, it kept losing height and shortly after it had reached out over the North Sea eight parachutes were seen to open. The escorting fighters transmitted for a radar fix and circled over the rubber dinghies until relieved by others. Although the sea was rather rough it is most likely that the airmen were rescued.

Because of unsuitable weather that winter and early spring there was not much operational flying of the type that suited us, so we concentrated mainly on training. We were however, sent on a few operational flights that we were not particularly enthusiastic about, that is we escorted Beaufighters and Mosquitos in search of shipping along the enemy coast from Belgium up to the northern tip of Jutland. This meant flying at low altitudes, and often in poor visibility, and it was not very exciting sitting in a single-engined plane over the ocean for up to four hours at a time, with small chance of being rescued should something go wrong. One was inclined to listen very closely to the engine on these flights and the wags declared that our ears grew noticeably larger during this period! By now I had become the 'owner' of my own aircraft, YT-B, and it was a comfort to know that its engine had been treated as gently as possible.

But now that we were into April 1944, noticeable changes began to take place in our operational deployment.

X   IN THE TEMPLE OF LEARNING

It did not escape our notice that preparations were being made for the invasion of the Continent, and indeed it was unthinkable that yet another year could pass before it took place. It was about time that the Nazis were beaten and an end put to the war. Also the Soviet demands for a 'Second Front' grew ever louder. However when, and especially where, this invasion was to take place was known only to a handful of people. It was of course imperative to keep strictly secret exactly where the Allies intended to land, and much was done to deceive and lead the Germans astray regarding this. These measures were so successful that at first Hitler insisted that the landings in Normandy were mere deceptions and the actual invasion would take place further north-east in the Pas de Calais area.

Hitler had put much effort into fortifying every part of the European coastline where landings could possibly be made, and proudly called this Festung Europa—Fortress Europe. These fortifications could no doubt cause the invading forces untold losses, and it was imperative to weaken them as much as possible before the landings started. Also his lines of communication to the coastal areas must be crippled to hamper the movement of central reserves. But now the Allies faced certain difficulties, for an obvious concentration of softening-up attacks on the intended landing areas would give the game away, so such attacks must therefore be carried out along the whole of the coast.

Our role in the early stages was to escort the bombers doing these attacks, but because of the Mustang's range and carrying capacity, a decision was taken to form us into an independent offensive unit, and we were named 122 Wing of the 2nd Tactical Air Force. In place of the drop-tanks, two 500-lb bombs were hung under the wings and we were dispatched to attack either planned targets or to search for targets of opportunity.

Before we could begin on our new role we had to learn the art of dropping bombs, and to that effect we launched into a concentrated training programme. We moved from Gravesend to Ford near the south coast, not far from Bognor Regis. Ford airfield was a Royal Navy establishment and as all billets were occupied by naval personnel we had to make do with tents. A year or two earlier we would not have met any difficulties finding accommodation, but the South of England was now very overcrowded due to the impending invasion.

There are two methods for dropping bombs from a fighter—dive-bombing and skip-bombing. The former method calls for an approach to the target at a height of about 10,000 feet when the aircraft is rolled over and dives vertically towards the target. At around 4000 feet the bombs are released. Because of the speed reached in the dive, 4000 feet were needed to pull out safely. Skip-bombing called for a low-level approach to the target with the bombs travelling nearly horizontally after being released, even bouncing on the ground towards it. In this case the bombs had to be fitted with a fuse that delayed the explosion by a few seconds so that the aircraft could get out of range of the flying debris. We practised both these methods on a bombing range and after a while we began to obtain reasonably good results.

In the beginning we were understandably not very pleased with being 'downgraded' into the role of 'bomber pilots' for we emphatically looked upon ourselves as fighter pilots. Also many of us considered this a much more dangerous task than flying around the skies looking for Jerries to shoot down. Most worthwhile targets were well guarded with Flak guns, and a pilot's flying skill was of no avail to him if a bullet had his name on it. Many a first class fighter pilot who could fight his way out of a furious dog-fight, lost his life to the ack-ack guns.

But then it dawned upon us that carrying bombs might not be such a drawback after all. Lately our German opponents had shown a reluctance to come up and fight. We had roamed widely over France, Belgium and the Netherlands in search of prey and found very little. But now the Jerries would be forced to meet us in the air, as otherwise we could just drop our bombs where we pleased.

However, our hopes of enticing the Germans to come up and fight were not fulfilled on the first bomb-carrying expedition. On April 19 we were given the task of dive-bombing the great railway marshalling yards at Tours, about 120 miles west of Paris. The three squadrons flew at 10-, 11- and 12,000 feet in ideal weather conditions; a thin layer of cloud high above us and scattered fair-weather wisps below. There could be no doubt that we were clearly visible from the ground. Surely the Huns would seize the opportunity and send up a strong force of fighters to oppose us.

Nothing happened. We flew unhindered except for a few Flak guns that occasionally sent us greetings. The German commanders controlling the defences in the area probably thought we were just a bunch of fighters capable of doing only limited damage, and it was not worthwhile risking any of their precious Fws or Messerschmitts on this occasion. Well, they were now about to discover these fighters were not quite so harmless after all.

On arrival at Tours we formed up and delivered the attack in such a deliberate way that it resembled nothing more than a wing training exercise. The only difference was that we became acutely aware of the Flak. Black smoke-puffs appeared in the sky around us as we neared the target, and one shell exploded so close to my aircraft that it was jolted. I heard a loud bang over the engine noise and felt the thud of shrapnel hitting metal, but I was not aware of any changes in the handling of the plane.

As the large workshops were disappearing under the nose of my aircraft, I rolled over and pulled back the stick to go into a vertical dive and followed this up with the usual procedures practised during training: keep the centre of the gunsight on one of the sheds and watch the altimeter unwind rapidly ... through 5000 feet ... pull slightly on the stick and count to three ... press the button ... the bombs are away ... pull hard on the stick to come out of the dive—gravity forces pressing hard ... try to turn a little to avoid the Flak ... climb steeply ... re-form on the leader.

Looking down at the target crowded with wagons, engines, workshops and other structures it became clear that the results of our efforts might have been better; bombs had been scattered over a fairly wide area, but several sheds were on fire and considerable damage appeared to have been done to rolling-stock and railway lines, and on the whole the outcome could be considered reasonable.

The Wingco was leading 65 Squadron on this occasion and now his voice could be heard on the R/T:

'OK boys, that wasn't too bad. Let's do a little scouting around. DOG-

WOOD Squadron, you stay at 10,000 and JERICO, you descend to five and we TOMBOYS will go lower. Keep your eyes skinned.'

We descended to 1000 feet and followed the railway in a south-westerly direction. We were now flying in the 'finger four' formation with a good spread between the sections so as to give each other cross-cover. After a short while we caught sight of smoke from a railway engine and prepared to go down to destroy it, but as we drew closer we could see that it was a passenger train and the Wingco told us to leave it alone. We continued south-west and after a while we could see the town of Bordeaux and its airport with a few aircraft spread around the perimeter.

'Alright, TOMBOY, we'll attack in sections. I'll go first, then Red section followed by Blue. We'll make only one pass and then reform north of the aerodrome. Happy hunting!'

Having said that, Pete and his section turned to the right and started the dive towards the airfield, and we in Red section followed them a few seconds later. We closed rapidly on the aerodrome and saw tracer shells rising from various points around the perimeter, first towards the section ahead of us but before long they started curling towards us in red arcs. Now I became too busy to take much notice of them; on the ground ahead of me stood a black Ju 88 and I approached it rapidly with a finger squeezing the trigger on the control column. I clearly saw the explosive shells from my guns straddle the aircraft and suddenly just before passing it I saw flames leap into the air. Before I knew it the airfield lay behind and I was zooming up again. The return flight was without incident and we all reached home safely after well over three hours in the air.

Debriefing revealed that we had left three twin-engined aircraft burning and a few others had been badly damaged. The Germans would have to start taking notice of these fighters with the deadly sting.

During the following weeks the Wing sallied frequently across the Channel carrying bombs and such sorties were called Armed Reconnaissances. We roamed the northern part of the Continent from Holland to the Cherbourg Peninsula looking for ways to harass the Germans. The most common targets comprised road transport of any kind, trains, river barges and military convoys. Any type of military equipment that was sighted was mercilessly attacked, making all movement during the hours of daylight very hazardous for the Germans and forcing them to do most of their transportation under cover of darkness. German fighters were rarely seen during this period, giving the impression they were being saved for a later day. Flak guns were the principal defences against our attacks, and because most of these were delivered at low altitudes, the guns took their toll. On many occasions the pilots shot down did not die and some of them even managed, with the aid of the underground, to get back to England.

About the middle of May I was taken off these operations and sent on a course at the Royal Air Force College, Cranwell, in Lincolnshire. The course bore the grand name: 'Junior Commanders' Course', and I was undeniably a little self-complacent over having been chosen for what obviously pointed to advancement. At the same time however, I was a little annoyed with the timing, as the invasion appeared to be imminent and I certainly did not want to miss out on that momentous event. I discussed this with our CO, Squadron Leader Westenra, and he declared that as far as he was concerned I was free to return to the Squadron as soon as the invasion started, even though the course was not over.

No doubt it was an honour to be enrolled in this venerable temple of learning, so steeped in traditions and history—but in fact I was bored stiff. I was bored with the discipline and ceremonious atmosphere, so different from life in the Squadron. I was bored with sitting in a classroom listening to endless lectures on military law and King's Regulations. None of my classmates were pilots; they were officers from various administrative branches and, contrary to me, they took all this legal mumbo-jumbo most seriously. Instead of concentrating on the instructor's rigmarole I stared out the window at the flower beds where the sun shone, and let my mind drift to my comrades at Ford. They would either be lying idly around in the grass discussing aeroplanes, girls and other interesting subjects, or they would be flying up in the blue sky free as the birds. Were they now beginning to encounter the Jerries across the Channel? Who was now flying my 'B'? Hopefully he treated her well. The long-awaited 'D-Day' must surely be close...

This flight of fancy from the classroom must have been conspicuous for I gave a start when I heard the instructor say in a loud and clear voice: 'Mister Jonsson, you are clear to land!' The classroom burst into laughter.

However, I had no cause to complain about my relations with the instructors as they were on the whole most amiable. One afternoon towards the latter part of the course I was honoured by an invitation to tea with the Commanding Officer in his quarters, and no doubt I owed this to my nationality. He was an elderly Air Vice-Marshal who had been a fighter pilot in the First World War and the rows of ribbons under his wings bore witness to valour and long service. His conversation was bright and amusing, and surprisingly he knew much about my country. He had carefully followed Grierson's flight to Iceland in 1933 and the difficulties he had encountered, and he wished to learn more about the nation and the land. He lamented being too old to take an active part in the present war. I told him about my wishes to return to my squadron as soon as it became obvious that the invasion was about to start, and he said no obstacles would be placed in my way. In my shoes he would have done the same.

Then, about a week later, on the morning of 6 June 1944, the news broke that the invasion had commenced during the night. I cursed—I had already missed the first day. Because of tremendous traffic on the roads and railways—all south bound—I did not manage to get to Ford until the evening.

XI   INVASION

It was still dark, and heavy blasts of wind shook our aircraft and the rain pounded on them as we sat in our cockpits and awaited the green flare that would be the signal to start engines. We had drunk our morning cup of tea in a chilly mess-tent, and in the ops-room we had studied the invasion area marked with coloured crayons on a large wall map. The landing beaches had been given names such as Utah, Omaha, Gold, Sword and Juno. We had listened to Spy's report on the situation as it was 24 hours after the landings had commenced. Fighting on the beaches was still ferocious but there seemed no doubt that the Allied forces had secured bridgeheads in most places. It was now our task to search out the German supply routes to these bridgeheads and do all we could to delay their efforts to move up reinforcements. So far there had been no undue evidence of the Luftwaffe over the invasion fleet and the beaches, no doubt because of the overwhelming superiority the Allies had in the air.

There was only a faint hint of grey light in the eastern sky when the flare went up and cast a mouldy glow on the base of the low-lying clouds and the rivulets of rain on the canopy over my head glimmered in the green light. The met officer had said that even though the wind was less severe on the other side of the Channel, the area of rain stretched inland from the beaches and we could expect drizzle and poor visibility. Not a very encouraging prospect. Now our engines were started and in the growing light we taxied into position and took off according to plan, and the Wing set course due south.

The blanket of cloud lay depressingly low over the sea and the drizzle greatly reduced our vision. We passed many ships in the Channel, some sailing south and others north, but it was not until after about fifteen minutes flying that we entered the Baie de la Seine and caught sight of the main invasion fleet. In spite of our low altitude and the poor visibility limiting our radius of vision we could see hundreds of ships in this wide bay.

In the choppy sea landing craft were darting between the large transport ships and shore, and further out to sea flashes from the warships' guns were visible through the murk. Fires were scattered along the beaches and the smoke from them blended with the drizzle and low clouds and certainly did nothing to improve visibility.

Now the Wing Commander's voice came over the R/T: 'Alright, TOMBOY and DOGWOOD, we'd better split up here. The visibility is too poor for a wing formation. Each squadron to carry on independently. Good luck!'

Onward we flew at 500 feet and as we passed the coast tracer bullets rose to meet us, but in a short while we were safely beyond the coastal defences.

Our hopes of improvement in visibility and cloud conditions, once the coast had been passed, did not materialize. We roamed around at a low altitude but saw no transport on the roads except a couple of tractors and a horse cart. At one moment we met a bunch of Spitfires at the same height, and it was only by the grace of God that collisions were averted. This incident was, however, sufficiently unnerving to convince our leader that flying around the treetops in limited visibility in close vicinity to other groups of friendly aircraft was only asking for trouble and only served the enemy's interests. Westenra, our CO, now set course for home, and a short while later we heard Pete Wickham ordering the Wing to return to base.

The only squadron in the Wing to drop its bombs on this sortie was No 19. They had caught sight of a tank darting into a wood and considered it likely that others might be hiding there too, so they unloaded their bombs into the coppice. They were however, unable to ascertain whether they did any damage to the enemy.

On arrival back at Ford we faced landing with the bombs still hanging under our wings. This was the first time that such a situation had arisen and we were far from certain about what would happen if a landing was so heavy that a bomb fell off. The boffins had tried to assure us that there was no danger of the bomb exploding; that could only happen if the bombs were 'armed' by the release mechanism. But we pilots knew very well that the 'impossible' could happen in matters concerning aeroplanes (as became clearly evident in a closely related case, which will be recounted later on) and we were not at peace until all were safely down. As a matter of fact one bomb did fall from an aircraft during landing and bounced along the ground ahead of the plane and came harmlessly to rest by the perimeter.

So, my first invasion flight had been abortive, and a bit of an anticlimax, but the same could not be said about the next one. Around midday the cold front passed over and conditions improved greatly. The Squadron flew two sorties that afternoon and I went on the second. A decision had been reached that a Wing formation was too unwieldy for the type of operation that was now our lot, to search for and destroy enemy transport and military equipment. Each squadron was therefore dispatched as an independent unit, and as we approached enemy territory we broke up into sections of four planes. I flew in a section under the leadership of Ron Barrett, and we headed for the area north of the city of Caen, where bloody battles were later fought between British and German armies. Now the weather was ideal; good visibility and scattered clouds at around 3000 feet. We roamed around under the clouds in search of targets and at first we had trouble finding any. There could however, be no doubt that a variety of military equipment must be concealed somewhere in this area so close to the battle front, but the German Army, having learned from experience, had become highly proficient at hiding from aerial attacks, and generally managed to avoid being caught on the roads during daylight hours.

Now, once again, my sharp eyesight came in handy. We had just flown over some woods when I had second thoughts—something I'd seen below had aroused my suspicions. I asked Ron to lead us back over the woods, this time a little lower. We dived down to about 1000 feet and had only just reached the edge of the woods when a string of tracer bullets rose to meet us. There could no longer be any doubts that something was hidden there, and after further search we found a long line of trucks and armoured vehicles in a narrow alley between the trees. They were skilfully hidden under camouflage nets and cut-off tree branches, and had not a trigger-happy soldier fired tracer bullets, this lucrative prey would probably have evaded us.

We immediately set-to, attacking the convoy, first with bombs and then with our guns. We also called up the rest of the Squadron and within a short while they had joined in the fray. By the time we had finished, seven lorries were burning and most of the rest were damaged if not completely wrecked. Not much Flak had been visible, but it must be kept in mind that rifles and hand-held machine guns are not normally loaded with tracer ammunition and a lot of bullets could have been flying through the air without us being aware of them. Indeed it later transpired that a few aircraft had been hit by stray bullets, but without suffering too much damage.

During the following days we continued our raiding, admittedly with mixed results, but most of the time we managed to cause the Germans considerable damage and harassment. At last, on the third day of the invasion the Squadron encountered German fighters. The affray was short and sharp, and three Fw 190s were shot out of the sky, one each by Sutherland, Milton and our CO. All our aircraft returned this time, but the results of such encounters were not always so much in our favour. On the very next sortie we were back in the same neighbourhood and we had just finished lobbing our bombs on a group of armoured vehicles when we suddenly discovered a gaggle of Me 109s in among us and they shot down Anderson, Milton and Driscoll before zooming up into the clouds. The only Australian in the Squadron, 'Ned' Kelly managed to clobber one of the Messerschmitts before they disappeared.

As on many previous occasions my guardian angels were kept busy shielding me. This time the shield was only just barely wide enough, as bullets squeezed by it, shattering the canopy over my head, and one lodged in my instrument panel. Our Armed Reccies continued, and in the period which followed, the Squadron flew across to France two or three times a day whenever weather allowed, and not many days were lost. Now however, the German fighter pilots were obviously getting their second wind, because they were meeting us in greater numbers and with more determination than ever before.

XII   HE WAVED TO ME

The following weeks were so full of events and adventures that it would take too much time and space to portray them in detail, and I shall have to make do with mentioning just a few, although it is difficult to pick and choose. One day however, towards the end of June, remains especially memorable. Our Squadron was given the task of cutting a railway line by bombing an embankment near the town of Dreux, a little to the west of Paris. A section of four Mustangs carrying bombs was considered sufficient for the job and the other two sections were to act as escorts. I was given the role of leading the bomb-carrying section.

We crossed the Normandy coast at 10,000 feet in nearly ideal weather conditions; a thin layer of altostratus clouds high above, no clouds below and the fair-weather haze only slightly reducing the horizontal visibility. The invasion armada rode at anchor on a calm sea and barges plied between ships and the beaches, which were nearly invisible under a layer of smoke. As usual the Flak guns near the coast sent us their greetings, and as usual the first volley was uncomfortably close, with black puffs appearing in the sky amongst us. We then altered slightly our heading and altitude, and before the gunners below had finished working out our new course and height, we made another change. It really was like a game of chess with the gunners having to guess our next move, and sometimes their guesses were a little too good for our liking.

To the south we could see a group of tiny dots moving in a westerly direction. Without doubt this was a cluster of fighters, but from this distance it was impossible to tell whether they were friend or foe. Could they be the Abbeville Boys? We had other fish to fry this time but it was always best to keep an eye on these rascals. After a while we could see Paris and then Dreux slightly further west.

The R/T crackled: 'TOMBOY Yellow, TOMBOY leader calling. The target is straight ahead, you'd better start nosing down.'

The intention was to skip-bomb the embankment and I led my section in a long descending arc so we could approach the built-up part of the railway at right-angles and at a low level. To our great disappointment all our bombs bounced over the lines and some of them hit a factory building on the other side. We were given no time to investigate what sort of factory this was because we were now warned that a large group of 'bogies' was approaching from the south and likely to be 'bandits'. I led my section in as steep a climb as possible to rejoin our comrades. As we got closer we saw them turn towards a group of approximately thirty Fw 190s which were swooping down on them.

The enemy split into smaller groups and now a typical aerial battle commenced with aircraft twisting and turning all over the sky. We had only a short distance to go to join our companions, who were fighting great odds, when I searched the sky above and caught sight of another group of Fws approaching from the south and obviously about to join the battle. The R/T channel was so choked with shouts, oaths and yells of elation that there was no time to give warning. This was a situation fraught with danger but experience had taught me that offence is usually the best form of defence and with that in mind I continued to climb to engage the enemy above. And an extraordinary thing happened—when they saw us coming they turned tail. They probably thought we were part of a larger formation which they did not want to mix with.

Now I felt it appropriate that we make use of the advantage we had gained. We were at 12,000 feet and the Fws climbed for all they were worth, but we gradually caught up with them, and at 22,000 feet we were close enough to open fire. As so often on previous occasions my marksmanship was poor. However, my tracers went close enough to the aircraft I was shooting at to frighten the pilot, for suddenly he rolled over on his back and pulled the nose down into a vertical dive, followed by his wingman.

The Focke Wulf 190 could outdive a Spitfire, but with the Mustang it was a different story. I told Yellow 3 and 4 to continue chasing the other planes, then rolled over and followed the silly fellow, who thought he could leave a Mustang behind in a dive. I told Basil Clapin, my No 2, to follow the Fw on the right and I'd take care of the one on the left. We quickly caught up with them and I was able to direct a long stream of bullets at my adversary before I was forced to pull over to one side as I was about to pass him. I saw that I had obviously hit the plane as one of the landing wheels was halfway extended. Now he would be a sitting duck, I triumphantly thought; the enemy plane was damaged and surely would not fly as well as an undamaged one.

The dog-fight down by the treetops started in the traditional manner with my adversary on one side of a circle in a steep turn and I on the other, each intent on out-turning the other. In the beginning I entered into this game rather placidly, even a little carelessly—this was going to be easy, and I was not going to take any needless risks of stalling out at this low altitude. But, watch out! The German was beginning to gain on me, I'd have to steepen my turn. Bloody hell! I didn't like the look of this; he kept turning still tighter! My engine was now at full power, my wings vertical just above the treetops and the aircraft shuddering on the verge of a stall. I was perspiring and had a tight feeling in my chest. This was unbelievable, and really should not be possible. The Mustang ought to be able to out-turn the Fw 190. This must be an outstanding pilot, or else the Focke Wulf's flying qualities improved with a wheel hanging down! Whatever the reason I now faced disaster. My adversary continued to gain advantage and in a short time it would be my fate either to be shot down or crash due to stalling. Neither choice was very desirable and time was running out. But now my wonderful guardian angels came to my aid once again, and none too soon. The enemy was just about to disappear behind me and I could expect his bullets to start slamming into my aircraft very soon.

A voice whispered in my ear: Use your flaps. In a Spitfire (and Hurricane) such action was unthinkable as in those aircraft the flaps were designed to be either fully up, or fully down (as for landing), but in the Mustang the pilot had the choice of intermediate flap positions. By extending 10 degrees of flap the lift of the wings could be increased without adding too much drag. I wasted no time in selecting 10 degrees and instantly the effect became apparent. The aircraft stopped trembling and I was able to tighten the turn so that the circle became smaller. Slowly but surely the situation reversed and I now started creeping up behind my foe, and after a while I was able to open fire on him. When my tracer bullets started shooting past him the pilot no doubt decided that the game was up for he suddenly straightened out, zoomed upwards and baled out just at the moment his aircraft stalled. His parachute only just managed to open before he hit the ground. I was now able to start breathing normally again and rejoice over the outcome. While naturally I was pleased with getting out of this tight spot, it also gladdened me that this plucky and brilliant pilot had also escaped with his life. He had shown amazing skill in handling his damaged aircraft, and had fought courageously to the end.

I flew a circle and watched the pilot land in the middle of a field where he gathered his parachute, slung it over his shoulder and waved to me. I decided to make a low pass to salute him. I flew towards him as he stood there in the field and as I passed him just a few feet off the ground I waggled my wings and he threw me a salute. Although I had aimed my aircraft at the downed pilot he had made no attempt to run, nor had he shown any signs of fear, and I suppose that was typical of the respect fighter pilots bore for each other no matter on which side they were. Militarily, I suppose, I had every right to kill this enemy, as it was most likely that within a short time he would be back in the air again as a dangerous adversary. But it never entered my mind to fire my guns at him where he stood there in the open. Obviously the German's attitude was the same—he had not considered himself to be in any danger of being shot at by another pilot in such a situation.

The same attitude was valid regarding enemy pilots suspended defence-lessly under their parachutes—generally they were inviolable. I use the word generally because, regretfully, there were a few cases of villains, on both sides, that violated this unwritten law, and I shall tell of an example of this later.

I have often been asked by people who never played any active part in warfare how I felt after having killed human beings. This is a mindless question and there is no simple answer to it. The easiest response is to say that in war you must either kill or be killed. The enemy is an adversary who will knock you off given a chance, so usually the best thing to do is to beat him to it. Killing is of course the most repulsive side of warfare, and will probably never be avoided until man has learned to live in peace and harmony with his neighbours. Very little points to this prerequisite ever being reached on this planet of ours; for that to happen Homo Sapiens will have to change greatly.

Man's nature of course has deep roots in his past when as a hunter he had to kill other animals to support himself and his family. I myself derive no pleasure from killing animals, yet I pursue various types of hunting and feel gratified when I successfully vanquish the prey, either fish or fowl. In such cases the joy of the hunt overpowers my distaste for killing. We excuse this slaughter of God's creatures by calling it hunting instinct, inherited from ancient times. To be sure this may be so, but it does not justify the killing of human beings. That act can usually be traced to greed, power struggle or arrogance, which are the most common grounds for the loss of peace. But then, in most cases, it becomes the lot of the common soldier to carry the sword and die, and rarely of those that were the cause of the war.

As a fighter pilot I did my utmost to destroy enemy planes and other military objects, and in the heat of battle it never even entered my head that I might be shooting at human beings. I had no lust to kill. Although the Germans were my enemies I harboured no hidden desire to kill them. Of course I detested Nazism and all it stood for, and I was prepared to do my bit to wipe it out, but this did not arouse in me a desire to kill. Furthermore, we knew that by no means all Germans were Nazis and that many of our adversaries were just doing their patriotic duty fighting for their Father-land. I and my colleagues had sound respect for our foes in the air. We were fully aware of the fact that many of them were outstanding pilots, although during the latter part of the war an increasing number of poorly trained recruits were filling their ranks. We knew that life in Luftwaffe fighter squadrons was little different from the life in our own fighter squadrons, which was characterized by brotherhood, lust for life and love of flying. Ideally we would have wanted nobody to be killed, and that at the end of the day we could all lift our beer mugs to drink a toast to worthy adversaries. Regretfully, reality was not so romantic or simple.

The reactions of the vanquished enemy pilot as I flew past him, however, served to confirm what I have said about the mutual respect between fighter pilots wherever they came from.

I now gave Basil a call and got an instant reply. After chasing the other Fw for a while he lost it, but said he could now see me and was on his way to join me. At that moment I caught sight of him approaching from the south, and together we took up a northerly course, and kept low in the hope of coming across some worthwhile target on the way home. Suddenly I became aware of tracer bullets shooting past me on the left so I made a sharp right turn as I called a warning to Basil. We now found ourselves among a group of Fw 190s which had caught us unaware, and once again we faced a 'dance of life and death'. We were now in a critical plight as we were only two Mustangs against a greater number of Fw 190s being flown by determined pilots. I quickly felt very exposed and lonely—I couldn't see my companion anywhere, but spotted Germans wherever I looked. All I could do was to keep making tight turns and throwing my aircraft all over the sky to avoid the tracers that seemed to be coming at me from all directions. In this mad melee I was never given the chance to take aim at an adversary— I was too busy taking avoiding action.

And then suddenly the sky was empty; one moment there were enemy planes everywhere, and an instant later, as I emerged from a complicated evasive manoeuvre, they were all gone. I flew a couple of tight circles to make sure I was alone and then called Basil. To my surprise he replied. He said his aircraft had been hit in the engine cooling system and he expected the engine to seize at any moment. He was heading south to get as far from the Germans as possible before baling out. Fortunately, all went well for him. The French Resistance smuggled him through the front line and within a fortnight he was back with the Squadron.

I continued homewards and after a while I caught sight of two Fw 190s heading towards me from the east and immediately turned to meet them. To my amazement they split up when they saw me coming and I set off to chase one of them. He headed south and after a short while I decided that my fuel supply was running too low to continue. I was just about to turn back when, for some inexplicable reason, the pilot of the Fw threw his aircraft into a sharp turn to the right. As a parting gesture I sent him a deflection shot from long range. I had no hopes of hitting him, and in fact saw my tracer bullets pass behind the aircraft. I was therefore astonished when I saw the pilot of the Fw bale out and hang suspended under his parachute. I am convinced that it was only fear that caused him to take such drastic action, and this confirmed our belief that the Germans were now having to make do with very inexperienced pilots. The amazing fact remained, however, that within a short period I had caused the destruction of two Fw 190s without actually having shot them down!

The needles of my fuel gauges were now pointing at uncomfortably low figures, and it would be touch and go whether I got safely back to base. The Army Engineers had, however, been busy bulldozing temporary landing strips in the bridgehead area, and we had been told that one of them, B-6, could be used for landings, but should only be used in dire emergency, as it was still within range of the German artillery. I considered the situation I found myself in could truthfully be classified as dire emergency, and decided to put down on this strip. The landing went without a hitch and soldiers led me into a sandbagged pen. I had hardly switched off the engine when we heard the hair-raising whistling sound that precedes an oncoming artillery shell, followed by a loud explosion nearby. Obviously the Germans had seen me land and were letting us know. I ran with the soldiers into a slit trench, where we had to crouch for a few minutes whilst shells landed in the neighbourhood. However, they all fell harmlessly in the fields around, the closest one about thirty yards away, throwing earth and dust over us. After a while the shelling stopped and we hurriedly poured petrol from cans into my aircraft. I wished to get away from this hell as quickly as I could, and the soldiers also wanted to be rid of me so the artillery would leave them in peace.

On arrival back at base I discovered that four of our pilots were missing: Webb, E. Williams, Sumners and Clapin, but I was able to supply the good news that Basil Clapin was most likely alive and well. That day the Wing shot down nine enemy fighters and damaged many more.

*

XIII BEER, HORSES AND FRIED CHICKEN

On June the 27th, three weeks after the first landings, the Wing moved to France. In the fields at Martragny, north of Caen, and only about 2000 yards from the German lines, Army Engineers had levelled the ground and covered it with metal plating to form a runway. This was identified as B-7. Here we were joined by our ground crews, who had suffered a most uncomfortable crossing on a tank landing craft, the voyage having taken four days due to bad weather. The first night we slept in slit trenches. However, we did not get much sleep as the Germans shelled us during the hours of darkness, and to our dismay we discovered next morning that many of our aircraft, dispersed in a nearby orchard, were wrecked or damaged. Also three of our ground crews had been killed. The Wing was moved to another airstrip nearer the coast, but within 48 hours, after the Germans had been pushed further inland, we were back at B-7. We camped in the shade of some tall conifer trees and raised our large mess tent in a coppice near by. Two specially outfitted trucks served as headquarters, housing operations, flying control and the Wing Commander's quarters. Unlike North Africa, our ground staff followed close on our heels, so our circumstances were much better this time.

We kept up our sorties without interruption, and as we were so much closer to the battle area we usually flew many times a day. Because we flew mostly low level the light Flak guns were our greatest menace. Many of our aircraft were hit by shells from these, and it was comforting to be able to land on a runway just inside the battle front rather than having to nurse a damaged aircraft across the Channel.

At this point we were given a new type of target to deal with. Around about the middle of June the Germans sent their first flying bombs (V-1) to London, and naturally considerable alarm was caused among the citizens of the metropolis and the population of south-east England, over which these missiles passed. These flying bombs were really small aeroplanes powered by a simple jet engine, and flew at a low altitude with a speed of about 400 mph. A large explosive charge was carried in the nose and it exploded on hitting the ground, after the engine stopped in accordance with a timing device.

By the nature of things it was practically impossible to place these bombs with any great accuracy, and they were only suitable for use against large sprawling targets such as London. They were therefore of only very limited application against military targets, and their main purpose was to have a paralysing effect on the population's will to fight. This aim was, however, never attained—the Londoners took these bombs in their stride as any other nuisance, and with their renowned humour nicknamed them 'Doodle-bugs'. Certainly these bombs could have done considerably more damage if they had been aimed at closer targets, when their track would be less affected by the wind, such as the invasion fleet or even Portsmouth and other ports crowded with military hardware. But Hitler was only intent on revenge for the raids being carried out against the cities in Germany.

This also applied to the rockets (V-2) which descended on London a few weeks later. The only difference was that you could not hear them come.

The V-1s were launched off mobile platforms, mostly in the Pas de Calais, and because they could be moved around they were difficult to locate, but whenever they were found they were attacked, and frequently it became our task to carry out such raids. On the other hand the V-2s were launched off specially constructed concrete pads, which were mostly located in Holland. These launching-pads were exceptionally well-defended by anti-aircraft guns, and were among the most dangerous targets we attacked, and cost us considerable sacrifices.

Life in our camp was really quite pleasant and comfortable. Admittedly, we missed the luxury of being able to pop into a pub at the end of a day's work for a pint of beer, and to mix with the ladies that were usually to be found there to add spice to our existence. At the beginning of the invasion and for the next few weeks beer was severely rationed in Normandy. This was understandable as no doubt most other things had priority for space in the holds of the cargo ships. But some bright lad in our Wing had an excellent brain wave; why not bring beer over from England in the large auxiliary tanks that could be hung under the wings of our Mustangs? Each tank could carry 75 gallons—this would make an excellent addition to our meagre ration. Action was immediately taken.

Four tanks were sent to a factory for their insides to be coated with a substance to prevent the taste of metal, as is done with preserving cans, and taps were fitted. A contract was made with a brewery in London, and on an appointed day every week a Mustang flew with two empty 'beer' tanks to Croydon aerodrome and brought back two full ones; one containing mild and the other bitter. These tanks were placed on trestles in our mess-tent, which quickly became known as the best pub in Normandy. It did not take long for the word to spread to nearby military units that we had a good supply of beer, and our mess was frequently a very popular and crowded place in the evenings. The fact that nurses from a military hospital in the neighbourhood were regulars only helped to boost the attendance. Furthermore, someone was usually found who could play an accordion or a guitar for a sing-song or dancing. It was not long before the beer trips were increased to two a week. Although most pilots liked to nip over to England whenever possible, to contact families and loved ones, the beer-run was not in demand. The reason was that a full beer tank could easily fall off if the landing was not perfectly smooth. The 'beer kite's' arrival was watched by all available personnel, and woe to the poor pilot who was unlucky enough to bounce!

But life those days was not all fun and games; our friends and companions were constantly being removed from our midst, and the pilots of the Wing daily laid their lives on the line. The dangers came from many directions. For example, one day I flew behind my CO on a strafing attack on a convoy of lorries. I watched him make a low approach towards a large truck with his guns blazing, and when he was only a short distance from it there was an enormously bright flash and neither the truck nor the aircraft were seen again. The explosion was so powerful that my aircraft, 200 yards away, was thrown upwards by the blast. There can be no doubt that the truck was loaded with some very powerful explosives.

Combat with German fighters was practically a daily occurrence during this period, for their pilots did their utmost to protect their fellow country-men on the ground against our attacks. As I now turn the pages of my log book I come across accounts of many sorties that ended in aerial battles, but it would only become tedious for the reader if I tried to narrate them all. The following entry in my log book for July 29 is fairly typical for this period:

"Armed Recco Dreux-Evreux. An exciting trip. We met a formation of a/c in the Evreux area going in the opposite direction. At first they were reported as Spits, but turned out to be 109s. This left us at a disadvantage, but we jettisoned our bombs in a hurry and engaged them. We were outnumbered 3 to 1. The CO shot down a 109 and Sgt. Holland was seen to be hit and blew up in the air. After a while the Huns withdrew, but a few moments later we met another large formation of 109s and 190s, and again we had a dog-fight. We (only five of us) were badly outnumbered and therefore no-one had a chance to keep his sights on a Hun for any length of time. I had snapshots at about 4 different Huns, but each time I had to brake away because I was being attacked myself. During this I got hit in the tail plane, fuselage and port wing. At last I managed to get three bursts into a 190 and he went vertically into the ground. Ned Kelly and Ashworth each got a 109 damaged. Maxie Lloyd got hit in the spinner from a 109 in a head-on attack, but got back OK."

I will not tire the reader with further accounts of this type. It is sufficient to say that this was an extremely eventful and exciting period, during which the Wing won many victories but also lost many pilots, as did the Luftwaffe.

As we moved into August the great Allied advance commenced with the breakout of American units from the most westerly bridgeheads. They advanced from the town of St Lo, first south and then to the east in an attempt to entrap most of the German forces south of Caen. This move started off well with the Americans making rapid progress, and in desperation the Germans mounted a counter-attack in the hopes of splitting up the Allied forces. Fortunately for the Allies the weather remained good for the next few days and they were able to make the best use of their overwhelming air supremacy. At the end of the first day of the German counter-attack, their wrecked and scorched trucks, armoured vehicles, artillery and tanks lay strewn about the fields and roads. A decisive role in this destruction was played by Typhoon fighters armed with armour-piercing rockets which could destroy even the heaviest of tanks. However, Mustangs and many other types of aircraft also did a great deal of damage with bombs and cannons. There can be no doubt that air power played a large part in halting the German counter-attack. The spearhead of their army units now withdrew rapidly eastwards, but on the banks of the river Seine they faced great difficulties because so many bridges had been destroyed. They tried to cross the river on barges, and it became our task to do our damndest to delay them.

We now entered a trying period caused by a mysterious phenomenon, which I shall explain and which sadly terminated the lives of many of our comrades. As I have previously stated we frequently carried two 500 lb bombs, but the authorities decided we should drop 1000 lb bombs on these barges. Now, a 1000 lb bomb is no baby—nearly the size of an oil barrel—but because the flying distance was so short we only needed to carry a small amount of fuel, and it was no problem for us to carry a 2000 lb bomb-load.

We reached the target at 10,000 feet, and in line astern we dived in the traditional way to 4000 ft to release our bombs. All this was normal procedure for dive-bombing, but now strange things began to take place. During the dive our aircraft took to blowing up for no apparent reason. Certainly, the Flak was unusually heavy over these barges. More than once I actually heard the shells exploding above the noise of the engine, and when that happens they are getting uncomfortably close. But this was not a sufficient reason for an aircraft to blow up into smithereens when carrying 1000 pounders but not when 500 lb bombs were being carried. I myself witnessed two occasions when aircraft ahead of me simply disappeared in such explosions. On one of these occasions the ack-ack guns had not even opened fire, so they were not to be blamed.

Bomb specialists were flown over from England to examine our equipment and they emphatically asserted that the bombs could not explode until after they had been released. The arming mechanism for the bombs consisted of a small propeller on the nose of the bomb which had to turn a few times to make it 'live', but this was prevented from happening by a pin which was only pulled out when the bomb was released. After that the bomb needed a heavy blow on the nose to make it explode. All this was clear to us, and we knew that what was happening was technically impossible; and yet it happened! Experiments were made by hanging 500 lb bombs on some aircraft and 1000 lb bombs on others, but it all came to the same thing; only the aircraft carrying the larger bombs blew up.

The pilots were now becoming distinctly uneasy—it was bad enough having to fly through concentrated Flak, without the added risk of our own bombs killing us in some inexplicable way. In three days the Squadron lost two pilots, Ashburn and Wills, and all together seven or eight pilots of the Wing were killed in this manner.

A decision was thus taken to revert to 500 lb bombs, but before that happened I experienced an incident, which while in retrospect was rather comical, at the time was not so amusing and caused me much embarrass-ment. During a bombing raid on the barges one of my bombs 'hung up'—i.e., did not fall off when I pressed the release button. At first this caused me no anxiety; I would simply fly out to sea and shake it off. On arrival there I started pulling out of dives so that gravity would pull the bomb free, but no matter how I threw my aircraft around the sky, it was of no avail; the bomb wouldn't budge. I experimented to see how slowly I could fly with a 1000 lb bomb under a wing and discovered that below a speed of 220 mph I was unable to hold the wings level, so obviously landing with the bomb was out of the question.

I was in a real dilemma. As we had not intended to fly over water I had neither a dinghy nor a 'Mae West' so baling out over the sea was not a very feasible choice. Neither was it desirable to bale out over enemy-held territory and risk becoming a prisoner of war. If I baled out over the congested area held by the Allies I risked causing considerable damage, and even killing some of my comrades-in-arms. The same was valid if I managed to cross the Channel to England, which was rather doubtful considering the small amount of fuel I carried.

I flew around off the coast making repeated and unsuccessful attempts to get rid of the bloody bomb, and to tell the truth I was beginning to get very worried. What the hell was I to do!? Suddenly I had a brain wave—fire my guns. When these powerful guns were fired they caused considerable vibration, and perhaps that would be enough to loosen the bomb. Without further ado I took off the safety catch and pressed the firing button. To my delight the right wing shot upwards as the bomb fell free, and I started breathing again. But my elation was short lived when I looked over the side and discovered where I was.

I was flying at about 4000 feet and below me there were a few scattered cloud-tufts and between them I could see dozens of ships riding at anchor. In dealing with my problem I had, without noticing it, drifted in over the invasion fleet. I waited breathlessly to see where my bomb would land, and by the grace of God it fell harmlessly in the sea between two ships. But my trials were far from over yet. I suddenly found myself in the midst of the most concentrated anti-aircraft fire I had ever experienced. Every ship in the fleet must have opened fire on me, and who could blame them. The Flak over the barges was bad enough, but that was peanuts compared with this. How I ever got out of this unscathed I do not know, but I did, with my aircraft peppered with shrapnel.

When not flying we found various means of passing the time. We played a lot of card games and chess; throwing horseshoes and other such activities were also popular. In the evenings when the weather was good we often lay around a camp-fire and chatted about whatever came to mind. As we were a group from many different countries and continents this small-talk was often both enjoyable and interesting. It was also a strange feeling to be able to lie in the grass besides an open fire and stare up into the starry sky without having to worry about an attack from the air, and nobody to yell at us to 'put out that bloody light'. It was not so very long ago that such a light might have brought on trouble, but now German night-raiders were rare species and caused us little worries.

During the daytime we sometimes went on hikes or drives in the neighbourhood and bought eggs, cheese, vegetables and fruit from local farmers. This was mostly done by bartering, as the locals were eager to exchange their wares for cigarettes, tea, coffee and various other items which by then were luxuries on the continent of Europe. Furthermore, these people were glad to receive something of value; the Germans had forced them to accept worthless occupation money.

And I must mention the blessed horses. On a large estate near our airfield we came across a man who claimed to be the manager. His erstwhile employer had been friendly with the Germans and a group of their officers had been billeted in the mansion. However, the squire had fled in a hurry with his proteges when the paratroops appeared during the invasion. The manager pointed to some stately looking horses grazing in a field and said they had belonged to the German officers, who had been members of a famous cavalry regiment, and had used the horses for riding pleasure. Seeing that all the necessary bridles and saddles were hanging in the stables he saw no reason why we should not avail ourselves of these horses. We didn't have to be told twice, for amongst us there were Australians and Canadians, in addition to Englishmen who had equestrian backgrounds and now thankfully accepted this offer. We negotiated with the manager to have the horses corralled in the afternoons ready for riding, and most evenings groups of noisy airmen were to be seen in the neighbourhood behaving like cowboys. It did not seem to make any difference to the horses whether they were spoken to in English, Icelandic or German, and I adopted a brown gelding which I called Sörli (an Icelandic horse-name), and derived much pleasure from riding him on occasions for the remainder of our stay at B-7. I was sorry to have to leave Sörli behind when we moved on to new pastures in mid-July.

One sultry evening in July a rather comical incident took place. After dinner, Bill and I had gone for a long ride. The weather was glorious; a full moon high in a cloudless sky lit up the countryside so that it was almost like daytime. Towards the battle front in the south a few flares hung in the sky, the occasional flash from an explosion could be seen, and a subdued sound like surf breaking on a distant shore reached our ears. After having returned our mounts to the stable we strolled to our tent, sat down in deck-chairs, lit our pipes, sipped our whisky and chatted. Life was pleasant and uncomplicated. After a while we agreed that a little bite to eat would do no harm so we strolled over to the mess marquee. It was getting on a bit so the lights were out and everyone had left. The cook-house tent was attached to the mess, and Bill and I decided to search it for something edible. Although it was nearly as bright as daylight outside, it was pitch black inside the tents. Neither of us had brought along flashlights or matches, so we had to feel our way forward in the dark. We weren't being very successful finding anything to eat, however. The refrigerators proved to be locked and there did not seem to be any food on the shelves we could finger in the dark. As I was feeling my way along a top shelf rather high up my hand touched a bowl covered with a dish. Gingerly I took it down, lifted the plate and sniffed. Well, well, we had certainly struck it rich—the bowl was full of pieces of fried chicken.

We each took a couple of pieces and replaced the bowl onto the shelf. On our way out through the tents we started gnawing the meat off the bones with great relish. However, before we reached the entrance to the marquee I suddenly remembered that I had failed to replace the plate on top of the bowl, so I returned to take care of this. As I felt my way out through the tents again I heard something that sounded like a cry of anguish from my pal, followed by sounds of puking. When I emerged into the bright moon-light I saw he was ejecting a jet of vomit. I took a look at the chicken leg I was holding. It was crawling with big fat maggots.

*

XIV   MY GUARDIAN ANGELS ARE BUSY

After the heavy fighting of June and July, the German defences south of Caen crumbled. The Allies had the enemy on the run and destroyed and captured a large part of their forces. The bloodiest area was near the town of Falaise. In his memoirs General Eisenhower says: 'The battlefield at Falaise was unquestionably one of the greatest "killing grounds" of any of the war areas. Roads, highways and fields were so choked with destroyed equipment and with dead men and animals that passage through the area was extremely difficult.'[1]

The bulk of this destruction was caused by the Allied Air Forces. The Germans now concentrated on trying to save whatever they could of their armour. The advance of some of the Allied columns was so rapid that co-ordination became a problem, and at times the columns had to be halted to prevent comrades shooting at each other. The Germans were able to take advantage of this and effect the escape of a considerable amount of their armour. However, the front moved rapidly eastwards, and consequently we were also moved forward and took up position on another temporary airstrip called B-12. This was a step in the right direction, but we were loath to have to leave our four-legged friends behind.

Day after day we roamed over enemy territory in sections of four in search of targets. We were making it practically impossible for the Germans to move along the roads or railways during daylight hours. Without doubt they were now experts at clearing off the roads and hiding at the first sound of aircraft, but at the same time we were becoming adept at spotting their hiding places. During the following weeks our Wing destroyed hundreds of road transports, railway engines, river barges and other military equipment. As an example, we found a train in the neighbourhood of Trier transporting something like fifty tanks. We blew up the engine and then flew a protective patrol while a wing of Typhoons destroyed the tanks with rocket fire. It must be borne in mind that we were just a small unit in a large force of British and American predators, all hunting the same prey. It was remarkable that the Germans continued to be able to find means of transport in spite of all this destruction.

But alongside this 'transport bashing' our Wing was also engaged in shooting down the enemy aircraft that had the audacity to venture into 'our territory'. On one occasion our new CO, Dickie Lamb, destroyed a Me 109, the Australian 'Ned' Kelly two Fw 190s, Dinsdale and Robinson one

---

[1] *Crusade in Europe*, p. 279, Doubleday & Co.

each and I myself claimed a victory and a probable. I should have done better, because my position as a section leader gave me frequent opportunities, but as before my poor shooting let me down.

But this activity of ours was not without cost. We suffered the losses of Metzler, Holland, Basil Scharff and Jimmy Muir. Also my pal Bill got shot down, but he was able to announce over the radio that he was about to force-land in a field, so we had good reasons to believe that he was still alive. And true enough, he turned up again at dispersal a couple of days later, and had an amusing tale to tell.

His aircraft had been hit in the glycol system and he had flown in a westerly direction until his engine was about to seize and he then belly landed in a field. Just before landing he had observed some German tanks in a wood he glided over, so he wasted no time and took to his heels to put more distance between himself and the enemy. He noticed a couple of French farm workers in a field, but when he approached them they threatened to stab him with pitchforks. However, he was able to convince them that he was 'Un aviateur Anglais'. They directed him to a nearby farm house on the edge of a village, and as he rounded a corner to approach the back door he was confronted with a woman who screamed loudly and nearly dropped the baby she was holding. He was however, let into the house by an elderly lady dressed in black, and it now transpired that the Germans had only a short time earlier left the village and retreated into the woods where he had seen them. The name of this village was Buneville and after a while all its residents turned up, headed by the local Resistance leader, to welcome Bill and proclaim him their liberator. Speeches were made, after which a little girl presented him with a painted egg. A jolly time was had by all with food and wine being passed around. Later that evening British troops arrived and Bill hitch-hiked back to our airfield.

It was also during this period that I think I came closest to being shot down by an enemy fighter. Our Squadron was given the task of bombing a bridge in Holland, and I led TOMBOY Yellow section. The outward flight was uneventful, but a lot of cumulus clouds were scattered around making the target difficult to find and also affecting our bombing. As usual we dived on the target from 10,000 feet, but none of us scored a direct hit, although a number of bombs fell close enough to the bridge to damage it.

We were re-forming at 8000 feet when the controller called us to say his radar indicated that 50 plus bandits were heading towards us from the south at 20,000 feet.

Our CO's voice came on the radio: 'OK TOMBOY Squadron, let's climb like the clappers and keep our eyes skinned!'

We were just reaching the tops of the highest clouds at around 15,000 feet when I caught sight of black dots in the sky to the south of us. No doubt they were the foes we were expecting, and I announced this on the R/T. We immediately turned towards them and kept on climbing, and had just reached the same height as the Messerschmitts and Focke-Wulfs when we met them head on. The ensuing melee was typical of the confusion that reigns when fighters meet fighters. Aeroplanes darted all over the sky, twisting and turning around each other, and wherever one looked there seemed to be fighters diving, turning and climbing. As we were only twelve against over fifty we had our work cut out, and we practically never had a chance to get onto an enemy's tail without having to break off immediately to avoid being shot down. The radio channel filled with shouts, calls, curses and warnings.

But through all this noise a voice was clearly heard: 'TOMBOY Red One calling! I'm on fire and baling out!' Shortly after this I caught sight of a vertical trail of smoke and close to it an airman swinging under his white parachute canopy. Thank God he is safe, I thought to myself as I threw my plane into a violent turn to avoid an attack from a Focke-Wulf. A little later I caught sight of the parachute again but at the same I saw something that I had hoped I would never live to witness. I felt sick in the stomach when I caught sight of a Messerschmitt with guns blazing, heading towards my helpless comrade. I saw the pilot jerk when the bullets hit him.

'You filthy swine!' I yelled. 'You shall be made to pay for this, you bastard!'

I went after the Messerschmitt. At that moment I was filled with red hot anger and hate—hate for this infamous bully that could sink so low as to shoot at a helpless airman hanging in a parachute. That Messerschmitt had the same effect on me as the red cloak has on a bull in the arena—I had only one thing in mind at that time: to nail the bloody wretch. I chased him with great determination, and I think he quickly became aware of being in great peril. I now dredged up all the technique and experience I had gained through the years, and to my satisfaction I found I had no difficulty getting the better of him. I delayed pressing the firing button until I was close enough to be absolutely sure of hitting him. At that moment I was aware of nothing but this devil whom I was going to kill—there was no room for any other thought.

And then disaster overtook me. Had I not been so preoccupied, I would have realised that I was in danger. Suddenly the control column jerked in my hands, and I felt bullets hitting my aeroplane. I had given all my attention to chasing this villain, completely ignoring the fact that I was surrounded by enemy planes. Until now I had survived because I had followed the golden rule: 'watch your tail'. In my rage I had forgotten this truism, and was now having to pay for the oversight. My desperate reactions at that moment remain unclear to me, but in some way or another

I managed to twist my aircraft out of the hail of bullets and dive into a cloud. I counted myself lucky, and breathed a sigh of relief. But my jubilation didn't last long as suddenly there was an explosion and the cockpit filled with smoke. The smoke was quickly sucked out through a hole in the canopy, and then I saw that where the instrument panel had been there was just a tangle of smoking wires, ripped metal and broken glass. At a quick glance the only complete instrument left appeared to be the clock up in the left-hand corner. My tormentor had doubtlessly followed me into the cloud and had been close enough to keep me in sight. By the grace of God he now seemed to have left.

So far the engine appeared to be undamaged, and the aircraft still reacted to the controls although the control column felt far from normal. But now I faced another problem—the blind-flying instruments were gone, and in the cloud I had no idea what my attitude was in relation to mother earth. There was no airspeed indicator, but judging from the sound of the engine I suspected we were fast losing speed so I jerked the stick forward. This had the effect of throwing dust, broken glass and other rubbish off the floor into the air, some of it getting into my eyes and temporarily blinding me. Suddenly I became aware my aircraft's movements were unusual and I was being pushed towards one side of the cockpit. I must be in a spin, but I had become so completely disorientated that I couldn't even tell in which direction I was spinning. I knew that the base of the cloud was around 2000 feet above ground, and if I came out of the cloud in a spin I would have precious little time to save the aircraft.

The remarkable thing about the situation was that I had no time to become really frightened—I was far too occupied with trying to discover what was up and what was down. Suddenly I emerged from the cloud with the horizon spinning around at high speed and I was alternatively looking at the ground or the sky. To tell the truth I have no idea what I did next; my reactions were purely automatic, but somehow or other I managed to get the aircraft flying on a level keel just above the fields and treetops. I was able to control it, but to maintain level flight I had to hold the control column in a most unusual position, and this indicated that the control surfaces were badly damaged. I was soaked with perspiration and I pulled off my oxygen mask so that I could wipe away the sweat that was pouring down my face.

I then sensed the smell of burning rubber in the smoke that was still coming from the ripped metal and tangled wires that had once been an instrument panel. I no longer had a compass and had lost all bearings, but shortly I was able to gather directions from the sun and take up a westerly heading, and after a while I began to recognize landmarks. I hoped desperately that a fire would not flare up as smoke was still pouring from the tangled mess in front of me. I also hoped that no enemy planes crossed my path; my trusted Mustang was certainly not in any condition for strenuous exertions. The R/T was completely dead, so even if I wanted to do so I could not call for help.

Suddenly a couple of Spitfires were flying alongside me and their leader waved to me. I felt relieved when I saw them but at the same time I received a shock. I had not seen them coming and realised that they could just as easily have been enemy planes and have finished me off.

Now I was glad that our wing had been moved to the B-12 landing strip, which was a good deal further east than our previous base, and I was greatly relieved when I caught sight of it and was able to wave goodbye to my escort. They waved back and broke off. With a sigh of relief I discovered that the undercarriage extended normally, and I guided my damaged Mustang down onto the runway.

On inspection it became perfectly clear that some time would pass before my beloved B flew again. In addition to the wrecked cockpit there was extensive damage to the tail control surfaces and the fuselage just behind the pilot's seat. Once again, my guardian angels had been severely taxed!

XV   DANCING IN THE STREETS

The Allied armies were now advancing rapidly, so we did not stay very long at B-12, and our next move was to the aerodrome at Beauvais, a town about 30 miles north of Paris. This was the first real airfield we had been based on since moving to France, and although most of its buildings and other structures had been destroyed the runways were in reasonable condition.

The town had only recently been liberated and we paid it a visit to join the residents in their celebrations. Crowds were everywhere in the streets and squares waving French, American and British flags. Everywhere joy and merrymaking prevailed, brass bands played and people danced in the streets. Moving along was difficult because of all the people that wanted to hug and kiss us, and present us with wine and fruit. This was tangible evidence of how overjoyed the population was to be free of German oppression, and we were, in no uncertain terms, made to feel their appreciation for the part we played in the liberation.

A few days later, after the jubilation had subsided a little, I took a companion with me into town in the A Flight jeep to buy some cheese, which was plentiful around here, and much of it very savoury. On emerging from the cheese-dealer we discovered we had a flat tyre, and as no tools were found in the jeep, I went to a nearby garage to borrow some. The foreman immediately sent a lad out to change the tyres for us and in the meantime offered me a glass of wine in his office. I cast my eyes around the workshop and caught sight of a streamlined, and highly polished coupé, a Voisine sports car. These were highly expensive buggies owned mainly by rich French tycoons. The foreman spoke very little English but I tried to explain to him my surprise at seeing a car of such calibre during times like this when petrol was so hard to come by. He spat on the floor and in an agitated tone delivered a long harangue in French, of which I only understood bits and pieces. However, the word 'collaborateur' cropped up now and again, and after much gesticulation, repetition and guess-work I gathered that the car belonged to a 'despicable collaborator' who fled with the Boche to escape the wrath of his countrymen, and had to leave the car behind due to lack of petrol. The foreman just wanted to be rid of this 'monument of treason', and indicated that he'd be pleased if I could have it removed.

I needed no more prompting. My companion and I tied a rope to it and towed it to the airfield. There we poured some petrol into it and tried to start the engine. At first we thought the starter was unserviceable as it wouldn't budge, but the mechanics quickly found a secret switch under the driver's seat and after that it gave no trouble. This was a beautiful, powerful car and a delight to drive. Around about this time many of our pilots acquired cars, mainly jalopies that the Germans had abandoned due to lack of petrol, but my sports car was in a class of its own, and was eyed with envy by many. Our CO, Lance Burra-Robinson, tried very hard to get me to relinquish it and offered me a Mercedes-Benz and a sizeable sum of money in exchange, but I resisted all pressures. Later, events were to prove that I'd have done better if I'd accepted his offer.

Shortly after our arrival at Beauvais, the Germans withdrew their last troops from Paris. At the time I was in temporary command of A Flight in the absence of Bob Tickner, our flight commander, and I obtained permission from the CO to drive a few of the lads to the capital to observe the celebrations. There was no problem getting six of us into the open jeep, and as there was very little traffic on the roads it took us less than an hour to reach the suburbs. The nearer we drew to the city centre the more difficult it became to move forward due to the throngs of joyous people singing and dancing in the streets. For political and diplomatic reasons, Supreme Command had agreed that French army units should be the first to march into the city. Consequently only French troops were to be seen in the streets at that time, and we airmen stood out rather conspicuously. When the people noticed us they showed us great friendliness in the same way as the good people of Beauvais had done.

As we sat in our parked jeep in one of the main streets in the centre of the city we were approached by a well-dressed, venerable elderly man who invited us to follow him into a nearby house to accept refreshments. The large and beautifully furnished flat we entered was crowded with dignified gentlemen, elegant ladies and high-ranking French officers, and the champagne flowed freely. It was noticed that among the six of us, four bore shoulder badges depicting far away countries: Australia, Canada, New Zealand and Iceland. It further emerged that of the other two, one came from England and the other, my pal Bill, was a Welshman. Now numerous toasts were drunk to all these countries and of course to America and the newly-liberated France.

There is no doubt that during the drive back to base that dark night the driver of the jeep and his passengers would be deemed unfit to be in charge of a motor vehicle in accordance with today's laws, and they certainly did not sober up on the way, as a goodly supply of champagne took care of that. But home they arrived unharmed, except possibly that their vocal chords may have suffered from gross misuse in producing sounds that were supposed to represent musical tones, but which were more like Tarzan calling his anthropoid brothers.

XVI   DAYS OF PLENTY IN BRUSSELS

The merciless war continued and our ruthless search for enemy transport and its destruction continued unabated. Encounters with the Luftwaffe were becoming fewer these days, and as before our greatest danger came from the Flak. Typical entries in my log book are as follows:

August 25. "Armed Recce Seine-Amiens. One armoured car and staff car damaged. Squadron got 8 flamers.

August 25. "Armed Recce and bombing tanks. One tank found by edge of wood and bombed. Wood suspected of hiding more tanks so it was bombed. Also strafed a truck.

August 25. "Armed Recce and bombing E of Seine. Bombed wood supposed to conceal tanks. Too hazy for strafing.

August 26. "Armed Recce Seine-Amiens. Knocked out a large tank carrier. Six bombed Gisors marshalling yards. Bombing good.

August 26. "Armed Recce. Attacked two lorries, one blew up.

August 28. "Armed Recce. We found a fairly large road convoy four miles east of Amiens and gave it a pounding. Squadron got 10 flamers and many damaged. My guns badly need harmonizing.

September 1. "Armed Recce NE of Lille. Good trip. The Sqdn. came across about 30 MT (Motor Transport) and left 9 flamers and 10 damaged, NO FLAK!

September 1. "Armed Recce NE of Lille. Again we found a lot of MT and left quite a few flamers and damaged. Much Flak."

I could go on...

Due to the very rapid advance of the ground forces we did not stay at Beauvais very long. On September 9, six days after our arrival there we were told that the Allies had liberated Brussels and we were to move to Grimbergen aerodrome on the outskirts of the city.

I had no intentions of leaving my beautiful car behind so I got one of the junior pilots to fly my Mustang to Brussels whilst I drove. I set off in the morning and because of the warm, sunny weather I drove with the top down. The distance was only about 125 miles, and although there were no modern motorways in those days I did not expect to take more than four hours at the outside to drive that distance in such a powerful sports car. There I was badly mistaken. Such a short time had passed since the area had been liberated from Nazi oppression that the citizens were still in a state of euphoria and celebration. In every village and town I drove through the whole population seemed to be in the streets singing, dancing and waving flags, and I had the greatest of difficulties driving through the throng. There were times when I was simply forced to stop and take part in the festivities.

The liberating forces had passed through so rapidly, on the heels of the enemy, that the people had not been given the opportunity to show them the appreciation and hospitality they so much longed to do, and I now became the 'victim' of their happiness. The citizens simply grabbed me and treated me as if I were the General who commanded the liberation forces that had thrown out the hated Boche (possibly the car helped to give that impression!) and they literally carried me on their arms. I, of course, sincerely shared their joy, and no doubt harboured a little pride and satisfaction over having, in my small way, helped to make these scenes possible. There is no knowing how many pretty girls kissed me that day nor how many dignified citizens hugged me, and how many glasses of wine were poured down my throat—I was certainly in a state of exhilaration and intoxication. In the evening when I eventually reached my destination, my car was full of wine bottles, fruit, farm products and flowers, and I myself was full to overflowing.

Now we entered a time of grandeur, but also one of great strain. The grandeur was the result of greatly improved living conditions and, even more so, the warmth and friendliness lavished on us by the grateful Belgians. The strain was mainly brought on by the concentrated and difficult flying we had to perform in connection with the attempt by airborne troops to capture the important bridges at Arnhem and Nijmegen in Holland. Unfortunately that operation was largely a failure, which I will come to later.

On the edge of Grimbergen airfield stands a large mansion—practically a palace—which the Luftwaffe had commandeered and turned into an officers' mess, and into which our Wing now moved. In fact the British authorities had told the owner that he could now move back into his mansion, but his reply was that it would give him pleasure if the RAF would accept the use of his humble home for the duration of the war. The wings of this mansion housed many bedrooms, which now became our billets, and in the centre section the kitchen, mess hall, lounge, billiard room and ball room were located. All were handsomely furnished and it was obvious that our colleagues in the Luftwaffe had left everything in good condition. And they had also left something else: in the basement we found thousands of bottles of champagne and cognac, and a large supply of good cigars. The mansion's owner said that all this belonged to the Germans—they had fled in such a hurry that they they'd left it all behind.

So we enjoyed a period of affluence. Every day thankful Belgian citizens delivered to our doorstep various coveted farm products, vegetables, fruit and other delicacies which our cooks turned into feasts to be washed down with generous amounts of champagne supplied with the compliments of the Luftwaffe! Furthermore, it was extremely pleasant to sip a glass, or two, of cognac and smoke a first-class cigar with our after-dinner cups of coffee. We frequently held banquets in the evenings, well attended needless to say by the local beauties. I became enamoured with a blond at the first of these balls, but like Adam, our Biblical forefather, we were not allowed to remain for very long in Paradise. Only nine days after arriving in Brussels we were to be whipped away from this haven of bliss.

We continued our assault on the enemy's transport system, but now the weight of our attack moved to a greater extent into the German Fatherland. There we paid special attention to the railways and particularly the locomotives and freight wagons. The Flak was at times fearfully heavy and, unavoidably, we lost quite a few of our comrades, but fortunately many of them were able to make forced landings or bale out.

And then in mid-September a large airborne force from Britain made a daring attempt to capture the important bridge at Arnhem in Holland. A great deal has been written about this military venture, and even a motion picture made about it, so I need not go into details here, but there can be no doubt that the war in Europe would have been over many months sooner had it succeeded. But, unfortunately, the operation was a failure, and the battle was bloody.

Throughout the eight-day engagement, our Wing flew incessantly in attempts to come to the aid of the paratroops, but the weather, bad enough in the beginning, constantly deteriorated. Because of low cloud the German aircraft used the opportunity to sneak in for darting attacks and then escape into the clouds. It was unlikely that these raids did much damage, but we felt very frustrated at not being able to help our troops on the ground with direct attacks on enemy positions. Low cloud and drizzle prevented us from being able to identify such targets, and we could not risk the chance of attacking our own troops.

I shall revert to copying a few entries from my log book, for they give a graphic description of the conditions at the time:

> **17 September:** "Patrol Arnhem area. The airborne lads are fighting for the bridges at Arnhem and Nijmegen, and under cover of low cloud the Huns have been busy trying to lob bombs at them and the bridges. In a flight earlier today the Squadron tangled with 30-40 Huns. Dave Metzler was shot down but was seen to bale out. Jimmy Muir was hit by Flak and dived into the ground. The Wing lost 4 pilots but claimed 6 Huns destroyed and a few probables. We lost Bill Scharff the day before yesterday."

Then come eight entries in a row, all as the following:

> **20-24 September:** "Patrol Arnhem-Nijmegen. Huns in the area but bad weather prevents us finding them. Much Flak."

And then the last entry:

> **25 September:** "Patrol Arnhem-Nijmegen. Immediately after take-off

the Squadron got split up due to low cloud. I found myself left with six aircraft. After some searching we found Nijmegen and came under heavy fire from light and medium ack-ack. A little later we spotted two 109s and chased them but lost them in cloud. On the way home we were ordered to land at Eindhoven for refuelling and then to return on patrol. While we were there some 109s and 190s attacked the airfield but none of us were hurt and only one aircraft was damaged."

These examples are sufficient to show the enormous difficulties we faced purely because of low cloud and poor visibility.

It is well known that paratroopers are especially well-trained in the art of unarmed combat. One evening in Brussels I was left in no doubt about this. I popped into a down-town night-club, and as I came out into the dark again I discovered two men tampering with my car. They had lifted the bonnet and with the aid of a flashlight were obviously intent on connecting the ignition leads past the switch in order to steal the car. When I got closer I could see from the red berets they wore that they were paratroopers, and I said in a stern voice: 'What the hell do you think you are doing lads? Are you trying to steal my car?'

One of them turned and shoved me away as he said: 'Shut up you ass, we have as much right to this bloody car as you. Piss off or you'll be sorry.' Having said that he turned back to helping his mate.

I walked to him, pulled his sleeve roughly and said: 'If you don't leave my car alone I'll call the police.' I then tried to pull him away.

I don't know exactly what he did but suddenly I found myself lying flat on my back on the cobblestones. Now I was mad. I stood up and walked to the rascal, fully intent upon giving him a hiding. However, as I brought up my fist I found myself gripped in such a way that I went flying over the top of the fellow and landed again in a heap on the ground. I felt dazed but heard one of my adversaries say in a shocked voice: 'My God, it's a bleeding officer. Let's piss off, mate.' I heard the clatter of their boots on the cobblestones as they ran away.

I had a sore shoulder and my left wrist hurt badly. Next morning it had become thickly swollen and when I showed it to our MO he took me to the nearest hospital to have it X-rayed. It turned out to be broken. The wrist was put in splints and I had to have my arm in a sling until the swelling subsided enough to have it wrapped in Plaster-of-Paris. I should have known better than to take on a couple of paratroopers in unarmed combat!

For the next three days I roamed around, inactive and restless, while my comrades continued their ceaseless patrols of the Nijmegen-Arnhem battle front. I constantly badgered the MO and the CO until at last they gave in and agreed to let me fly in spite of my wrist being encased in plaster. They were reluctant to do this as they thought the plaster might hamper my flying and possibly place myself, and even my companions, in unnecessary peril. I pointed out however, that the left hand was only used for controlling the throttle, and as my fingers stuck out of the plaster and were free, this should present no problem.

We certainly enjoyed life to the hilt—we flew relentlessly during the day and dallied without cares in the evenings. But then we had a bombshell. After only nine days in this blissful haven we were suddenly told that we had three hours to prepare for departure. The Wing was to return to England.

To leave Brussels so soon—this was unthinkable! To leave all this luxury and move to England where rationing, growing inflation and austerity were prevalent—this was terrible. And only three hours notice! Had the powers-that-be gone completely mad?

There was nothing we could do about it though; England it would have to be, and we'd have to make the best of it. We were given no time to say farewell to the various friends we had made in this friendly city, or to kiss our girlfriends good-bye. We hurriedly packed our bags and squeezed them into our Mustangs. The ground staff and those pilots that did not have planes to fly would be transported in Dakotas. I had a problem on my hands, of course, as I was loath to leave my delightful sports car behind. I had made enquiries and discovered that it would be easy to have it transported to England in an empty cargo vessel if only I could get it to the docks at Antwerp, but there was no time for that. The squadrons that were to replace us were equipped with Tempests and some of them had already arrived.

One of the pilots, an Australian, saw my car and asked me what I was going to do with it. I admitted to having a problem, and asked him if I could talk him into taking it to Antwerp for me. He just laughed and said he had no time for that but offered to buy it off me for 1000 Belgian Francs. I gasped with disbelief. One thousand Francs for such a magnificent car. Did he think I was a simpleton? He shrugged his shoulders and smiled; I could take it or leave it, but I would inevitably have to leave the car behind and then he would just grab it for nothing. He was really only doing me a favour by offering me 1000 Francs. I could see that I did not have much option, and with a feeling of frustration and a sense of loss I accepted these harsh conditions. I'd have been much better off if I'd taken my CO's offer three weeks earlier; and I would not have been injured.

So what? Providence had not endowed me with much business acumen, but surely had made up for that in other ways. I was still alive for one thing! I agreed to his offer.

The final act before departure was to have the mechanics stuff bottles of cognac and champagne all around us in the cockpit. Every available space was used, leaving us just enough room to move our arms and legs to fly the aircraft. Our CO expressed displeasure with this conduct and said that not only were we breaking the laws of Customs and Excise, but also putting ourselves in considerable peril. However he was not actually going to put a ban on it.

The Squadron took off with the CO in the lead and set course for Matlask aerodrome in Norfolk, which was to be our new base. We climbed in fairly close formation, and for the first 10,000 feet it looked reasonably tidy, but as we continued to climb the formation started to become a little straggled—we were expecting the corks of the champagne bottles to start popping. It dawned on us that in a playful way our CO was making us feel the blunder of our actions. Higher and higher we climbed and the formation was beginning to look as if the aeroplanes were being flown by a bunch of raw recruits. He took us up to 30,000 feet and in our minds we could see ourselves sitting in a bubbling champagne bath, and in a temperature of minus 30° Celsius this was not very inviting. We knew that the CO was having a very amusing time, and although he was a popular figure, most of us were by now cursing him heartily. Thankfully he now decided it was time to descend.

Nothing serious happened, and for that we can most likely thank the wire on the champagne corks. We now started to breath our oxygen a little more calmly; the danger had passed and our formation flying improved, and by the time we made a low pass over our new airfield it was good enough to have been applauded at an air show... well nearly!

XVII   FEAR CREEPS IN

Over the Ruhr at 35,000 feet the cold was piercing. Slightly to the north, and about 15,000 feet below us, 120 four-engined Halifax bombers flew in large formations and were approaching the target, which this time was Essen. Our role was to protect these bombers from being attacked by German fighters. For the first part of their route the bombers had been escorted by Spitfires, but near the German border we had taken over the escort duties; our Mustangs had so much greater range than the Spitfires. It was October 6 and we in 65 Squadron were top cover at 35,000 feet, the boys of 122 were medium cover, 5000 feet below us, and 19 Squadron flew close cover, just above the bombers. We flew a zig-zag course in a very open finger-four formation, two and two aircraft together. We kept a close look-out and carefully scanned the vast expanse of sky all around us. The large drop-tanks hung under our wings and would not be jettisoned unless we were about to engage the enemy.

Around the bombers far below us we could spot the black puffs of smoke made by exploding anti-aircraft shells, and these black dots became more numerous as the large industrial areas of the Ruhr came closer. It was no life of bliss for those poor lads down there in the Halifaxes. We could see smoke trailing from one of bombers in the leading formation and... oh, my God! Over there one of them had simply disintegrated in flame and smoke. Four white parachutes appeared—at least six young men had lost their lives in that doomed aeroplane. Someone had said the other day: 'The lesser of two evils is to have your brass monkeys frozen off at 35,000 feet than have your ass burned off in that target-shooting gallery down at 20,000,' I was certainly prepared to agree with him. Although I was frozen stiff I would not like to change places with a Halifax pilot.

Far to the south two white trails appeared in the blue sky; at first only faintly but gradually they became more distinct as they approached on a course that would intercept our own some distance ahead. Although the two aircraft were still too far away for us to identify, we were in no doubt about what they were. Because of their height and speed they could only be the new German jet fighters, the Messerschmitt 262, which were now appearing in increasing numbers. We kept a watchful eye on them. We knew that their tactics were to dive down on the bombers at great speed, make a passing attack and disappear. Because of their superior speed there was very little we could do to fight them off unless their pilots were foolish enough to turn back for another attack. As soon as these jet planes started making steep turns they lost speed and thereby their superiority. Only a few days ago one of the pilots of 122 Squadron had fought a duel with one of them and shot it down.

These two adversaries of ours were about 5000 feet above us and flew in a sweeping arc ahead of the bombers' course, and now we could clearly identify them. They kept up a gentle left turn and we expected them at any moment to start their dive towards the bombers; we prepared ourselves to try to intercept them and get a quick shot at them as they passed by at high speed. To our amazement they kept on turning until they were heading south again and gradually disappeared from sight.

We flew large circles around the target while the train of bombers 'laid their eggs' and set course for home again. Oh, how dreadfully cold it was up there at 35,000 feet. We sat there motionless for over three hours in biting frost and no matter how many items of clothing one wore, the cold seeped through them and into one's bones and marrow so that one's arms and legs felt like frozen logs. All feeling, except that of discomfort, had long since left our extremities. How we envied our American colleagues their electrically heated flying suits. The Mustang was designed to accommodate such suits, and the authorities kept promising to supply us with them, but so far we had been kept waiting.

We saw two more Halifaxes go down as burning wrecks after being hit by Flak, but no more enemy planes appeared this time. Near the border a group of Spitfires met us to take over the duty of shepherding our flock home, and we were free to leave.

After departure from Matlask our leader had been forced to return to base because of trouble with his landing gear, and I had taken over command of the Squadron. Now that our escort role was over we still had a good supply of petrol left in our tanks, so I put into effect a plan I had in mind. It had become evident that most of our pilots were becoming fed up with the rather uneventful, and unrewarding escort flying that had been our lot since arriving at Matlask three weeks ago. Oh, to be sure there was a sort of excitement when we occasionally got caught up in terrifying Flak that had us sweating in spite of the cold, but enemy fighters were rarely seen and most of us had not had an opportunity to fire our guns since leaving Brussels. We had been whisked away from the excitement of close proximity, day-to-day fighting, and now suddenly found ourselves in the totally different role of cruising around an empty sky at high altitude with nothing happening except the occasional alarm of a closely bursting ack-ack shell. We missed the excitement of low flying and the thrill of firing one's cannons at a tangible enemy.

I decided that now was an opportunity to do something about this. I called the Wingco on R/T and requested permission for TOMBOY to make a detour on the way home, and received immediate consent.

Below us there were only some thin sheets of cloud to the south-west, so the weather was ideal. After a short while we were down to 2000 feet, and ahead of us to the north-east lay a fairly large town which I figured to be Osnabrück. The important thing was that on the outskirts of the town we could see a very large railway marshalling yard with rows of freight cars, and here and there jets of steam indicated the presence of locomotives. I told each of the section leaders to pick his target, make one attack and then reform north of the town at 2000 feet.

Followed by my section I dived down on a locomotive that was just about to disappear into a shed. At the very moment I opened fire I became aware of tracer bullets heading for us from many directions and I felt the control column twitch in my hand and my aircraft jerk as it was hit. I pulled back on the stick, shoved the throttle forward and climbed for all I was worth to get out of this hell-hole. I felt that my aircraft was not responding to the controls in a normal way, and I observed that a part of the right wing-tip and aileron were missing. The engine seemed to run normally, and the aircraft was controllable, so I counted myself lucky.

I informed my companions of my predicament and that I was heading for home by the shortest route. Within a short time they were by my side and, apart from a few Flak gunners taking pot shots at us, the flight home was uneventful.

It was probably after this flight that the seeds of fear were surreptitiously planted within me. To start with they were not really noticeable, no more than the first signs of cancer make themselves felt. However, slowly but surely they took control, and manifested themselves in many small but important ways. I stopped seeking to go on every flight, and made excuses to myself that as an acting flight commander, and frequently as a leader of the Squadron, in the CO's absence, I should not be greedy and hog too many trips. However, I continued to give myself a generous quota of flights, because I was not going to admit to myself, let alone others, that any changes were taking place. But there was no denying that 'fear had raised its ugly head'. I could not ignore the thoughts in the back of my mind telling me that the war was nearly over, and that it would be unforgiveable to get killed during the last days.

XVIII   POSTED TO ICELAND

In the beginning of November a new pilot by the name of Graham Pearson was posted to the Squadron and joined my flight. I simply must include him in my story for he was such a memorable and endearing character. He was a young man from the middle or upper classes, tall and slender with a mop of blond hair. His features were regular and he would be described as good-looking in spite of a large mouth, which appeared even larger because of being nearly permanently formed into a smile. He talked with what seemed a rather affected accent and his manner, at times, gave one reason to classify him as a likeable simpleton. Likeable he was, but certainly no simpleton. He was, however, on occasions rather accident prone. In many ways he reminded me of Bertie Wooster, the character created by P G Wodehouse.

His career with the Squadron did not start very favourably. As he had never flown a Mustang, I told him to contact Chiefy for an aircraft, and take it up for some familiarisation. It so happened that just then most of our aircraft were being worked on by the mechanics, but the CO's—standing in front of the dispersal hut—was free. This presented no problem as it was common practice for other pilots in the Squadron to fly the CO's plane when he himself was not flying. When Graham was about to climb into the cockpit he discovered the CO's parachute was there. He lifted it out and laid it on the wing while he replaced it with his own, but had the misfortune to see it slide down off the wing into a muddy puddle that rain had formed during the night. Graham tried hurriedly to jump off the wing to retrieve the parachute before it got thoroughly soaked, but unfortunately he had already put on his flying helmet, and the R/T cord attached to it now got tangled with something in the cockpit, with the consequence that Graham nearly broke his neck and finished up sitting in the puddle beside the parachute.

Eventually he got airborne, completed his practice flight and came in to land. However, it was not his lucky day. He undershot rather badly and the undercarriage caught a wire fence, dragging it for a considerable distance along the runway, and the Mustang eventually ended up on its nose.

Poor Graham was shattered, and now dreaded being introduced to the CO, who was absent on this day. It did not escape my attention that he was the main subject of conversation in the mess at dinner time that evening. Officers stood in small groups, tittered and cast amused glances in Graham's direction. I felt quite sorry for the poor fellow and tried to console him, and the upshot was that we decided to go on a pub crawl in Norwich, the nearest town. We drove there in Graham's car, a flashy, long-nosed Jaguar, which he drove as if he were competing in the Monte Carlo rally. After a good meal and numerous pints of beer—all paid for by him— he had regained his good humour, and on the way home he no doubt tried to impress me with his driving skills. The result was that I sat rigid with terror, holding on for dear life. As we went careering along the typical narrow English country lanes, the rear end of the car slid in one of the many bends and hit a tar-boiler standing on the verge. With much wrenching of the steering wheel and screeching of brakes Graham managed to stop the car within the next fifty yards or so. The tar-boiler was nowhere to be seen—it had no doubt taken a flying leap into a nearby pond—and inspection showed considerable damage to the rear end of the Jaguar. No, this certainly was not Graham's day.

At the aerodrome next day a police constable from the local village was seen riding his bike around the station. He went hither and thither apparently searching for something. We were given to understand that he was looking for a tar-boiling machine that had disappeared from the neighbourhood. Whatever gave him the idea that such a contraption might be found on a fighter station!?

In truth, of course, he had ample reason to think so. It was not uncommon for young pilots, full of spirits (and beer), to take home souvenirs from their pub crawls. They had a propensity for decorating their rather drab surroundings with certain borrowed 'objets d'art'. As an example of this I can say that for a period the entrance to our dispersal hut had a colourful sign hanging over it, depicting a group of merry men lifting frothy mugs of beer, underneath which stood the legend: 'The Jolly Bargeman'. That is to say, until a pub landlord in Norwich sent the police to collect it. We felt he was being rather stingy! The wind-sock at our dispersal consisted of a pair of pink bloomers that some unsuspecting lady had hung on her clothes line to dry. They were still being aired! Over the door to the WC in the officers' mess there was a sign that had once belonged to a well known railway station. It bore the name WATERLOO. And so on. There were many other examples of the station personnel's fondness for collecting souvenirs.

Our task of escorting the heavy bombers to Germany continued, the raids being carried out whenever the weather over the targets allowed. My log book contains such names as Hannover, Berlin, Gelsenkirchen, Cologne, Dortmund, Frankfurt, Hamm and many more. These flights were mostly long and tedious, flown at great height in extreme cold, leaving us chilled to the bones. We rarely saw any enemy planes, but the monotony was occasionally broken up when we got caught up in some alarmingly heavy Flak. Certainly none of us were enthusiastic about these trips, and to create some variety, and to satisfy the longing for action, inherent in young, adventurous fighter pilots, the authorities decided to allow 'rhubarbs' to be carried out when we were not otherwise engaged.

Now and again I found myself in charge of the Squadron, a situation that happened with increasing frequency during this time. The CO was absent for long periods, and as I was now the Squadron's most experienced pilot it became my task to hold the reins. All the pilots who had been in the Squadron when I joined it were gone. Even my pal Bill was now engaged in other activities.

Of course the first person to approach me with proposals for a rhubarb was Graham. He was itching to have a go and was worried about the war ending before he had had an opportunity to meet a foe in the air. He contrived a plan to fly to Bavaria in the south of Germany in search of enemy planes to shoot down. There were flying schools in the neighbourhood of Munich that might possibly present some good hunting, and he wanted me to lead a section of four aircraft for this purpose.

To be truthful, I was not exactly overjoyed at the prospect. A few months earlier no bonds would have held me back, but now the poison of fear was gradually seeping into my veins. Needless to say I kept this well-hidden and put on a brave front. I was the bold and experienced fighter pilot that the young recruits looked up to as a leader!

Although the weather over south-east England was rather murky, the MET officer said that there would be broken cloud and good visibility over southern Germany and therefore no reason not to go.

The four Mustangs that consequently took off from Matlask that gloomy December day, and headed south, were heavy, with full tanks of petrol, including drop-tanks. At first we climbed up through thick cloud, but at 10,000 feet we broke out of it and continued under a clear sunny sky. Over the continent the clouds below started breaking up, and near Luxembourg we were able to dive down and continue our journey at around 2000 feet under scattered fluffy clouds. With a map on my knees I tried to keep track of our progress.

There ahead of us lay a large river which had to be the Mosel, and shortly after that we should reach the Rhine. Yes, it was all falling into place. We would fly along the Rhine until we reached Mannheim and then set course for Munich. I thought about how greatly things had changed during the last three years. There was a time when four aircraft flying over enemy territory would have tried to avoid encountering enemy fighters and stay as close to cloud-cover as possible. This no longer applied. We now flew provocatively, challenging the enemy to come up and fight. Suddenly tracer bullets arose from the ground and puffs of black smoke appeared in the sky close to us. We had probably come too close to some town or military object, but this did not worry us unduly; we just changed height and direction slightly every fifteen seconds or so.

Now I could see Mannheim in the distance and steered us well clear of the city—coming close to the ack-ack guns of large towns was not very healthy. After leaving Mannheim and Heidelberg behind, I was able to perceive Stuttgart through a heavy rain shower that was descending on the city. Furthermore, the mountains beyond the city appeared to be in clouds, and this caused me some apprehension. As we drew closer it became obvious that flying around that area would be foolhardy. Large thunderclouds lay on the hilltops, reaching high into the sky and heavy rain showers were spread far and wide, with intermittent flashes of lightning visible.

I advised my comrades that this was as far as we were going, and we would have to look for action somewhere else. We started a turn to the left but just then I caught sight of a group of fighters approaching from the west and diving down towards us.

'TOMBOY section!' I called on the R/T. 'Twenty plus bogeys at 10 o'clock above, diving. Be prepared to drop tanks and break sharply into them when I give the word.'

When the aircraft drew closer I was able to identify them as P-47s of the US Army Air Force and informed my companions of this. I advised them, however, to be on guard as the Yanks were known to shoot first and ask questions afterwards. Fortunately their leader realized in time that we were friends, and there can be little doubt that the white stripes painted on the wings of all Allied aircraft played a part in helping identification.

By now I'd had enough and informed my charges that we were taking the shortest route home. During the last half hour we flew in thick cloud which demanded some very close formation flying. My mates performed this skilfully, and with the aid of the control tower's radar we landed in rain and murk at Matlask after three hours flying.

After this abortive flight I couldn't escape doing some soul-searching, and deliberating whether I was really and truly fit to continue in this position. I had to admit to myself that I had felt anxiety whilst over Germany. The keenness, offensive spirit and confidence of my former days was gone. In those days I would hardly have returned home from a flight like this without having fired my guns. Although my companions had not said so I could feel that they were disappointed with how little offensive spirit I had shown. Yes, they certainly deserved somebody more fit to lead them. I had already flown more than the 200 operational hours, which the Air Force stipulated as the limit for a tour of duty, and fatigue was no doubt setting in. I decided to discuss this with my CO, Sqdn Ldr Burra-Robinson, on his return from leave.

During the following days I escorted bombers to Germany on a few more raids, and suffered anxiety on each occasion. Never before had the engine seemed to run so unevenly, nor the time pass with such slowness. And then, on December 18, came my last flight, although I did not know it at the time.

That this flight turned out to be most unsatisfactory and incomplete was not of my making, and I felt dissatisfied with ending my career as a fighter pilot in the way I did, although at the same time I had to admit feeling relieved that it was all over. The Wing went on a sweep of the Hannover-Bremen area. After take-off I was unable to retract my undercarriage, so I had to land and change aircraft. I took off again and flew to Germany in search of the Wing, but after a while I gave up the search as unbroken cloud below me prevented me from ascertaining my position.

A few days later the Wing Commander called me to his office and informed me it had come to his attention that I had already exceeded the maximum hours for a tour of operations. I would have to give it up and take a long vacation. He also asked me if I had any special preferences for a posting for further duties after my vacation.

Without hesitating I said: 'Yes sir, to a squadron stationed in Iceland.' I immediately regretted saying this, as it seems to be a principle in the military services to grant the opposite to what is requested. I visualized myself being posted to some remote spot, such as the Falkland Islands, or flying a desk at a recruiting centre somewhere in the Midlands.

The unbelievable happened—I was posted to Iceland!

XVIIII   THIS IS YOUR SON

It was an optimistic young lad who, on 18 April 1940, had stepped onto a trawler in the small town of Hafnarfjördur in Iceland and set off to the uncertainty and perils of war. He intended to learn to fly, and was even prepared to fight in the war to reach his goal. Now, at last, on 14 February 1945 this same young man stepped back onto Icelandic soil. He had achieved his goal—he was a pilot.

I returned to Iceland as a passenger in a Dakota transport plane of the Royal Air Force and landed on Reykjavik aerodrome, which had not existed when I left nearly five years earlier. Here in the marshland known as Vatnsmýri, I had, as a youngster, searched for sticklebacks in the drainage ditches. And here too I had actually touched a real aeroplane for the first time, when I ran errands for the Dutch pilots flying their biplanes on weather-recording flights one summer, those many years ago. And here I had nursed dreams of one day becoming a pilot.

Yes, a great deal of changes had taken place here in these marshes since those days, and I was soon to discover that the country and the nation had also undergone many transformations.

I had not harboured much hope of the Air Ministry finding a job for me in Iceland, for the RAF no longer had any fighters based there, and it therefore came as a pleasant surprise when I received orders to proceed to Prestwick to catch a plane to Reykjavik. I had been given the job of flying an aircraft called a Martinet, which was a single-engined two-seater plane designed as a trainer. My task was to fly around the sky towing a drogue for the air gunners of bombers and anti-submarine planes to practice shooting at.

I had not advised anyone of my pending arrival in Iceland, so I looked forward excitedly to surprising my family and friends. I got the transport to drop me off at Lækjatorg, the main square in the centre of the town. From there I walked along the main street, Austurstræti, towards my father's bookshop. I knew that my sister, Betty, was serving in the shop so I planned to start my homecoming there, where, as a youngster I had spent so much time doing odd jobs and running errands. On my walk along Austurstræti I was left in no doubt about being home. All the old familiar shops, banks, restaurants, the Post Office and other establishments were still there. As I walked along the street—oh, how short and narrow it now seemed—I notice that many people stared with surprise at the word Iceland on the shoulders of this fellow wearing the uniform of a Royal Air Force officer, and I also noticed that one or two were about to greet me but hesitated, probably due to uncertainty, and looked away.

As I entered the bookshop my sister stared at me for a moment, open-eyed with disbelief, yelled 'STEINI!' (the common diminutive of my name), ran from behind the counter and threw her arms around me. It was an unforgettable moment.

Betty and I agreed that it would be advisable to call my father on the phone to prepare him and my stepmother, whom I had never met, for my arrival. The telephone rang once and then I heard the familiar voice say: 'One-nine-three-four.'

'Well, how do you do,' I said as calmly as I could.

There was a moment of silence on the line and then the voice said: 'Eh... who is that, please?'

'This is your son returning from the wars,' I said solemnly, having the greatest difficulty not bursting out laughing.

As Betty had done shortly before he exclaimed: 'STEINI!'

I am not about to go into details of all the joyful reunions that lay ahead. It is sufficient to say they were many and happy.

And it also pleased me immensely that even people that I didn't know showed me good-will and friendliness. An example of this was the taxi driver that drove Betty and me home that day. When she was about to pay him he refused to take the money and said it had been a pleasure to have been allowed to drive us.

I stayed in Iceland for the next three months, or until shortly after the war in Europe was over, as then there was no longer any need for target towing. All that time I dwelt in my father's house and cycled the two miles to the aerodrome when I had to fly, which on average was about three times a week. The job was not very demanding and I had a great deal of time off.

However, my first flight in this new role was rather memorable, as it was the first—and only—time in my flying career that I had an accident during take-off. Admittedly I had an excuse for this misfortune, but even so it hurt my pride. During take-off in single-engined aircraft with a powerful engine, the twisting momentum (torque) of the propeller tends to turn the aircraft off a straight line. This is normally compensated for by trimming the aircraft, i.e. applying mechanical pressure to the rudder to counter-balance the torque of the propeller. Up to now I had only flown aircraft powered with British engines (the engines in the Mustangs were of British design, although built in the USA), but this aeroplane was powered with an American engine, and no-one remembered to tell me that they rotate in the opposite way to the British. I therefore applied rudder trim in the wrong direction with the effect that the propeller and the rudder worked together to deflect the aircraft on take-off, and although I applied full rudder I was unable to prevent the plane from swinging, and it caught one of the runway lights with the right-hand wheel, bending the leg, just as I was leaving the ground.

There was nothing else to do but land on the left wheel and hold the right wing off the ground as long as possible. This was fairly successfully accomplished, causing only minor damage to the aircraft, which was back in service a few days later.

During the coming years I was destined to land hundreds of times on Reykjavik airport and I could never forget that my first landing there was a 'crash-landing'.

These were really blissful days at home in Iceland. I enjoyed the company of family members and old friends, went skiing, deep-sea fishing, hunting and travelled a good deal around the country. As I was an officer in the RAF I had the privilege of access to all the various officers' clubs and messes of both the British and American occupation forces, and these privileges were unstintingly used. I had girlfriends galore, but after a while one became special, and I spent most of my spare time with her. If I hadn't already been engaged to a girl in England, who later became my first wife, I am sure that our association would have become more permanent.

Then in late May this joyful period of my life came to an end, and I was sent back to England. With the future in mind I had applied for a transfer to Transport Command, and I was now sent on a course to learn to fly twin-engined aircraft. At the end of that, I found myself on a course in a Transport Command school to be trained to fly Dakotas.

As a qualified Dakota pilot I joined 187 Squadron stationed on Membury airfield, a short distance west of London. The Squadron's task was to transport soldiers to and from India, and that was my job for the next year or so. The Dakota's crew consisted of two pilots, a navigator and a radio operator. These flights to India were in many ways memorable and enjoyable, but at times they could be quite arduous and difficult, for in those days there were few navigational aids to help us on our routes. Transit stops for crew changes were made at numerous locations, and we got to see many interesting places.

For most of us these flights were also most profitable, as much business was conducted at many of the places we visited. Because of the war there was a shortage of many commodities in various places, and the distribution of goods was still very poor in many parts of the world. There might be an abundance of certain items in one place and a shortage of the same items in the next. For example we usually left England with a good supply of cigarettes and coffee-beans, amongst other things. In Cagliari in Sardinia, usually our first transit stop, we would exchange these for various silk goods or cameras. Some of this we might sell for cash in some of the Arab countries we passed through. In Karachi, which was then part of the Indian Empire under the British Crown, a great variety of goods could be purchased to be sold at a profit in other places. We all bought carpets because a profit of over 100 per cent could be made when selling them in England. Actually a bit of a problem arose when the authorities imposed a ban on transporting carpets, following an incident when an aircraft was unable to maintain height after losing an engine, and had to belly-land in the desert. Twenty-four carpets were found on board that had not been entered on the load-sheet. But quickly ways and means were found to smuggle carpets on board, and this profitable business continued. Jewels and precious stones were also popular merchandise. A roaring trade was done in bicycle tyres at various stops en route, and many other items could be mentioned, but it is sufficient to say that I was more affluent during this period than at any other time in my career in the Air Force.

In the late summer of 1946 I sat for examinations that secured me a civil flying licence; the 'B' licence as it was then called. As we newly-baked civil pilots emerged from the Ministry of Civil Aviation with our licences in hand we were waylaid by scouts from many of the top European airline companies and offered instant jobs. Even if they'd offered me fortunes I would have had no difficulties turning them down—I had made up my mind to return home to Iceland as soon as the Air Force let go of me.

Marianne and I got married in July. We had been together since shortly after I joined 65 Squadron in Gravesend in January 1944, and from that time I had spent most of my leaves with her.

The marriage ceremony took place at the Registry Office in the town of Chatham in Kent, and of course my pal Bill was best-man. The ceremony was also attended by my sister Betty and her husband James. She had recently married a British Naval Officer who had been stationed in Iceland, where he travelled around the coast and had the nasty job of defusing mines that drifted ashore. Now they were living in Beckenham on the southern outskirts of London.

A comical incident happened on the way from Gravesend to the Chatham Registry Office. The ancient jalopy we drove had a puncture in one of the rear tyres. As there was no jack in the car Jimmy and I had to hold it up while Bill did the tyre-change. It was a scorching hot day, so the two RAF officers and the Naval Lieutenant that turned up at the Registry Office fifteen minutes late were rather sweaty and dirty, but the officiating dignitary took it all in his stride and tied the knot.

We spent our honeymoon as guests of the mayor of Douglas on the Isle of Man. The Island enjoys a limited autonomy under the Crown, and the Islanders regard their old Legislative Assembly, the Tynwald, as being closely related to Thingvellir, the Icelandic Legislative Assembly of the Middle Ages (the Viking period), when Nordic people resided on the Island. Through the media it had come to the attention of administrators on the Island that an Icelander was serving in the RAF, and with the aid of the Air Ministry they had managed to dig me up and invite me to visit the Island. Needless to say we greatly enjoyed the hospitality lavished on us.

And now the time approached when it became my turn to say farewell to the Air Force and return to wearing civvies. In mid-December I received orders to report to a Demobilization Centre about 60 miles west of London. Arriving there I found a group of cheerful officers, who, like me, had been engaged for the duration of the war (or 'The Present Emergency' as it was worded), and now awaited dismissal. As far as I could see, all seemed to welcome the fact that they were leaving the service. It was now peacetime and the rigid discipline of the regular forces was beginning to become onerous. This discipline was no doubt natural for the real soldiers, but we did not see ourselves as being such any longer. We were just civilians wearing uniforms which we now wanted to be rid of. Some time had now passed since the end of the war, and we understood well enough that unavoidably it took quite a while to return such a large number of persons back to civil life, in an orderly fashion. But now the moment had arrived when we should say good-bye to the King's men and set out into the world as just ordinary 'Misters'.

The King gave me two civilian suits—unbelievably unfashionable and unattractive. Also a mackintosh, two shirts, a necktie, a hat and a pair of shoes. I was thanked for loyal service and handed a cheque for £350 Sterling as a token of gratitude. This chapter of my life was over and I was about to start a new one. I had been engaged as a pilot with Iceland Airways and looked forward to start work in the New Year. I now held an Icelandic professional pilot's licence—No. 13. It amused me, that when I applied for this licence I was told that it would be number 24, unless of course I would care for No. 13, which had been by-passed by all my predecessors. I didn't have to think twice—13 has always been a lucky number for me.

Now all that remained to be done was to get myself home. My wife, Marianne, was already there, and had started work in my father's book-shop. I had booked a passage for myself and my car, a small 10hp Ford, on a Polish tramp steamer, leaving Hull early next morning. I had a long night drive ahead of me, so I'd better get going. I threw my suitcase onto the back seat and set off. I had been on the go since early morning and felt tiredness creeping in. After about four hour's drive I was past Birmingham and sped along a winding road in the Pennines. I yawned incessantly and had the greatest difficulty keeping my eyes open. The next thing I knew, I had a jarring start when the car suddenly took a leap and shot up a hill on the right-hand side of the road where, after about ten yards, it came to a halt. The left-hand door stood wide open and my suitcase was gone. I had fallen asleep on a bend in the road. I climbed out and found my suitcase lying open on the road, its contents strewn all over the place. I walked over to the left-hand side of the road and looked into a void. The steep slope disappeared into the darkness. I shivered. I could so easily have been lying somewhere down there in that black pit.

My guardian angels had still not forsaken me.

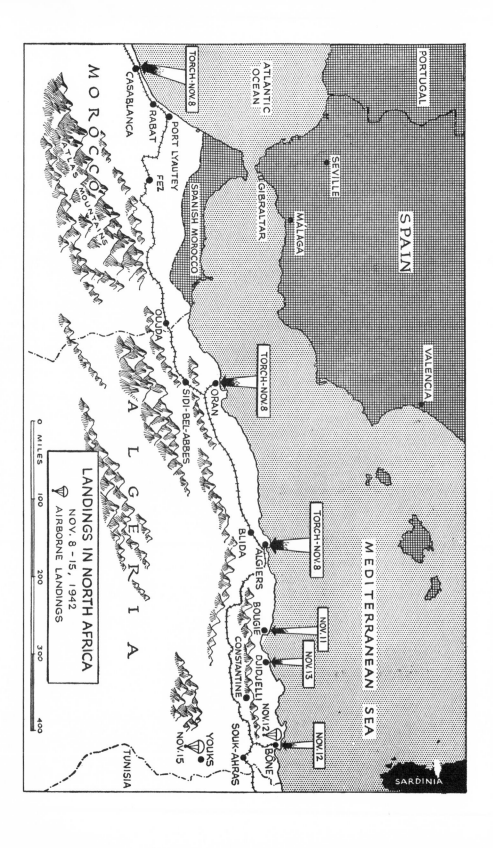

LANDINGS IN NORTH AFRICA
NOV. 8 - 15, 1942
AIRBORNE LANDINGS

MILES
0   100   200   300   400

MOROCCO

ATLAS MOUNTAINS

CASABLANCA
RABAT
PORT LYAUTEY
FEZ

SPANISH MOROCCO

TORCH-NOV. 8

ATLANTIC OCEAN

PORTUGAL

SPAIN

SEVILLE
MÁLAGA
VALENCIA

GIBRALTAR

A L G E R I A

OUJDA
SIDI-BEL-ABBES
ORAN

TORCH-NOV. 8

BLIDA
ALGIERS

TORCH-NOV. 8

BOUGIE
NOV. 11

CONSTANTINE
DJIDJELLI
NOV. 13

NOV. 12
BÔNE
NOV. 12

SOUK-AHRAS
YOUKS
NOV. 15

TUNISIA

MEDITERRANEAN SEA

SARDINIA

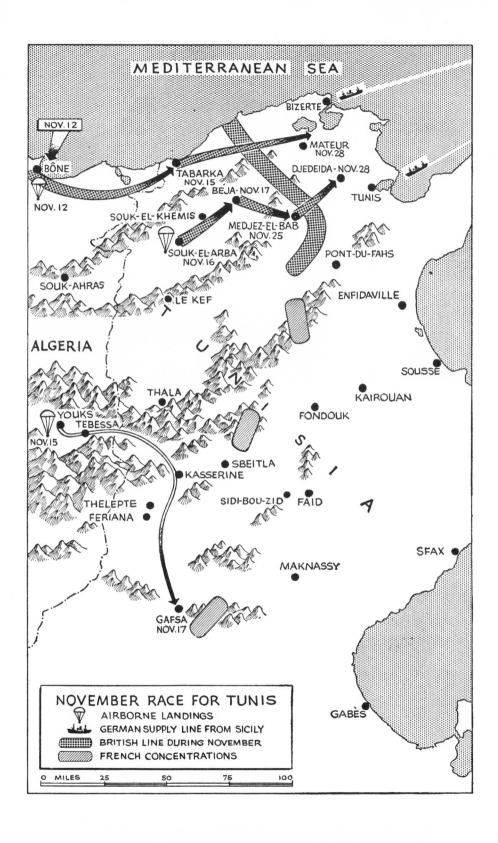

MEDITERRANEAN SEA

BIZERTE

NOV. 12

BÔNE
NOV. 12

MATEUR
NOV. 28

DJEDEIDA – NOV. 28

TABARKA
NOV. 15

BEJA – NOV. 17

TUNIS

SOUK-EL-KHEMIS

MEDJEZ-EL-BAB
NOV. 25

SOUK-EL-ARBA
NOV. 16

PONT-DU-FAHS

SOUK-AHRAS

LE KEF

ENFIDAVILLE

ALGERIA

T
U
N
I
S
I
A

THALA

SOUSSE

KAIROUAN

YOUKS
TEBESSA
NOV. 15

FONDOUK

SBEITLA

KASSERINE

SIDI-BOU-ZID FAID

THELEPTE
FERIANA

MAKNASSY

SFAX

GAFSA
NOV. 17

NOVEMBER RACE FOR TUNIS

AIRBORNE LANDINGS
GERMAN SUPPLY LINE FROM SICILY
BRITISH LINE DURING NOVEMBER
FRENCH CONCENTRATIONS

GABÈS

0 MILES   25   50   75   100

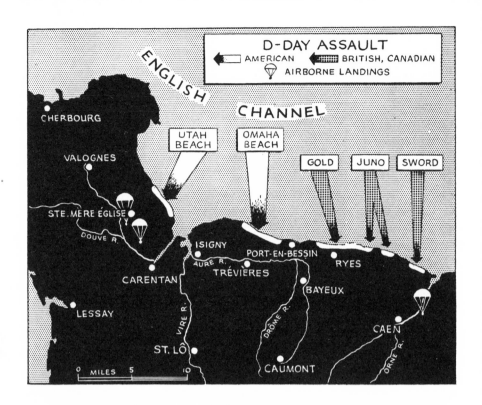

INDEX